The Essential Keto Diet Cookbook 2022

500

Quick And Delicious Low-Carb Recipes With **21-Days Meal Plan** For Busy People To Keep A Ketogenic Diet Lifestyle

Brady Brown

CONTENTS

Chapter 3. Pork, Beef & Lamb Recipes...31

Chapter 5. Fish And Seafood Recipes..66

Chapter 6. Sauces And Dressing Recipes..82

Chapter 7. Soups, Stew & Salads.. 87

Chapter 8. Vegan, Vegetable & Meatless Recipes... 100

Chapter 9. Desserts And Drinks **117**

Introduction

As you probably know, losing weight is not that easy.

If you're like most people who have tried many different weight loss programs, you'll find that it's not difficult to get positive results in the beginning.

After a couple of weeks, you'd start to drop a few pounds, and you'd be happy about it.

But the real challenge lies in keeping the weight off.

This is why, many experts suggest getting into a weight loss program that can become a lifestyle for you.

This way, you can achieve your ideal weight and maintain it for a long time.

One example of such weight loss program is the ketogenic diet.

Also known as the keto diet, this one can eventually become a lifestyle for you if you are able to do it right.

And this does not only keep the pounds off, it also improves your overall health.

Are you ready to get to know more about this amazing diet program?

Then let's get started.

Chapter 1. The KETO Lifestyle

Proven Benefits of a KETO Diet

1. A keto diet leads to weight loss. When you avoid carbohydrates, your body starts burning stored fat; it will automatically cause decreased appetite. On the other hand, you will experience higher energy levels.

2. Mental clarity and better concentration. On a keto diet, our brain uses ketones as the main fuel; consequently, it reduces the levels of toxins. It will significantly improve your cognitive functions, mental focus, concentration, and mental performance.

3. Health benefits. A keto diet restricts carbohydrates; they can be found in unhealthy sugary foods, refined grains such as bread, pasta and white rice. On the other hand, it promotes foods that are loaded with high-quality protein (it is essential for building muscle), good fat, and healthy veggies. Many studies have proven that low-carb diets can significantly improve health. They measured the main outcomes such as LDL cholesterol, HDL cholesterol, blood sugar levels, triglycerides, and weight loss. Fatty fish such (for example, tuna and salmon) is well known for its ability to lower triglycerides; consequently, it can reduce the risk of stroke. Unsaturated fat-packed foods such as seeds, nuts and unrefined vegetable oils can help your body to lower triglycerides, too. In addition, cutting out carbs can reduce insulin levels and regulate blood sugar. Not only can keto diets improve your physical performance and boost weight loss, but they also treat some serious conditions. Keto diets have proven beneficial in treating several brain disorders such as epilepsy in children. Moreover, ketogenic diets are incredibly effective in treating metabolic syndrome.

Go Shopping

It's time to restock your pantry, refrigerator, and freezer with delicious, keto-friendly foods that will help you lose weight, become healthy, and feel great!

1. The Basics

With these basics on hand, you'll always be ready to prepare healthy, delicious, and keto-friendly meals and snacks.

- Water, coffee, and tea

- All spices and herbs

- Sweeteners, including stevia and erythritol

- Lemon or lime juice

- Low-carb condiments like mayonnaise, mustard, pesto, and sriracha

- Broths (chicken, beef, bone)

- Pickled and fermented foods like pickles, kimchi, and sauerkraut

- Nuts and seeds, including macadamia nuts, pecans, almonds, walnuts, hazelnuts, pine nuts, flaxseed, chia seeds, and pumpkin seeds.

2. Meats

Any type of meat is fine for the keto diet, including chicken, beef, lamb, pork, turkey, game, etc. It's preferable to use grass-fed and/or organic meats if they're available and possible for your budget. You can and should eat the fat on the meat and skin on the chicken.

All wild-caught fish and seafood slide into the keto diet nicely. Try to avoid farmed fish.

Go crazy with the eggs! Use organic eggs from free-range chickens, if possible.

3. Veggies

You can eat all nonstarchy veggies, including broccoli, asparagus, mushrooms, cucumbers, lettuce, onions, peppers, tomatoes, garlic (in small quantities—each clove contains about 1 gram of carbs), Brussels sprouts, eggplant, olives, zucchini, yellow squash, and cauliflower.

Avoid all types of potatoes, yams and sweet potatoes, corn, and legumes like beans, lentils, and peas.

4. Sweeteners

The sweeteners may sound strange if you haven't heard of them before. They both come from natural sources and are safe to use in any quantity.

Stevia is extracted from the leaves of a plant called Stevia rebaudiana. Stevia has zero calories and contains some beneficial micronutrients like magnesium, potassium, and zinc. It's readily available in liquid or powder form online and in most supermarkets. It's much sweeter than sugar, so containers are usually very small—you won't need nearly as much.

Erythritol is a sugar alcohol that is low in calories, about 70 percent as sweet as sugar, and can be found naturally in some fruits and vegetables. Sugar alcohols are indigestible by the human body, so erythritol cannot raise your blood sugar or insulin levels. Several studies have proven it to be safe. Sugar alcohols can sometimes cause temporary digestive discomfort, but out of the few available sugar alcohols like xylitol, maltitol, and sorbitol, erythritol is considered to be the most forgiving and best for everyday use.

5. Fruits

You can eat a small amount of berries every day, such as strawberries, raspberries, blackberries, and blueberries. Lemon and lime juices are great for adding flavor to your meals. Avocados are also low in carbs and full of healthy fat.

Avoid other fruits, as they're loaded with sugar. A single banana can contain around 25 grams of net carbs.

6. Dairy

Eat full-fat dairy like butter, sour cream, heavy (whipping) cream, cheese, cream cheese, and unsweetened yogurt. Although not technically dairy, unsweetened almond and coconut milks are great as well.

Avoid milk and skim milk, as well as sweetened yogurt, as it contains a lot of sugar. Avoid any flavored, low-fat, or fat-free dairy products.

7. Fats and Oils

Avocado oil, olive oil, butter, lard, and bacon fat are great for cooking and consuming. Avocado oil has a high smoke point (it does not burn or smoke until it reaches 520°F), which is ideal for searing meats and frying in a wok. Make sure to avoid oils labeled "blend"; they commonly contain small amounts of the healthy oil and large amounts of unhealthy oils.

KETO Cooking

The ketogenic diet can seem complicated at first, but it is really about simplifying your eating habits. A "plan" can be different for everyone. For example, I always pack keto-friendly snacks when I go out of town and when I have all-day meetings. Otherwise, it is easy to give in to what is available. For others, preparing an entire week's worth of food on the weekend may be the best plan for success.

1. Use the highest-quality ingredients you can afford. Processed and lower-quality foods can cause inflammation in your body, which is what a ketogenic diet is fighting against. So do what you can to keep your diet as clean as possible with real, high-quality foods.

2. Remove non-keto foods from your home. Give away your carb-filled pantry items to your friends, neighbors, coworkers, or a charity. Just get them out of the house to set yourself up for success.

3. Keep your food as simple as possible. Stick to recipes like the ones in this book that use real food and do not have lots of ingredients. Keto is made to be simple.

4. Track your food throughout the day. Get in the habit of entering your meals into an app like Carb Manager. Not every meal has to add up to perfect keto macros, but the more mindful you are throughout the day, the easier it will be to reach your goals. The macro goals you are aiming for every day are in fat, protein, carbs, and calories.

5. Plan your meals. Prepping meals ahead of time so you always have food on hand is the key to success for many people. Make sure your refrigerator and pantry are stocked with staples so that when those cravings hit, you can satisfy them with an appropriate low-carb, high-fat option.

6. Prep and store ingredients ahead of time. Hardboiled eggs make perfect last-minute snacks that you can prepare ahead of time and have ready in the refrigerator. I also like to prepare small zip-top bags of veggies, nuts, slices of cheese, and other keto-friendly snacks, and keep them available in the fridge for grab and go. Also, you will find that rinsing and cutting up vegetables you plan to use for the next week's recipes is a helpful way to cut down on your evening meal-prep time.

7. Cook in bulk. It is usually cheaper to buy meat and poultry in larger quantities, so don't be reluctant to cook a week's worth at one time and store it in the refrigerator and freezer. It will save you a lot of time throughout the week.

8. Don't be afraid of new food combinations. The ketogenic diet gives you the opportunity to get creative with delicious high-fat ingredients you may not be very familiar with.

9. Don't be afraid of salt and seasoning. You can give a dish as simple as eggs a totally different taste profile simply by using different seasonings. Have fun with flavors.

10. Commit. It takes about a month to become fully keto-adapted, which is when your body has fully switched over and has become super-efficient at using fat/ketones as fuel. Keto is meant to be a long-term way of eating, so give your body time to heal and adjust.

Top KETO Diet Tips

1. Decreasing Stress

Chronic stress will severely hinder your body's ability to enter ketosis.

This is because the stress hormone cortisol elevates your blood sugar levels, which prevents your body from burning fats for energy because there is too much sugar in the blood.

If you are currently going through a high stress period in your life, starting the ketogenic diet may not be the best idea.

It's best to begin this nutrition plan when you can keep stress to a minimum and you're able to devote a large portion of your waking hours towards staying in ketosis.

If you definitely want to start a keto diet now, it's still doable.

Just be sure to take steps to reduce the stress in your life such as getting enough sleep, exercising regularly, taking time to do something you enjoy (like listening to your favorite podcast) or adopting relaxation techniques like deep breathing, meditation or yoga.

2. Add More Salt to Your Diet

Many people have a negative stigma when it comes to how much sodium you should be consuming daily.

We have been taught that our sodium intake should be very low but this is typically only the case on high carbohydrate diets.

This is because higher carb diets means naturally higher levels of insulin. When insulin levels are high, your kidneys begin to retain sodium.

When you adopt a low carb, high fat diet like the keto diet, insulin levels are much lower and your body excretes more salt since there are no carbohydrates present in your body to spike insulin and hold onto the sodium.

When you're in ketosis, add an extra three to five grams (3,000 to 5,000 mg) of sodium in your diet.

3. Exercise Frequently

Maintaining a regular exercise schedule while on the keto diet can boost your ketone levels and help you transition into a low carb, high fat lifestyle much quicker than without exercise.

To get into ketosis, your body needs to get rid of any glucose present in the body. Exercising uses different types of energy for fuel including carbohydrates, fats and amino acids.

The more frequently you exercise, the quicker your body depletes its glycogen stores.

Once your body has gotten rid of its glycogen storages, it will seek out other forms of fuel and will turn to fat for energy through ketosis.

Be sure to incorporate a workout regimen that includes both high intensity exercises in conjunction with low intensity steady state exercises like walking or jogging.

This will help you balance your blood sugar and aid your body in entering ketosis.

4. Drink Plenty of Water

Staying hydrated is important no matter what diet you're on but you must pay extra attention when starting out on the ketogenic diet.

This is because your body excretes more water from your body when carbohydrates aren't present.

Aim to drink half of your bodyweight in ounces of water at the minimum.

Be sure to drink more on days where you are sweating more often such as hot summer days or after intense workouts.

5. Count Your Carbs

Measuring your carbohydrate intake is extremely important. Be careful of hidden carbohydrates in certain foods that may seem keto-friendly but are actually loaded with sugars.

Here are some examples of keto foods that may have hidden carbohydrates:

- Chicken wings loaded with barbecue or buffalo sauce
- Milk
- Most fruits (blueberries are fine in small amounts)
- Low-fat foods like yogurt
- Breaded meats

Make sure to look at the nutrition facts of everything you eat until you understand where those hidden carbs are coming from.

You should only be consuming 50 grams maximum in carbohydrates on the ketogenic diet.

When calculating your carb count, you want to determine the net carbs of your total daily intake.

Total carbs – Fiber = Net Carbs

The general rule of thumb is to consume 20 to 30 net carbs daily. If you exercise more frequently, you can get away with the upper threshold and still stay in ketosis.

Chapter 2. Appetizers, Snacks & Side Dishes

Sweet And Hot Nuts

Servings: 12
Cooking Time: 4 Hours
Ingredients:

- ½ pound assorted nuts, raw
- 1/3 cup butter, melted
- 1 teaspoon cayenne pepper or to taste
- 1 tablespoon MCT oil or coconut oil
- 1 packet stevia powder
- ¼ tsp salt

Directions:
1. Place all ingredients in the crockpot.
2. Give it a good stir to combine everything.
3. Close the lid and cook on low for 4 hours.

Nutrition Info:

- Per Servings 2.9g Carbs, 7.0g Protein, 21.6g Fat, 271 Calories

Soy Garlic Mushrooms

Servings: 8
Cooking Time: 10 Minutes
Ingredients:

- 2 pounds mushrooms, sliced
- 3 tablespoons olive oil
- 2 cloves of garlic, minced
- ¼ cup coconut aminos
- 4 tablespoons butter
- Salt and pepper to taste

Directions:
1. Place all ingredients in a dish except for the butter and mix until well-combined.
2. Allow marinating for 2 hours in the fridge.
3. In a large saucepan on medium fire, melt the butter and add mushrooms and sauté for 8 minutes. Season with pepper and salt to taste.
4. Serve and enjoy.

Nutrition Info:

- Per Servings 4.7g Carbs, 3.8g Protein, 11.9g Fat, 152 Calories

Pecorino-mushroom Balls

Servings: 4
Cooking Time: 20 Minutes
Ingredients:

- 2 tbsp butter, softened
- 2 garlic cloves, minced
- 2 cups portobello mushrooms, chopped
- 4 tbsp blanched almond flour
- 4 tbsp ground flax seeds
- 4 tbsp hemp seeds
- 4 tbsp sunflower seeds
- 1 tbsp cajun seasonings

- 1 tsp mustard
- 2 eggs, whisked
- ½ cup pecorino cheese

Directions:
1. Set a pan over medium-high heat and warm 1 tablespoon of butter. Add in mushrooms and garlic and sauté until there is no more water in mushrooms.
2. Place in pecorino cheese, almond flour, hemp seeds, mustard, eggs, sunflower seeds, flax seeds, and Cajun seasonings. Create 4 burgers from the mixture.
3. In a pan, warm the remaining butter; fry the burgers for 7 minutes. Flip them over with a wide spatula and cook for 6 more minutes. Serve while warm.

Nutrition Info:

- Per Servings 7.7g Carbs, 16.8g Protein, 30g Fat, 370 Calories

Cheesy Green Bean Crisps

Servings: 6
Cooking Time: 30 Minutes
Ingredients:

- Cooking spray
- ¼ cup shredded pecorino romano cheese
- ¼ cup pork rind crumbs
- 1 tsp garlic powder
- Salt and black pepper to taste
- 2 eggs
- 1 lb green beans, thread removed

Directions:
1. Preheat oven to 425ºF and line two baking sheets with foil. Grease with cooking spray and set aside.
2. Mix the pecorino, pork rinds, garlic powder, salt, and black pepper in a bowl. Beat the eggs in another bowl. Coat green beans in eggs, then cheese mixture and arrange evenly on the baking sheets.
3. Grease lightly with cooking spray and bake for 15 minutes to be crispy. Transfer to a wire rack to cool before serving. Serve with sugar-free tomato dip.

Nutrition Info:

- Per Servings 3g Carbs, 5g Protein, 19g Fat, 210 Calories

Middle Eastern Style Tuna Salad

Servings: 6
Cooking Time: 0 Minutes
Ingredients:

- ¼ cup chopped pitted ripe olives
- ¼ cup drained and chopped roasted red peppers
- 2 green onions, sliced
- 2 pcs of 6-oz cans of tuna in water, drained and flaked
- 6 cups salad greens like lettuce
- ¼ cup Mayonnaise

Directions:

1. Except for salad greens, mix all the ingredients in a bowl.
2. Arrange salad greens on the bottom of the bowl and top with tuna mixture.
3. Serve and enjoy.
Nutrition Info:
- Per Servings 3g Carbs, 3g Protein, 8g Fat, 92 Calories

Roasted String Beans, Mushrooms & Tomato Plate

Servings: 4
Cooking Time: 32 Minutes
Ingredients:
- 2 cups strings beans, cut in halves
- 1 lb cremini mushrooms, quartered
- 3 tomatoes, quartered
- 2 cloves garlic, minced
- 3 tbsp olive oil
- 3 shallots, julienned
- ½ tsp dried thyme
- Salt and black pepper to season

Directions:
1. Preheat oven to 450°F. In a bowl, mix the strings beans, mushrooms, tomatoes, garlic, olive oil, shallots, thyme, salt, and pepper. Pour the vegetables in a baking sheet and spread them all around.
2. Place the baking sheet in the oven and bake the veggies for 20 to 25 minutes.
Nutrition Info:
- Per Servings 6g Carbs, 6g Protein, 2g Fat, 121 Calories

Mixed Roast Vegetables

Servings: 4
Cooking Time: 40 Minutes
Ingredients:
- 1 large butternut squash, cut into chunks
- ¼ lb shallots, peeled
- 4 rutabagas, cut into chunks
- ¼ lb Brussels sprouts
- 1 sprig rosemary, chopped
- 1 sprig thyme, chopped
- 4 cloves garlic, peeled only
- 3 tbsp olive oil
- Salt and black pepper to taste

Directions:
1. Preheat the oven to 450°F.
2. Pour the butternut squash, shallots, rutabagas, garlic cloves, and brussels sprouts in a bowl. Season with salt, pepper, olive oil, and toss them. Pour the mixture on a baking sheet and sprinkle with the chopped thyme and rosemary. Roast the vegetables for 15–20 minutes.
3. Once ready, remove and spoon into a serving bowl. Serve with oven roasted chicken thighs.
Nutrition Info:
- Per Servings 8g Carbs, 3g Protein, 3g Fat, 65 Calories

Parmesan Crackers With Guacamole

Servings: 4
Cooking Time: 10 Minutes
Ingredients:
- 1 cup finely grated Parmesan cheese
- ¼ tsp sweet paprika
- ¼ tsp garlic powder
- 2 soft avocados, pitted and scooped
- 1 tomato, chopped
- Salt to taste

Directions:
1. To make the chips, preheat oven to 350°F and line a baking sheet with parchment paper.
2. Mix parmesan cheese, paprika, and garlic powder. Spoon 8 teaspoons on the baking sheet creating spaces between each mound. Flatten mounds. Bake for 5 minutes, cool, and remove to a plate.
3. To make the guacamole, mash avocado, with a fork in a bowl, add in tomato and continue to mash until mostly smooth. Season with salt. Serve crackers with guacamole.
Nutrition Info:
- Per Servings 2g Carbs, 10g Protein, 20g Fat, 229 Calories

Walnut Butter On Cracker

Servings: 1
Cooking Time: 0 Minutes
Ingredients:
- 1 tablespoon walnut butter
- 2 pieces Mary's gone crackers

Directions:
1. Spread ½ tablespoon of walnut butter per cracker and enjoy.
Nutrition Info:
- Per Servings 4.0g Carbs, 1.0g Protein, 14.0g Fat, 134 Calories

Coconut And Chocolate Bars

Servings: 6
Cooking Time: 30 Minutes
Ingredients:
- 1 tbsp Stevia
- ¾ cup shredded coconut, unsweetened
- ½ cup ground nuts (almonds, pecans, or walnuts)
- ¼ cup unsweetened cocoa powder
- 4 tbsp coconut oil
- Done

Directions:
1. In a medium bowl, mix shredded coconut, nuts, and cocoa powder.
2. Add Stevia and coconut oil.
3. Mix batter thoroughly.
4. In a 9x9 square inch pan or dish, press the batter and for a 30-minutes place in the freezer.
5. Serve and enjoy.
Nutrition Info:

- Per Servings 2.3g Carbs, 1.6g Protein, 17.8g Fat, 200 Calories

Stuffed Jalapeno

Servings: 4
Cooking Time: 20 Minutes
Ingredients:
- 12 jalapeno peppers, halved lengthwise and seeded
- 2-oz cream cheese softened
- 2-oz shredded cheddar cheese
- ¼ cup almond meal
- Salt and pepper to taste

Directions:
1. Spray a cookie sheet with cooking spray and preheat oven to 400oF.
2. Equally fill each jalapeno with cheddar cheese, cream cheese, and sprinkle almond meal on top. Place on a prepped baking sheet.
3. Pop in oven and bake for 20 minutes.
4. Serve and enjoy.

Nutrition Info:
- Per Servings 7.7g Carbs, 5.9g Protein, 13.2g Fat, 187 Calories

Parmesan Crackers

Servings: 6
Cooking Time: 25 Minutes
Ingredients:
- 1 ⅓ cups coconut flour
- 1 ¼ cup grated Parmesan cheese
- Salt and black pepper to taste
- 1 tsp garlic powder
- ⅓ cup butter, softened
- ⅓ tsp sweet paprika
- ⅓ cup heavy cream
- Water as needed

Directions:
1. Preheat the oven to 350°F.
2. Mix the coconut flour, parmesan cheese, salt, pepper, garlic powder, and paprika in a bowl. Add in the butter and mix well. Top with the heavy cream and mix again until a smooth, thick mixture has formed. Add 1 to 2 tablespoon of water at this point, if it is too thick.
3. Place the dough on a cutting board and cover with plastic wrap. Use a rolling pin to spread out the dough into a light rectangle. Cut cracker squares out of the dough and arrange them on a baking sheet without overlapping. Bake for 20 minutes and transfer to a serving bowl after.

Nutrition Info:
- Per Servings 0.7g Carbs, 5g Protein, 3g Fat, 115 Calories

Tasty Cream Cheese Stuffed Mushrooms

Servings: 2
Cooking Time: 0 Mins

Ingredients:
- 12 mushrooms, keto-friendly
- 1 package cream cheese, softened; low-carb
- 1/4 cup grated Parmesan cheese
- 1/4 teaspoon ground black pepper
- 1/4 teaspoon ground cayenne pepper
- What you'll need from the store cupboard:
- 1 tablespoon olive oil
- 1 tablespoon minced garlic
- 1/4 teaspoon onion powder

Directions:
1. Preheat oven to 350 degrees F.
2. Clean mushrooms; chop stems and discard the cut ends.
3. Heat oil in a large skillet over medium heat, sauté garlic and chopped stems until crispy. Set aside.
4. In a bowl, combine mushroom mixture with cream cheese, Parmensan cheese, black pepper, onion powder and cayenne pepper, stir well.
5. Scoop the filling into each mushroom cap and transfer to a greased baking sheet.
6. Bake for 20 minutes or until liquid has formed under caps.

Nutrition Info:
- Per Servings 1.5g Carbs, 2.7g Protein, 8.2g Fat, 88 Calories

Ricotta And Pomegranate

Servings: 3
Cooking Time: 12 Minutes
Ingredients:
- 1 cup Ricotta cheese
- 3 tablespoons olive oil
- 1/2 cup pomegranate Arils
- 2 tsp thyme, fresh
- 2 cups arugula leaves
- Pepper and salt to taste
- 1/2 tsp grated lemon zest

Directions:
1. Mix all ingredients in a bowl.
2. Toss until well combined.
3. Season with pepper and salt.
4. Serve and enjoy.

Nutrition Info:
- Per Servings 9g Carbs, 11g Protein, 25g Fat, 312 Calories

Apricot And Soy Nut Trail Mix

Servings: 20
Cooking Time: 10 Minutes
Ingredients:
- ¼ cup dried apricots, chopped
- 1 cup pumpkin seeds
- ½ cup roasted cashew nuts
- 1 cup roasted, shelled pistachios
- Salt to taste

- 3 tbsp MCT oil or coconut oil

Directions:
1. In a medium mixing bowl, place all ingredients.
2. Thoroughly combine.
3. Bake in the oven for 10 minutes at 3750F.
4. In 20 small zip-top bags, get ¼ cup of the mixture and place in each bag.
5. One zip-top bag is equal to one serving.
6. If properly stored, this can last up to two weeks.

Nutrition Info:
- Per Servings 4.6g Carbs, 5.2g Protein, 10.75g Fat, 129 Calories

Old Bay Chicken Wings

Servings: 4
Cooking Time: 30 Minutes

Ingredients:
- 3 pounds chicken wings
- ¾ cup almond flour
- 1 tablespoon old bay spices
- 1 teaspoon lemon juice, freshly squeezed
- ½ cup butter
- Salt and pepper to taste

Directions:
1. Preheat oven to 400oF.
2. In a mixing bowl, combine all ingredients except for the butter.
3. Place in an even layer in a baking sheet.
4. Bake for 30 minutes. Halfway through the cooking time, shake the fryer basket for even cooking.
5. Once cooked, drizzle with melted butter.

Nutrition Info:
- Per Servings 1.6g Carbs, 52.5g Protein, 59.2g Fat, 700 Calories

Choco And Coconut Bars

Servings: 9
Cooking Time: 30 Minutes

Ingredients:
- 1 tbsp Stevia
- ¾ cup shredded coconut, unsweetened
- ½ cup ground nuts (almonds, pecans, or walnuts)
- ¼ cup unsweetened cocoa powder
- 4 tbsp coconut oil

Directions:
1. In a medium bowl, mix shredded coconut, nuts, and cocoa powder.
2. Add Stevia and coconut oil.
3. Mix batter thoroughly.
4. In a 9x9 square inch pan or dish, press the batter and for a 30-minutes place in the freezer.
5. Evenly divide into suggested servings and enjoy.

Nutrition Info:
- Per Servings 2.7g Carbs, 1.3g Protein, 9.3g Fat, 99.7 Calories

Balsamic Brussels Sprouts With Prosciutto

Servings: 4
Cooking Time: 40 Minutes

Ingredients:
- 3 tbsp balsamic vinegar
- 1 tbsp erythritol
- ½ tbsp olive oil
- Salt and black pepper to taste
- 1 lb Brussels sprouts, halved
- 5 slices prosciutto, chopped

Directions:
1. Preheat oven to 400ºF and line a baking sheet with parchment paper. Mix balsamic vinegar, erythritol, olive oil, salt, and black pepper and combine with the brussels sprouts in a bowl.
2. Spread the mixture on the baking sheet and roast for 30 minutes until tender on the inside and crispy on the outside. Toss with prosciutto, share among 4 plates, and serve with chicken breasts.

Nutrition Info:
- Per Servings 0g Carbs, 8g Protein, 14g Fat, 166 Calories

Turkey Pastrami & Mascarpone Cheese Pinwheels

Servings: 4
Cooking Time: 40 Minutes

Ingredients:
- Cooking spray
- 8 oz mascarpone cheese
- 10 oz turkey pastrami, sliced
- 10 canned pepperoncini peppers, sliced and drained

Directions:
1. Lay a 12 x 12 plastic wrap on a flat surface and arrange the pastrami all over slightly overlapping each other. Spread the cheese on top of the salami layers and arrange the pepperoncini on top.
2. Hold two opposite ends of the plastic wrap and roll the pastrami. Twist both ends to tighten and refrigerate for 2 hours. Unwrap the salami roll and slice into 2-inch pinwheels. Serve.

Nutrition Info:
- Per Servings 0g Carbs, 13g Protein, 24g Fat, 266 Calories

Zucchini And Cheese Gratin

Servings: 8
Cooking Time: 15 Minutes

Ingredients:
- 5 tablespoons butter
- 1 onion, sliced
- ½ cup heavy cream
- 4 cups raw zucchini, sliced
- 1 ½ cups shredded pepper Jack cheese

- Salt and pepper to taste

Directions:
1. Place all ingredients in a mixing bowl and give a good stir to incorporate everything.
2. Pour the mixture in a heat-proof baking dish.
3. Place in a 350F preheated oven and bake for 15 minutes.
4. Serve and enjoy.

Nutrition Info:
- Per Servings 5.0g Carbs, 8.0g Protein, 20.0g Fat, 280 Calories

Chicken Enchilada Dip

Servings: 16
Cooking Time:240 Minutes

Ingredients:
- 2 pounds cooked rotisserie chicken, shredded
- 1 cup enchilada sauce
- ½ cup cheddar cheese
- 2 stalk green onions, sliced
- 3 tbsp olive oil
- Salt and pepper to taste

Directions:
1. Place all ingredients in the crockpot except for the green onions.
2. Give a good stir to combine everything.
3. Close the lid and cook on low for 4 hours. Mix well and adjust seasoning to taste.
4. Garnish with green onions.

Nutrition Info:
- Per Servings 1.5g Carbs, 16.2g Protein, 13.6g Fat, 178 Calories

Crispy Keto Pork Bites

Servings: 3
Cooking Time: 30 Minutes

Ingredients:
- ½ pork belly, sliced to thin strips
- 1 tablespoon butter
- 1 onion, diced
- 4 tablespoons coconut cream
- Salt and pepper to taste

Directions:
1. Place all ingredients in a mixing bowl and allow to marinate in the fridge for 2 hours.
2. When 2 hours is nearly up, preheat oven to 400oF and lightly grease a cookie sheet with cooking spray.
3. Place the pork strips in an even layer on the cookie sheet.
4. Roast for 30 minutes and turnover halfway through cooking.

Nutrition Info:
- Per Servings 1.9g Carbs, 19.1g Protein, 40.6g Fat, 448 Calories

Baked Cheese & Spinach Balls

Servings: 8
Cooking Time: 30 Minutes

Ingredients:
- ⅓ cup crumbled ricotta cheese
- ¼ tsp nutmeg
- ¼ tsp pepper
- 3 tbsp heavy cream
- 1 tsp garlic powder
- 1 tbsp onion powder
- 2 tbsp butter, melted
- ⅓ cup Parmesan cheese
- 2 eggs
- 1 cup spinach
- 1 cup almond flour

Directions:
1. Place all ingredients in a food processor. Process until smooth. Place in the freezer for about 10 minutes. Make balls out of the mixture and arrange them on a lined baking sheet. Bake at 350ºF for about 10-12 minutes.

Nutrition Info:
- Per Servings 0.8g Carbs, 8g Protein, 15g Fat, 160 Calories

Fat Burger Bombs

Servings: 6
Cooking Time: 20 Minutes

Ingredients:
- 12 slices uncured bacon, chopped
- 1 cup almond flour
- 2 eggs, beaten
- ½ pound ground beef
- 3 tablespoons olive oil
- Salt and pepper to taste

Directions:
1. In a mixing bowl, combine all ingredients except for the olive oil.
2. Use your hands to form small balls with the mixture. Place in a baking sheet and allow it to set in the fridge for at least 2 hours.
3. Once 2 hours is nearly up, preheat oven to 400oF.
4. Place meatballs in a single layer in a baking sheet and brush the meatballs with olive oil on all sides.
5. Cook for 20 minutes.

Nutrition Info:
- Per Servings 1.9g Carbs, 19.1g Protein, 40.6g Fat, 448 Calories

Tuna Topped Pickles

Servings: 5
Cooking Time: 0 Minutes

Ingredients:
- 1 tbsp fresh dill, and more for garnish
- ¼ cup full-fat mayonnaise
- 1 can light flaked tuna, drained
- 5 dill pickles
- ¼ tsp pepper

Directions:

1. Slice pickles in half, lengthwise. With a spoon, deseed the pickles and discard seeds.
2. In a small bowl, mix well the mayo, dill, and tuna using a fork.
3. Evenly divide them into 10 and spread over deseeded pickles.
4. Garnish with more dill on top and sprinkle black pepper.
5. Evenly divide into suggested servings and enjoy.

Nutrition Info:
- Per Servings 4g Carbs, 11g Protein, 14g Fat, 180 Calories

Keto-approved Trail Mix

Servings: 8
Cooking Time: 3 Minutes
Ingredients:
- ¼ cup salted pumpkin seeds
- ½ cup slivered almonds
- ¾ cup roasted pecan halves
- ¼ cup unsweetened cranberries
- ¾ cup toasted coconut flakes

Directions:
1. In a skillet, place almonds and pecans. Heat for 2-3 minutes and let it cool.
2. Once cooled, in a large resealable plastic bag, combine all ingredients.
3. Seal and shake vigorously to mix.
4. Serve and enjoy.

Nutrition Info:
- Per Servings 8.0g Carbs, 4.4g Protein, 14.4g Fat, 184 Calories

Spicy Devilled Eggs With Herbs

Servings: 4
Cooking Time: 30 Minutes
Ingredients:
- 12 large eggs
- 1 ½ cups water
- 6 tbsp mayonnaise
- Salt and chili pepper to taste
- 1 tsp mixed dried herbs
- ½ tsp sugar-free Worcestershire sauce
- ¼ tsp Dijon mustard
- A pinch of sweet paprika
- Chopped parsley to garnish
- Ice water Bath

Directions:
1. Pour the water into a saucepan, add the eggs, and bring to boil on high heat for 10 minutes. Cut the eggs in half lengthways and remove the yolks into a medium bowl. Use a fork to crush the yolks.
2. Add the mayonnaise, salt, chili pepper, dried herbs, Worcestershire sauce, mustard, and paprika. Mix together until a smooth paste has formed. Then, spoon the mixture into the piping bag and fill the egg white holes with it. Garnish with the chopped parsley and serve immediately.

Nutrition Info:
- Per Servings 0.4g Carbs, 6.7g Protein, 9.3g Fat, 112 Calories

Garlic And Basil Mashed Celeriac

Servings: 4
Cooking Time: 30 Minutes
Ingredients:
- 2 lb celeriac, chopped
- 4 cups water
- 2 oz cream cheese
- 2 tbsp butter
- ⅓ cup sour cream
- ½ tsp garlic powder
- 2 tsp dried basil
- Salt and black pepper to taste

Directions:
1. Bring the celeriac and water to boil over high heat on a stovetop for 5 minutes and then reduce the heat to low to simmer for 15 minutes. Drain the celeriac through a colander after.
2. Then, pour the celeriac in a large bowl, add the cream cheese, butter, sour cream, garlic powder, dried basil, salt, and pepper. Mix them with a hand mixer on medium speed until well combined. Serve with pan-grilled salmon.

Nutrition Info:
- Per Servings 6g Carbs, 2.4g Protein, 0.5g Fat, 94 Calories

Bacon-wrapped Jalapeño Peppers

Servings: 6
Cooking Time: 30 Minutes
Ingredients:
- 12 jalapeños
- ¼ cup shredded colby cheese
- 6 oz cream cheese, softened
- 6 slices bacon, halved

Directions:
1. Cut the jalapeno peppers in half, and then remove the membrane and seeds. Combine cheeses and stuff into the pepper halves. Wrap each pepper with a bacon strip and secure with toothpicks.
2. Place the filled peppers on a baking sheet lined with a piece of foil. Bake at 350ºF for 25 minutes until bacon has browned, and crispy and cheese is golden brown on the top. Remove to a paper towel lined plate to absorb grease, arrange on a serving plate, and serve warm.

Nutrition Info:
- Per Servings 0g Carbs, 14g Protein, 17g Fat, 206 Calories

Italian-style Chicken Wraps

Servings: 8
Cooking Time: 20 Minutes
Ingredients:
- ¼ tsp garlic powder
- 8 ounces provolone cheese
- 8 raw chicken tenders
- Salt and black pepper to taste
- 8 prosciutto slices

Directions:
1. Pound the chicken until half an inch thick. Season with salt, black pepper, and garlic powder. Cut the provolone cheese into 8 strips. Place a slice of prosciutto on a flat surface. Place one chicken tender on top. Top with a provolone strip.
2. Roll the chicken and secure with previously soaked skewers. Grill the wraps for 3 minutes per side.

Nutrition Info:
- Per Servings 0.7g Carbs, 17g Protein, 10g Fat, 174 Calories

Baba Ganoush Eggplant Dip

Servings: 4
Cooking Time: 80 Minutes
Ingredients:
- 1 head of garlic, unpeeled
- 1 large eggplant, cut in half lengthwise
- 5 tablespoons olive oil
- Lemon juice to taste
- 2 minced garlic cloves
- What you'll need from the store cupboard:
- Pepper and salt to taste

Directions:
1. With the rack in the middle position, preheat oven to 350°F.
2. Line a baking sheet with parchment paper. Place the eggplant cut side down on the baking sheet.
3. Roast until the flesh is very tender and pulls away easily from the skin, about 1 hour depending on the eggplant's size. Let it cool.
4. Meanwhile, cut the tips off the garlic cloves. Place the cloves in a square of aluminum foil. Fold up the edges of the foil and crimp together to form a tightly sealed packet. Roast alongside the eggplant until tender, about 20 minutes. Let cool.
5. Mash the cloves by pressing with a fork.
6. With a spoon, scoop the flesh from the eggplant and place it in the bowl of a food processor. Add the mashed garlic, oil and lemon juice. Process until smooth. Season with pepper.

Nutrition Info:
- Per Servings 10.2g Carbs, 1.6g Protein, 17.8g Fat, 192 Calories

Spicy Chicken Cucumber Bites

Servings: 6

Cooking Time: 5 Minutes
Ingredients:
- 2 cucumbers, sliced with a 3-inch thickness
- 2 cups small dices leftover chicken
- ¼ jalapeño pepper, seeded and minced
- 1 tbsp Dijon mustard
- ⅓ cup mayonnaise
- Salt and black pepper to taste

Directions:
1. Cut mid-level holes in cucumber slices with a knife and set aside. Combine chicken, jalapeno pepper, mustard, mayonnaise, salt, and black pepper to be evenly mixed. Fill cucumber holes with chicken mixture and serve.

Nutrition Info:
- Per Servings 0g Carbs, 10g Protein, 14g Fat, 170 Calories

Cheesy Lettuce Rolls

Servings: 6
Cooking Time: 10 Minutes
Ingredients:
- ½ pound gouda cheese, grated
- ½ pound feta cheese, crumbled
- 1 tsp taco seasoning mix
- 2 tbsp olive oil
- 1 ½ cups guacamole
- 1 cup buttermilk
- A head lettuce

Directions:
1. Mix both types of cheese with taco seasoning mix. Set pan over medium heat and warm olive oil. Spread the shredded cheese mixture all over the pan. Fry for 5 minutes, turning once.
2. Arrange some of the cheese mixture on each lettuce leaf, top with buttermilk and guacamole, then roll up, folding in the ends to secure and serve.

Nutrition Info:
- Per Servings 4.9g Carbs, 19.5g Protein, 30g Fat, 370 Calories

Squid Salad With Mint, Cucumber & Chili Dressing

Servings: 4
Cooking Time: 30 Minutes
Ingredients:
- 4 medium squid tubes, cut into strips
- ½ cup mint leaves
- 2 medium cucumbers, halved and cut in strips
- ½ cup coriander leaves, reserve the stems
- ½ red onion, finely sliced
- Salt and black pepper to taste
- 1 tsp fish sauce
- 1 red chili, roughly chopped
- 1 tsp swerve
- 1 clove garlic

- 2 limes, juiced
- 1 tbsp chopped coriander
- 1tsp olive oil

Directions:

1. In a salad bowl, mix mint leaves, cucumber strips, coriander leaves, and red onion. Season with salt, pepper and a little drizzle of olive oil; set aside. In the mortar, pound the coriander stems, red chili, and swerve into a paste using the pestle. Add the fish sauce and lime juice, and mix with the pestle.

2. Heat a skillet over high heat on a stovetop and sear the squid on both sides to lightly brown, about 5 minutes. Pour the squid on the salad and drizzle with the chili dressing. Toss the ingredients with two spoons, garnish with coriander, and serve the salad as a single dish or with some more seafood.

Nutrition Info:

- Per Servings 2.1g Carbs, 24.6g Protein, 22.5g Fat, 318 Calories

Reese Cups

Servings: 12
Cooking Time: 1 Minute
Ingredients:

- ¼ cup unsweetened shredded coconut
- 1 cup almond butter
- ½ cup dark chocolate chips
- 1 tablespoon Stevia
- 1 tablespoon coconut oil

Directions:

1. Line 12 muffin tins with 12 muffin liners.

2. Place the almond butter, honey, and oil in a glass bowl and microwave for 30 seconds or until melted. Divide the mixture into 12 muffin tins. Let it cool for 30 minutes in the fridge.

3. Add the shredded coconuts and mix until evenly distributed.

4. Pour the remaining melted chocolate on top of the coconuts. Freeze for an hour.

5. Carefully remove the chocolates from the muffin tins to create perfect Reese cups.

6. Serve and enjoy.

Nutrition Info:

- Per Servings 10.7g Carbs, 5.0g Protein, 17.1g Fat, 214 Calories

Onion Cheese Muffins

Servings: 6
Cooking Time: 20 Minutes
Ingredients:

- ¼ cup Colby jack cheese, shredded
- ¼ cup shallots, minced
- 1 cup almond flour
- 1 egg
- 3 tbsp sour cream
- ½ tsp salt

- 3 tbsp melted butter or oil

Directions:

1. Line 6 muffin tins with 6 muffin liners. Set aside and preheat oven to 350oF.

2. In a bowl, stir the dry and wet ingredients alternately. Mix well using a spatula until the consistency of the mixture becomes even.

3. Scoop a spoonful of the batter to the prepared muffin tins.

4. Bake for 20 minutes in the oven until golden brown.

5. Serve and enjoy.

Nutrition Info:

- Per Servings 4.6g Carbs, 6.3g Protein, 17.4g Fat, 193 Calories

Roasted Stuffed Piquillo Peppers

Servings: 8
Cooking Time: 20 Minutes
Ingredients:

- 8 canned roasted piquillo peppers
- 1 tbsp olive oil
- 3 slices prosciutto, cut into thin slices
- 1 tbsp balsamic vinegar
- Filling:
- 8 ounces goat cheese
- 3 tbsp heavy cream
- 3 tbsp chopped parsley
- ½ tsp minced garlic
- 1 tbsp olive oil
- 1 tbsp chopped mint

Directions:

1. Mix all filling ingredients in a bowl. Place in a freezer bag, press down and squeeze, and cut off the bottom. Drain and deseed the peppers. Squeeze about 2 tbsp of the filling into each pepper.

2. Wrap a prosciutto slice onto each pepper. Secure with toothpicks. Arrange them on a serving platter. Sprinkle the olive oil and vinegar over.

Nutrition Info:

- Per Servings 2.5g Carbs, 6g Protein, 11g Fat, 132 Calories

Bacon Mashed Cauliflower

Servings: 6
Cooking Time: 40 Minutes
Ingredients:

- 6 slices bacon
- 3 heads cauliflower, leaves removed
- 2 cups water
- 2 tbsp melted butter
- ½ cup buttermilk
- Salt and black pepper to taste
- ¼ cup grated yellow cheddar cheese
- 2 tbsp chopped chives

Directions:

1. Preheat oven to 350ºF. Fry bacon in a heated skillet over medium heat for 5 minutes until crispy. Remove to a paper towel-lined plate, allow to cool, and crumble. Set aside and keep bacon fat.
2. Boil cauli heads in water in a pot over high heat for 7 minutes, until tender. Drain and put in a bowl.
3. Include butter, buttermilk, salt, black pepper, and puree using a hand blender until smooth and creamy. Lightly grease a casserole dish with the bacon fat and spread the mash in it.
4. Sprinkle with cheddar cheese and place under the broiler for 4 minutes on high until the cheese melts. Remove and top with bacon and chopped chives. Serve with pan-seared scallops.

Nutrition Info:
- Per Servings 6g Carbs, 14g Protein, 25g Fat, 312 Calories

Boiled Stuffed Eggs

Servings: 6
Cooking Time: 30 Minutes
Ingredients:
- 6 eggs
- 1 tbsp green tabasco
- ⅓ cup mayonnaise
- Salt to taste

Directions:
1. Place the eggs in a saucepan and cover with salted water. Bring to a boil over medium heat. Boil for 10 minutes. Place the eggs in an ice bath and let cool for 10 minutes.
2. Peel and slice in half lengthwise. Scoop out the yolks to a bowl; mash with a fork. Whisk together the tabasco, mayonnaise, mashed yolks, and salt, in a bowl. Spoon this mixture into egg white.

Nutrition Info:
- Per Servings 5g Carbs, 6g Protein, 17g Fat, 178 Calories

Cobb Salad With Blue Cheese Dressing

Servings: 6
Cooking Time: 2 Hours 40 Minutes
Ingredients:
- ½ cup buttermilk
- 1 cup mayonnaise
- 2 tbsp sugar-free Worcestershire sauce
- ½ cup sour cream
- 1 ½ cup crumbled blue cheese
- Salt and black pepper to taste
- 2 tbsp chopped chives
- 6 eggs
- 1 cup water
- Ice bath
- 2 chicken breasts, boneless and skinless
- Salt and black pepper to taste
- 5 strips bacon
- 1 iceberg lettuce, cut into chunks
- 1 romaine lettuce, chopped
- 1 bibb lettuce, cored and leaves removed
- 2 avocado, pitted and diced
- 2 large tomatoes, chopped
- ½ cup crumbled blue cheese
- 2 scallions, chopped

Directions:
1. In a bowl, whisk the buttermilk, mayonnaise, Worcestershire sauce, and sour cream. Stir in the blue cheese, salt, pepper, and chives. Place in the refrigerator to chill for 2 hours.
2. Bring the eggs to boil in salted water over medium heat for 10 minutes. Once ready, drain the eggs and transfer to the ice bath. Peel and chop the eggs. Set aside.
3. Preheat the grill pan over high heat. Season the chicken with salt and pepper. Grill for 3 minutes on each side. Remove to a plate to cool for 3 minutes, and cut into bite-size chunks.
4. Fry the bacon in another pan set over medium heat until crispy, about 6 minutes. Remove, let cool for 2 minutes, and chop.
5. Arrange the lettuce leaves in a salad bowl and in single piles, add the avocado, tomatoes, eggs, bacon, and chicken. Sprinkle the blue cheese over the salad as well as the scallions and black pepper.
6. Drizzle the blue cheese dressing on the salad and serve with low carb bread.

Nutrition Info:
- Per Servings 2g Carbs, 23g Protein, 14g Fat, 122 Calories

Nutty Avocado Crostini With Nori

Servings: 4
Cooking Time: 12 Minutes
Ingredients:
- 8 slices low carb baguette
- 4 nori sheets
- 1 cup mashed avocado
- ⅓ tsp salt
- 1 tsp lemon juice
- 1 ½ tbsp coconut oil
- ⅓ cup chopped raw walnuts
- 1 tbsp chia seeds

Directions:
1. In a bowl, flake the nori sheets into the smallest possible pieces.
2. In another bowl, mix the avocado, salt, and lemon juice, and stir in half of the nori flakes. Set aside.
3. Place the baguette on a baking sheet and toast in a broiler on medium heat for 2 minutes, making sure not to burn. Remove the crostini after and brush with coconut oil on both sides.
4. Top each crostini with the avocado mixture and garnish with the chia seeds, chopped walnuts, Serve the snack immediately.

Nutrition Info:

- Per Servings 2.8g Carbs, 13.7g Protein, 12.2g Fat, 195 Calories

Basil Keto Crackers

Servings: 6
Cooking Time: 15 Minutes
Ingredients:
- 1 ¼ cups almond flour
- ½ teaspoon baking powder
- ¼ teaspoon dried basil powder
- A pinch of cayenne pepper powder
- 1 clove of garlic, minced
- What you'll need from the store cupboard:
- Salt and pepper to taste
- 3 tablespoons oil

Directions:
1. Preheat oven to 350oF and lightly grease a cookie sheet with cooking spray.
2. Mix everything in a mixing bowl to create a dough.
3. Transfer the dough on a clean and flat working surface and spread out until 2mm thick. Cut into squares.
4. Place gently in an even layer on the prepped cookie sheet. Cook for 10 minutes.
5. Cook in batches.
6. Serve and enjoy.

Nutrition Info:
- Per Servings 2.9g Carbs, 5.3g Protein, 19.3g Fat, 205 Calories

Spinach Turnip Salad With Bacon

Servings: 4
Cooking Time: 40 Minutes
Ingredients:
- 6 turnips, cut into wedges
- 1 tsp olive oil
- 1 cup baby spinach chopped
- 3 radishes, sliced
- 3 bacon slices, sliced
- 4 tbsp sour cream
- 2 tsp mustard seeds
- 1 tsp Dijon mustard
- 1 tbsp red wine vinegar
- Salt and black pepper to taste
- 1 tbsp chopped chives

Directions:
1. Preheat the oven to 400ºF. Line a baking sheet with parchment paper, toss the turnips with pepper, drizzle with the olive oil, and bake for 25 minutes, turning halfway. Let cool.
2. Spread the baby spinach in the bottom of a salad bowl and top with the radishes. Remove the turnips to the salad bowl. Fry the bacon in a skillet over medium heat until crispy, about 5 minutes.
3. Mix the sour cream, mustard seeds, Dijon mustard, vinegar, and salt with the bacon. Add a little water to deglaze the bottom of the skillet and turn off the heat.

4. Pour the bacon mixture over the vegetables, scatter the chives over it, and season with black pepper.Serve the salad with grilled pork chops.
Nutrition Info:
- Per Servings 3.1g Carbs, 9.5g Protein, 18.3g Fat, 193 Calories

Mozzarella & Prosciutto Wraps

Servings: 6
Cooking Time: 15 Minutes
Ingredients:
- 6 thin prosciutto slices
- 18 basil leaves
- 18 mozzarella ciliegine

Directions:
1. Cut the prosciutto slices into three strips. Place basil leaves at the end of each strip. Top with mozzarella. Wrap the mozzarella in prosciutto. Secure with toothpicks.
Nutrition Info:
- Per Servings 0.1g Carbs, 13g Protein, 12g Fat, 163 Calories

Simple Tender Crisp Cauli-bites

Servings: 3
Cooking Time: 10 Minutes
Ingredients:
- 2 cups cauliflower florets
- 2 clove garlic minced
- 4 tablespoons olive oil
- ¼ tsp salt
- ½ tsp pepper

Directions:
1. In a small bowl, mix well olive oil salt, pepper, and garlic.
2. Place cauliflower florets on a baking pan. Drizzle with seasoned oil and toss well to coat.
3. Evenly spread in a single layer and place a pan on the top rack of the oven.
4. Broil on low for 5 minutes. Turnover florets and return to the oven.
5. Continue cooking for another 5 minutes.
6. Serve and enjoy.

Nutrition Info:
- Per Servings 4.9g Carbs, 1.7g Protein, 18g Fat, 183 Calories

Garlic Flavored Kale Taters

Servings: 4
Cooking Time: 20 Minutes
Ingredients:
- 4 cups kale, rinsed and chopped
- 2 cups cauliflower florets, finely chopped
- 2 tbsp almond milk
- 1 clove of garlic, minced
- 3 tablespoons oil
- 1/8 teaspoon black pepper

- cooking spray

Directions:

1. Heat oil in a large skillet and sauté the garlic for 2 minutes. Add the kale until it wilts. Transfer to a large bowl.
2. Add the almond milk. Season with pepper to taste.
3. Evenly divide into 4 and form patties.
4. Lightly grease a baking pan with cooking spray. Place patties on pan. Place pan on the top rack of the oven and broil on low for 6 minutes. Turnover patties and cook for another 4 minutes.
5. Serve and enjoy.

Nutrition Info:

- Per Servings 5g Carbs, 2g Protein, 11g Fat, 117 Calories

Cranberry Sauce Meatballs

Servings: 2
Cooking Time: 25 Mins
Ingredients:

- 1 pound lean ground beef
- 1 egg
- 2 tablespoons water
- 1/2 cup cauliflower rice
- 3 tablespoons minced onion
- 1 can jellied cranberry sauce, keto-friendly
- 3/4 cup chili sauce

Directions:

1. Preheat oven to 350 degrees F.
2. Mix the ground beef, egg, water, cauliflower rice and minced onions together until well combined. Form into small meatballs and place on a rack over a foil-lined baking sheet.
3. Bake the meatballs for 20 to 25 minutes, turning halfway through.
4. Combine sauce ingredients in a large saucepan over low heat, toss with meatballs and allow to simmer on low for 1 hour.
5. Serve and garnish with parsley if desired.

Nutrition Info:

- Per Servings 8.6g Carbs, 9.8g Protein, 10.2g Fat, 193 Calories

Dill Pickles With Tuna-mayo Topping

Servings: 12
Cooking Time: 40 Minutes
Ingredients:

- 18 ounces canned and drained tuna
- 6 large dill pickles
- ¼ tsp garlic powder
- ⅓ cup sugar-free mayonnaise
- 1 tbsp onion flakes

Directions:

1. Combine the mayonnaise, tuna, onion flakes, and garlic powder in a bowl. Cut the pickles in half lengthwise. Top each half with tuna mixture. Place in the fridge for 30 minutes before serving.

Nutrition Info:

- Per Servings 1.5g Carbs, 11g Protein, 10g Fat, 118 Calories

Teriyaki Chicken Wings

Servings: 9
Cooking Time: 50 Minutes
Ingredients:

- 3 pounds chicken wings
- 1 onion, chopped
- 2 cups commercial teriyaki sauce
- 1 tablespoon chili garlic paste
- 2 teaspoons ginger paste
- Salt and pepper to taste

Directions:

1. In a heavy-bottomed pot, place on medium-high fire and lightly grease with cooking spray.
2. Pan fry chicken for 4 minutes per side. Cook in two batches.
3. Stir in remaining ingredients in a pot, along with the chicken.
4. Cover and cook on low fire for 30 minutes, stirring every now and then. Continue cooking until desired sauce thickness is achieved.
5. Serve and enjoy.

Nutrition Info:

- Per Servings 5.4g Carbs, 34.3g Protein, 5.4g Fat, 214 Calories

Duo-cheese Chicken Bake

Servings: 6
Cooking Time: 30 Minutes
Ingredients:

- 2 tbsp olive oil
- 8 oz cream cheese
- 1 lb ground chicken
- 1 cup buffalo sauce
- 1 cup ranch dressing
- 3 cups grated yellow cheddar cheese

Directions:

1. Preheat oven to 350ºF. Lightly grease a baking sheet with a cooking spray. Warm the oil in a skillet over medium heat and brown the chicken for a couple of minutes, take off the heat, and set aside.
2. Spread cream cheese at the bottom of the baking sheet, top with chicken, pour buffalo sauce over, add ranch dressing, and sprinkle with cheddar cheese. Bake for 23 minutes until cheese has melted and golden brown on top. Remove and serve with veggie sticks or low carb crackers.

Nutrition Info:

- Per Servings 3g Carbs, 14g Protein, 16g Fat, 216 Calories

Easy Garlic Keto Bread

Servings: 1
Cooking Time: 1 Minute 30 Seconds
Ingredients:
- 1 large egg
- 1 tbsp milk
- 1 tbsp coconut flour
- 1 tbsp almond flour
- ¼ tsp baking powder
- Salt to taste

Directions:
1. Mix all ingredients in a bowl until well combined.
2. Pour into a mug and place in the microwave oven.
3. Cook for 1 minute and 30 seconds.
4. Once cooked, invert the mug.
5. Allow to cool before slicing.

Nutrition Info:
- Per Servings 3g Carbs, 4g Protein, 7g Fat, 75 Calories

Air Fryer Garlic Chicken Wings

Servings: 4
Cooking Time: 25 Minutes
Ingredients:
- 16 pieces chicken wings
- ¾ cup almond flour
- 4 tablespoons minced garlic
- ¼ cup butter, melted
- 2 tablespoons Stevia powder
- Salt and pepper to taste

Directions:
1. Preheat oven to 400oF.
2. In a mixing bowl, combine the chicken wings, almond flour, Stevia powder, and garlic. Season with salt and pepper to taste.
3. Place in a lightly greased cookie sheet in an even layer and cook for 25 minutes.
4. Halfway through the cooking time, turnover chicken.
5. Once cooked, place in a bowl and drizzle with melted butter. Toss to coat.
6. Serve and enjoy.

Nutrition Info:
- Per Servings 7.8g Carbs, 23.7g Protein, 26.9g Fat, 365 Calories

Cheese-jalapeno Mushrooms

Servings: 8
Cooking Time: 20 Mins
Ingredients:
- 2 slices bacon
- 1 package cream cheese, softened; low-carb
- 3 tablespoons shredded Cheddar cheese
- 1 jalapeno pepper, ribs and seeds removed, finely chopped
- 8 mushrooms, stems removed and chopped and caps reserved; keto-friendly

- Salt and pepper to taste
- Cooking spray

Directions:
1. Preheat the oven to 400 degrees F.
2. In a large bowl, combine bacon, cream cheese, cheese, jalapenos, salt and pepper. Mix well.
3. Spoon the bacon filling into each mushroom cap. Then transfer the stuffed mushroom caps to a baking dish or sheet sprayed with cooking spray.
4. Bake until the mushroom caps are cooked, about 15-20 minutes.
5. Serve and enjoy.

Nutrition Info:
- Per Servings 2.5g Carbs, 6.1g Protein, 13.4g Fat, 151 Calories

Crab Stuffed Mushrooms

Servings: 3
Cooking Time: 25 Minutes
Ingredients:
- 2 tbsp minced green onion
- 1 cup cooked crabmeat, chopped finely
- ¼ cup Monterey Jack cheese, shredded
- 1 tsp lemon juice
- ¼ lb, fresh button mushrooms
- Pepper and salt to taste
- 3 tablespoons olive oil

Directions:
1. Destem mushrooms, wash, and drain well.
2. Chop mushroom stems.
3. Preheat oven to 400oF and lightly grease a baking pan with cooking spray.
4. In a small bowl, whisk well green onion, crabmeat, lemon juice, dill, and chopped mushroom stems.
5. Evenly spread mushrooms on prepared pan with cap sides up. Evenly spoon crabmeat mixture on top of mushroom caps.
6. Pop in the oven and bake for 20 minutes.
7. Remove from oven and sprinkle cheese on top.
8. Return to oven and broil for 3 minutes.
9. Serve and enjoy.

Nutrition Info:
- Per Servings 10g Carbs, 7.9g Protein, 17.3g Fat, 286 Calories

Grilled Cheese Bacon Jalapeno

Servings: 2
Cooking Time: 40 Mins
Ingredients:
- 8 ounces cream cheese
- 2 tablespoons grated Parmesan cheese
- 1 1/2 cups shredded Cheddar cheese
- 16 whole jalapeno peppers with stems
- 8 slices bacon, cut in half crosswise
- Oil spray
- 1 1/2 teaspoons garlic powder

Directions:

1. Preheat a grill over medium heat and brush grill grates with oil.
2. Combine cream cheese, Parmesan cheese, cheddar cheese and garlic powder in a small bowl, toss well.
3. Cut the jalapeños in half lengthwise. Using a small spoon, scrape out seeds & membranes.
4. Stuff the cheese mixture into the jalapeno halves. Wrap each jalapeno completely with bacon. Secure with toothpicks.
5. Place jalapenos on the grill and grill until cheese mixture is hot and bubbling around the edges, about 30 to 40 minutes.

Nutrition Info:

- Per Servings 1.6g Carbs, 5.8g Protein, 15g Fat, 164 Calories

Garlicky Cheddar Biscuits

Servings: 4
Cooking Time: 20 Minutes
Ingredients:

- ⅓ cup almond flour
- 2 tsp garlic powder
- Salt to taste
- 1 tsp low carb baking powder
- 5 eggs
- ⅓ cup butter, melted
- 1 ¼ cup grated sharp cheddar cheese
- ⅓ cup Greek yogurt

Directions:

1. Preheat the oven to 350ºF. Mix the flour, garlic powder, salt, baking powder, and cheddar, in a bowl.
2. In a separate bowl, whisk the eggs, butter, and Greek yogurt, and then pour the resulting mixture into the dry ingredients. Stir well until a dough-like consistency has formed.
3. Fetch half soupspoons of the mixture onto a baking sheet with 2-inch intervals between each batter. Bake them in the oven for 12 minutes to be golden brown and remove them after. Serve.

Nutrition Info:

- Per Servings 1.4g Carbs, 5.4g Protein, 14.2g Fat, 153 Calories

Jalapeno Popper Spread

Servings: 8
Cooking Time: 3 Mins
Ingredients:

- 2 packages cream cheese, softened; low-carb
- 1 cup. mayonnaise
- 1 can chopped green chilies, drained
- 2 ounces canned diced jalapeno peppers, drained
- 1 cup. grated Parmesan cheese

Directions:

1. Combine cream cheese and mayonnaise in a bowl until incorporated. Add in jalapeno peppers and green chilies. In a microwave safe bowl, spread jalapeno peppers mixture and sprinkle with Parmesan cheese.
2. Microwave jalapeno peppers mixture on High about 3 minutes or until warm.

Nutrition Info:

- Per Servings 1g Carbs, 2.1g Protein, 11.1g Fat, 110 Calories

Easy Baked Parmesan Chips

Servings: 10
Cooking Time: 10 Minutes
Ingredients:

- 1 cup grated Parmesan cheese, low fat
- 1 tablespoon olive oil

Directions:

1. Lightly grease a cookie sheet and preheat oven to 400°F.
2. Evenly sprinkle parmesan cheese on a cookie sheet into 10 circles. Place them about ½-inch apart.
3. Drizzle with oil
4. Bake until lightly browned and crisped.
5. Let it cool, evenly divide into suggested servings and enjoy.

Nutrition Info:

- Per Servings 1.4g Carbs, 2.8g Protein, 12.8g Fat, 142 Calories

Bacon-flavored Kale Chips

Servings: 6
Cooking Time: 25 Minutes
Ingredients:

- 2 tbsp butter
- ¼ cup bacon grease
- 1-lb kale, around 1 bunch
- 1 to 2 tsp salt

Directions:

1. Remove the rib from kale leaves and tear it into 2-inch pieces.
2. Clean the kale leaves thoroughly and dry them inside a salad spinner.
3. In a skillet, add the butter to the bacon grease and warm the two fats under low heat. Add salt and stir constantly.
4. Set aside and let it cool.
5. Put the dried kale in a Ziploc back and add the cool liquid bacon grease and butter mixture.
6. Seal the Ziploc back and gently shake the kale leaves with the butter mixture. The leaves should have this shiny consistency, which means that they are coated evenly with the fat.
7. Pour the kale leaves on a cookie sheet and sprinkle more salt if necessary.
8. Bake for 25 minutes inside a preheated 350oF oven or until the leaves start to turn brown as well as crispy.

Nutrition Info:

- Per Servings 6.6g Carbs, 3.3g Protein, 13.1g Fat, 148 Calories

Zucchini Gratin With Feta Cheese

Servings: 6
Cooking Time: 65 Minutes
Ingredients:
- Cooking spray
- 2 lb zucchinis, sliced
- 2 red bell peppers, seeded and sliced
- Salt and black pepper to taste
- 1 ½ cups crumbled feta cheese
- ⅓ cup crumbled feta cheese for topping
- 2 tbsp butter
- ¼ tsp xanthan gum
- ½ cup heavy whipping cream

Directions:
1. Preheat oven to 370ºF. Place the sliced zucchinis in a colander over the sink, sprinkle with salt and let sit for 20 minutes. Transfer to paper towels to drain the excess liquid.
2. Grease a baking dish with cooking spray and make a layer of zucchini and bell peppers in the dish overlapping one on another. Season with black pepper, and sprinkle with some feta cheese. Repeat the layering process a second time.
3. Combine the butter, xanthan gum, and whipping cream in a microwave dish for 2 minutes, stir to mix completely, and pour over the vegetables. Top with remaining feta cheese.
4. Bake the gratin for 45 minutes to be golden brown on top. Cut out slices and serve with kale salad.

Nutrition Info:
- Per Servings 4g Carbs, 14g Protein, 21g Fat, 264 Calories

Bacon Jalapeno Poppers

Servings: 8
Cooking Time: 10 Minutes
Ingredients:
- 4-ounce cream cheese
- ¼ cup cheddar cheese, shredded
- 1 teaspoon paprika
- 16 fresh jalapenos, sliced lengthwise and seeded
- 16 strips of uncured bacon, cut into half
- Salt and pepper to taste

Directions:
1. Preheat oven to 400oF.
2. In a mixing bowl, mix the cream cheese, cheddar cheese, salt, and paprika until well-combined.
3. Scoop half a teaspoon onto each half of jalapeno peppers.
4. Use a thin strip of bacon and wrap it around the cheese-filled jalapeno half.
5. Place in a single layer in a lightly greased baking sheet and roast for 10 minutes.
6. Serve and enjoy.

Nutrition Info:
- Per Servings 3.2g Carbs, 10.6g Protein, 18.9g Fat, 225 Calories

Tofu Stuffed Peppers

Servings: 8
Cooking Time: 10 Minutes
Ingredients:
- 1 package firm tofu, crumbled
- 1 onion, finely chopped
- ½ teaspoon turmeric powder
- 1 teaspoon coriander powder
- 8 banana peppers, top-end sliced and seeded
- Salt and pepper to taste
- 3 tablespoons oil

Directions:
1. Preheat oven to 400oF.
2. In a mixing bowl, combine the tofu, onion, coconut oil, turmeric powder, red chili powder, coriander powder, and salt. Mix until well-combined.
3. Scoop the tofu mixture into the hollows of the banana peppers.
4. Place the stuffed peppers in one layer in a lightly greased baking sheet.
5. Cook for 10 minutes.
6. Serve and enjoy.

Nutrition Info:
- Per Servings 4.1g Carbs, 1.2g Protein, 15.6g Fat, 187 Calories

Cajun Spiced Pecans

Servings: 12
Cooking Time: 10 Minutes
Ingredients:
- 1-pound pecan halves
- ¼ cup melted butter
- 1 packet Cajun seasoning mix
- ¼ teaspoon ground cayenne pepper
- Salt and pepper to taste

Directions:
1. Preheat oven to 400oF.
2. In a small bowl, whisk well-melted butter, Cajun seasoning, cayenne, salt, and pepper.
3. Place pecan halves on a cookie sheet. Drizzle with sauce. Toss well to coat.
4. Pop in the oven and roast for 10 minutes.
5. Let it cool completely, serve, and enjoy.

Nutrition Info:
- Per Servings 5.7g Carbs, 3.5g Protein, 31.1g Fat, 297.1 Calories

Lemony Fried Artichokes

Servings: 4
Cooking Time: 20 Minutes
Ingredients:
- 12 fresh baby artichokes
- 2 tbsp lemon juice
- 2 tbsp olive oil
- Salt to taste

Directions:
1. Slice the artichokes vertically into narrow wedges. Drain on paper towels before frying.
2. Heat olive oil in a cast-iron skillet over high heat. Fry the artichokes until browned and crispy. Drain excess oil on paper towels. Sprinkle with salt and lemon juice.

Nutrition Info:
- Per Servings 2.9g Carbs, 2g Protein, 2.4g Fat, 35 Calories

Baked Vegetable Side

Servings: 4
Cooking Time: 15 Minutes
Ingredients:
- 1 large zucchini, sliced
- 1 bell pepper, sliced
- ½ cup peeled garlic cloves, sliced
- A dash of oregano
- 4 tablespoons olive oil
- Salt and pepper to taste

Directions:
1. Place all ingredients in a mixing bowl. Stir to coat everything.
2. Place in a baking sheet.
3. Bake in a 350F preheated oven for 15 minutes.
4. Serve and enjoy.

Nutrition Info:
- Per Servings 10.0g Carbs, 3.0g Protein, 23.0g Fat, 191 Calories

Chocolate Mousse

Servings: 4
Cooking Time: 0 Minutes
Ingredients:
- 1 large, ripe avocado
- 1/4 cup sweetened almond milk
- 1 tbsp coconut oil
- 1/4 cup cocoa or cacao powder
- 1 tsp vanilla extract

Directions:
1. In a food processor, process all ingredients until smooth and creamy.
2. Transfer to a lidded container and chill for at least 4 hours.
3. Serve and enjoy.

Nutrition Info:
- Per Servings 6.9g Carbs, 1.2g Protein, 11.0g Fat, 125 Calories

Parsnip And Carrot Fries With Aioli

Servings: 4
Cooking Time: 40 Minutes
Ingredients:
- 4 tbsp mayonnaise
- 2 garlic cloves, minced
- Salt and black pepper to taste
- 3 tbsp lemon juice
- Parsnip and Carrots Fries:
- 6 medium parsnips, julienned
- 3 large carrots, julienned
- 2 tbsp olive oil
- 5 tbsp chopped parsley
- Salt and black pepper to taste

Directions:
1. Preheat the oven to 400ºF. Make the aioli by mixing the mayonnaise with garlic, salt, pepper, and lemon juice; then refrigerate for 30 minutes.
2. Spread the parsnip and carrots on a baking sheet. Drizzle with olive oil, sprinkle with salt, and pepper, and rub the seasoning into the veggies. Bake for 35 minutes. Remove and transfer to a plate. Garnish the vegetables with parsley and serve with the chilled aioli.

Nutrition Info:
- Per Servings 4.4g Carbs, 2.1g Protein, 4.1g Fat, 205 Calories

Cheddar Cheese Chips

Servings: 4
Cooking Time: 8 Minutes
Ingredients:
- 8 oz cheddar cheese or provolone cheese or Edam cheese, in slices
- ½ tsp paprika powder

Directions:
1. Line baking sheet with foil and preheat oven to 400F.
2. Place cheese slices on a baking sheet and sprinkle the paprika powder on top.
3. Pop in the oven and bake for 8 to 10 minutes.
4. Pay an attention when the timer reaches 6 to 7 minutes as a burnt cheese tastes bitter.
5. Serve and enjoy.

Nutrition Info:
- Per Servings 2.0g Carbs, 13.0g Protein, 19.0g Fat, 228 Calories

Cardamom And Cinnamon Fat Bombs

Servings: 10
Cooking Time: 3 Minutes
Ingredients:
- ¼ tsp ground cardamom (green)
- ¼ tsp ground cinnamon
- ½ cup unsweetened shredded coconut
- ½ tsp vanilla extract
- 3-oz unsalted butter, room temperature

Directions:
1. Place a nonstick pan on medium fire and toast coconut until lightly browned.
2. In a bowl, mix all ingredients.
3. Evenly roll into 10 equal balls.
4. Let it cool in the fridge.
5. Serve and enjoy.

Nutrition Info:
- Per Servings 0.4g Carbs, 0.4g Protein, 10.0g Fat, 90 Calories

Party Bacon And Pistachio Balls

Servings: 8
Cooking Time: 45 Minutes
Ingredients:
- 8 bacon slices, cooked and chopped
- 8 ounces Liverwurst
- ¼ cup chopped pistachios
- 1 tsp Dijon mustard
- 6 ounces cream cheese

Directions:
1. Combine the liverwurst and pistachios in the bowl of your food processor. Pulse until smooth. Whisk the cream cheese and mustard in another bowl. Make 12 balls out of the liverwurst mixture.
2. Make a thin cream cheese layer over. Coat with bacon, arrange on a plate and chill for 30 minutes.

Nutrition Info:
- Per Servings 1.5g Carbs, 7g Protein, 12g Fat, 145 Calories

Chapter 3. Pork, Beef & Lamb Recipes

Simple Pulled Pork

Servings: 4
Cooking Time: 25 Minutes
Ingredients:
- 4 pork chops, deboned
- 1 onion, sliced
- 5 cloves of garlic, minced
- 1 tbsp soy sauce
- 1 ½ cups water
- Salt and pepper to taste

Directions:
1. In a heavy-bottomed pot, add all ingredients and mix well.
2. Cover and cook on medium-high fire until boiling. Lower fire to a simmer and cook for 25 minutes undisturbed.
3. Turn off fire and let it cool a bit.
4. With two forks, shred meat.
5. Serve and enjoy.

Nutrition Info:
- Per Servings 2.4g Carbs, 40.7g Protein, 17.4g Fat, 339 Calories

Grilled Fennel Cumin Lamb Chops

Servings: 6
Cooking Time: 20 Minutes
Ingredients:
- 6 lamb rib chops
- 1 clove of garlic, minced
- ¾ teaspoon fennel seeds, crushed
- ¼ teaspoon ground coriander
- 5 tablespoons olive oil
- 1/8 teaspoon cracked black pepper
- Salt to taste

Directions:
1. Place the lamb rib chops in a shallow dish and rub onto the surface the garlic, fennel seeds, coriander, salt, and black pepper. Drizzle with olive oil. Allow to marinate in the fridge for 4 hours.
2. Heat the grill to medium and place the grill rack 6 inches above the heat source.
3. Grill the lamb chops for 10 minutes on each side or until well-done. For medium-rare lamb chops, cook for 6 to 8 minutes on each side.

Nutrition Info:
- Per Servings 0.5g Carbs, 17.0g Protein, 14.1g Fat, 190 Calories

Hot Pork With Dill Pickles

Servings: 4
Cooking Time: 20 Minutes
Ingredients:
- ¼ cup lime juice
- 4 pork chops
- 1 tbsp coconut oil, melted
- 2 garlic cloves, minced
- 1 tbsp chili powder

- 1 tsp ground cinnamon
- 2 tsp cumin
- Salt and black pepper, to taste
- ½ tsp hot pepper sauce
- 4 dill pickles, cut into spears and squeezed

Directions:

1. Using a bowl, combine the lime juice with oil, cumin, salt, hot pepper sauce, pepper, cinnamon, garlic, and chili powder. Place in the pork chops, toss to coat, and refrigerate for 4 hours.

2. Arrange the pork on a preheated grill over medium heat, cook for 7 minutes, turn, add in the dill pickles, and cook for another 7 minutes. Split among serving plates and enjoy.

Nutrition Info:

- Per Servings 2.3g Carbs, 36g Protein, 18g Fat, 315 Calories

Peanut Butter Pork Stir-fry

Servings: 4
Cooking Time: 23 Minutes

Ingredients:

- 1 ½ tbsp ghee
- 2 lb pork loin, cut into strips
- Pink salt and chili pepper to taste
- 2 tsp ginger- garlic paste
- ¼ cup chicken broth
- 5 tbsp peanut butter
- 2 cups mixed stir-fry vegetables

Directions:

1. Melt the ghee in a wok and mix the pork with salt, chili pepper, and ginger-garlic paste. Pour the pork into the wok and cook for 6 minutes until no longer pink.

2. Mix the peanut butter with some broth to be smooth, add to the pork and stir; cook for 2 minutes. Pour in the remaining broth, cook for 4 minutes, and add the mixed veggies. Simmer for 5 minutes.

3. Adjust the taste with salt and black pepper, and spoon the stir-fry to a side of cilantro cauli rice.

Nutrition Info:

- Per Servings 1g Carbs, 22.5g Protein, 49g Fat, 571 Calories

Pork Chops With Cranberry Sauce

Servings: 6
Cooking Time: 30 Minutes

Ingredients:

- 6-pieces bone-in pork loin chops
- 1 14-ounce fresh cranberries, pitted
- 5 tablespoons butter
- Salt and pepper to taste
- 1 cup water

Directions:

1. Add all ingredients in a pot on high fire and bring to a boil.

2. Once boiling, lower fire to a simmer and cook for 25 minutes.

3. Adjust seasoning to taste.
4. Serve and enjoy.

Nutrition Info:

- Per Servings 9.7g Carbs, 40.6g Protein, 27.6g Fat, 452 Calories

Pork Wraps

Servings: 6
Cooking Time: 40 Minutes

Ingredients:

- 6 bacon slices
- 2 tbsp fresh parsley, chopped
- 1 pound pork cutlets, sliced
- ⅓ cup ricotta cheese
- 1 tbsp coconut oil
- ¼ cup onion, chopped
- 3 garlic cloves, peeled and minced
- 2 tbsp Parmesan cheese, grated
- 15 ounces canned diced tomatoes
- ⅓ cup vegetable stock
- Salt and ground black pepper, to taste
- ½ tsp Italian seasoning

Directions:

1. Use a meat pounder to flatten the pork pieces. Set the bacon slices on top of each piece, then divide the parsley, ricotta cheese, and Parmesan cheese. Roll each pork piece and secure with a toothpick. Set a pan over medium heat and warm oil, cook the pork rolls until browned, and remove to a plate.

2. Add in the onion and garlic, and cook for 5 minutes. Place in the stock and cook for 3 minutes. Get rid of the toothpicks from the rolls and return them to the pan. Stir in the pepper, salt, tomatoes, and Italian seasoning, bring to a boil, set heat to medium-low, and cook for 20 minutes while covered. Split among bowls and enjoy.

Nutrition Info:

- Per Servings 2g Carbs, 34g Protein, 37g Fat, 435 Calories

Broccoli & Ground Beef Casserole

Servings: 6
Cooking Time: 4 Hours 15 Minutes

Ingredients:

- 1 tbsp olive oil
- 2 pounds ground beef
- 1 head broccoli, cut into florets
- Salt and black pepper, to taste
- 2 tsp mustard
- 2 tsp Worcestershire sauce
- 28 ounces canned diced tomatoes
- 2 cups mozzarella cheese, grated
- 16 ounces tomato sauce
- 2 tbsp fresh parsley, chopped
- 1 tsp dried oregano

Directions:

1. Apply pepper and salt to the broccoli florets, set them into a bowl, drizzle over the olive oil, and toss well to coat completely. In a separate bowl, combine the beef with Worcestershire sauce, salt, mustard, and pepper, and stir well. Press on the slow cooker's bottom.
2. Scatter in the broccoli, add the tomatoes, parsley, mozzarella, oregano, and tomato sauce. Cook for 4 hours on low; covered. Split the casserole among bowls and enjoy while hot.

Nutrition Info:
- Per Servings 5.6g Carbs, 51g Protein, 21g Fat, 434 Calories

Pork Burgers With Caramelized Onion Rings

Servings: 6
Cooking Time: 20 Minutes
Ingredients:
- 2 lb ground pork
- Pink salt and chili pepper to taste
- 3 tbsp olive oil
- 1 tbsp butter
- 1 white onion, sliced into rings
- 1 tbsp balsamic vinegar
- 3 drops liquid stevia
- 6 low carb burger buns, halved
- 2 firm tomatoes, sliced into rings

Directions:
1. Combine the pork, salt and chili pepper in a bowl and mold out 6 patties.
2. Heat the olive oil in a skillet over medium heat and fry the patties for 4 to 5 minutes on each side until golden brown on the outside. Remove onto a plate and sit for 3 minutes.
3. Meanwhile, melt butter in a skillet over medium heat, sauté the onions for 2 minutes to be soft, and stir in the balsamic vinegar and liquid stevia.
4. Cook for 30 seconds stirring once or twice until caramelized. In each bun, place a patty, top with some onion rings and 2 tomato rings. Serve the burgers with cheddar cheese dip.

Nutrition Info:
- Per Servings 7.6g Carbs, 26g Protein, 32g Fat, 445 Calories

One Pot Tomato Pork Chops Stew

Servings: 6
Cooking Time: 30 Minutes
Ingredients:
- 6 pork chops
- 1 onion, chopped
- 1 bay leaf
- ½ cup tomato paste
- 1 tsp oil
- Salt and pepper to taste
- 1/2 cup water

Directions:
1. Place a heavy-bottomed pot on medium-high fire and heat for 2 minutes. Add oil and heat for a minute more.
2. Add pork chops and sear for 3 minutes per side. Transfer to a chopping board and slice into bite-sized pieces.
3. In the same pot, sauté onion, bay leaf, and tomato paste for a minute. Add water and deglaze the pot.
4. Return chops to the pot, season with pepper and salt.
5. Cover and simmer for 20 minutes.

Nutrition Info:
- Per Servings 6.5g Carbs, 41.5g Protein, 17.5g Fat, 357 Calories

Pulled Pork With Avocado

Servings: 12
Cooking Time: 2 Hours 55 Minutes
Ingredients:
- 4 pounds pork shoulder
- 1 tbsp avocado oil
- ½ cup beef stock
- ¼ cup jerk seasoning
- 6 avocado, sliced

Directions:
1. Rub the pork shoulder with jerk seasoning, and set in a greased baking dish. Pour in the stock, and cook for 1 hour 45 minutes in your oven at 350ºF covered with aluminium foil.
2. Discard the foil and cook for another 20 minutes. Leave to rest for 30 minutes, and shred it with 2 forks. Serve topped with avocado slices.

Nutrition Info:
- Per Servings 4.1g Carbs, 42g Protein, 42.6g Fat, 567 Calories

Pancetta Sausage With Kale

Servings: 10
Cooking Time: 25 Minutes
Ingredients:
- ½ gallon chicken broth
- A drizzle of olive oil
- 1 cup heavy cream
- 2 cups kale
- 6 pancetta slices, chopped
- 1 pound radishes, chopped
- 2 garlic cloves, minced
- Salt and black pepper, to taste
- A pinch of red pepper flakes
- 1 onion, chopped
- 1½ pounds hot pork sausage, chopped

Directions:
1. Set a pot over medium heat. Add in a drizzle of olive oil and warm. Stir in garlic, onion, pancetta, and sausage; cook for 5 minutes. Pour in broth, radishes, and kale, and simmer for 10 minutes.

2. Stir in the, salt, red pepper flakes, pepper, and heavy cream, and cook for about 5 minutes. Split among serving bowls and enjoy the meal.

Nutrition Info:
- Per Servings 5.4g Carbs, 21g Protein, 29g Fat, 386 Calories

Lemon Pork Chops With Buttered Brussels Sprouts

Servings: 6
Cooking Time: 27 Minutes
Ingredients:
- 3 tbsp lemon juice
- 3 cloves garlic, pureed
- 1 tbsp olive oil
- 6 pork loin chops
- 1 tbsp butter
- 1 lb brussels sprouts, trimmed and halved
- 2 tbsp white wine
- Salt and black pepper to taste

Directions:
1. Preheat broiler to 400ºF and mix the lemon juice, garlic, salt, pepper, and oil in a bowl.
2. Brush the pork with the mixture, place in a baking sheet, and cook for 6 minutes on each side until browned. Share into 6 plates and make the side dish.
3. Melt butter in a small wok or pan and cook in brussels sprouts for 5 minutes until tender. Drizzle with white wine, sprinkle with salt and black pepper and cook for another 5 minutes.
4. Ladle brussels sprouts to the side of the chops and serve with a hot sauce.

Nutrition Info:
- Per Servings 2g Carbs, 26g Protein, 48g Fat, 549 Calories

Beef Steak Filipino Style

Servings: 6
Cooking Time: 25 Minutes
Ingredients:
- 2 tablespoons coconut oil
- 1 onion, sliced
- 4 beef steaks
- 2 tablespoons lemon juice, freshly squeezed
- ¼ cup coconut aminos
- 1 tsp salt
- Pepper to taste

Directions:
1. In a nonstick fry pan, heat oil on medium-high fire.
2. Pan-fry beef steaks and season with coconut aminos.
3. Cook until dark brown, around 7 minutes per side. Transfer to a plate.
4. Sauté onions in the same pan until caramelized, around 8 minutes. Season with lemon juice and return steaks in the pan. Mix well.
5. Serve and enjoy.

Nutrition Info:
- Per Servings 0.7g Carbs, 25.3g Protein, 27.1g Fat, 347 Calories

Beef Stew With Bacon

Servings: 6
Cooking Time: 1 Hour 15 Minutes
Ingredients:
- 8 ounces bacon, chopped
- 4 lb beef meat for stew, cubed
- 4 garlic cloves, minced
- 2 brown onions, chopped
- 2 tbsp olive oil
- 4 tbsp red vinegar
- 4 cups beef stock
- 2 tbsp tomato puree
- 2 cinnamon sticks
- 3 lemon peel strips
- ½ cup fresh parsley, chopped
- 4 thyme sprigs
- 2 tbsp butter
- Salt and black pepper, to taste

Directions:
1. Set a saucepan over medium-high heat and warm oil, add in the garlic, bacon, and onion, and cook for 5 minutes. Stir in the beef, and cook until slightly brown. Pour in the vinegar, pepper, butter, lemon peel strips, stock, salt, tomato puree, cinnamon sticks and thyme; stir for 3 minutes.
2. Cook for 1 hour while covered. Get rid of the thyme, lemon peel, and cinnamon sticks. Split into serving bowls and sprinkle with parsley to serve.

Nutrition Info:
- Per Servings 5.7g Carbs, 63g Protein, 36g Fat, 592 Calories

Cocoa-crusted Pork Tenderloin

Servings: 2
Cooking Time: 25 Minutes
Ingredients:
- 1-pound pork tenderloin, trimmed from fat
- 1 tablespoon cocoa powder
- 1 teaspoon instant coffee powder
- ½ teaspoon ground cinnamon
- ½ teaspoon chili powder
- 1 tablespoon olive oil
- Pepper and salt to taste

Directions:
1. In a bowl, dust the pork tenderloin with cocoa powder, coffee, cinnamon, pepper, salt, and chili powder.
2. In a skillet, heat the oil and sear the meat for 5 minutes on both sides over low to medium flame.
3. Transfer the pork in a baking dish and cook in the oven for 15 minutes in a 350F preheated oven.

Nutrition Info:
- Per Servings 2.0g Carbs, 60.0g Protein, 15.0g Fat, 395 Calories

Garlic Pork Chops

Servings: 4
Cooking Time: 30 Minutes
Ingredients:
- 1 ½ cups chicken broth
- 1 tablespoon butter
- 2 lemons, juiced
- 4 ¾ inch boneless pork chops
- 6 cloves garlic, minced
- Salt and pepper to taste
- 1 tablespoon olive oil

Directions:
1. Heat the olive oil in a large pot on medium-high fire.
2. Season the pork with salt, pepper, and garlic powder.
3. Place the pork in the Instant Pot and brown the sides. Set aside.
4. Add the garlic and sauté for a minute. Add the lemon juice and chicken broth. Stir in the butter.
5. Add the pork chops back to the pan. Cover the lid and simmer for 20 minutes.
6. Serve and enjoy.

Nutrition Info:
- Per Servings 4.8g Carbs, 50.2g Protein, 14.0g Fat, 355 Calories

Thai Beef With Shiitake Mushrooms

Servings: 6
Cooking Time: 30 Minutes
Ingredients:
- 1 cup beef stock
- 4 tbsp butter
- ¼ tsp garlic powder
- ¼ tsp onion powder
- 1 tbsp coconut aminos
- 1½ tsp lemon pepper
- 1 pound beef steak, cut into strips
- Salt and black pepper, to taste
- 1 cup shiitake mushrooms, sliced
- 3 green onions, chopped
- 1 tbsp thai red curry paste

Directions:
1. Melt butter in a pan over medium-high heat, add in the beef, season with garlic powder, pepper, salt, and onion powder and cook for 4 minutes. Mix in the mushrooms and stir-fry for 5 minutes.
2. Pour in the stock, coconut aminos, lemon pepper, and thai curry paste and cook for 15 minutes. Serve sprinkled with the green onions.

Nutrition Info:
- Per Servings 3g Carbs, 19g Protein, 15g Fat, 224 Calories

Pork Sausage With Spinach

Servings: 6
Cooking Time: 35 Minutes

Ingredients:
- 1 onion, chopped
- 2 tbsp olive oil
- 1½ pound Italian pork sausage, sliced
- 1 red bell pepper, seeded and chopped
- Salt and black pepper, to taste
- 4 pounds spinach, chopped
- 1 garlic, minced
- ¼ cup green chili pepper, chopped
- 1 cup water

Directions:
1. Set a pan over medium-high heat, warm oil and cook the sausage for 10 minutes. Stir in the onion, garlic and bell pepper, and fry for 3-4 minutes. Place in the spinach, salt, water, black pepper, chili pepper, and cook for 10 minutes. Split among serving bowls and enjoy.

Nutrition Info:
- Per Servings 6.2g Carbs, 29g Protein, 28g Fat, 352 Calories

Moroccan Beef Stew

Servings: 4
Cooking Time: 40 Minutes
Ingredients:
- 1 medium onion, chopped coarsely
- 2-lbs London broil roast, chopped into 2-inch cubes
- ¼ cup prunes
- 1 ¼ teaspoons curry powder
- ½ teaspoon ground cinnamon
- ½ teaspoon salt
- 2 cups water

Directions:
1. Add all ingredients in a pot on high fire and bring to a boil.
2. Once boiling, lower fire to a simmer and cook for 35 minutes.
3. Adjust seasoning to taste.
4. Serve and enjoy.

Nutrition Info:
- Per Servings 8.3g Carbs, 40.6g Protein, 49.6g Fat, 658 Calories

Warm Rump Steak Salad

Servings: 4
Cooking Time: 40 Minutes
Ingredients:
- ½ lb rump steak, excess fat trimmed
- 3 green onions, sliced
- 3 tomatoes, sliced
- 1 cup green beans, steamed and sliced
- 2 kohlrabi, peeled and chopped
- ½ cup water
- 2 cups mixed salad greens
- Salt and black pepper to season
- Salad Dressing

- 2 tsp Dijon mustard
- 1 tsp erythritol
- Salt and black pepper to taste
- 3 tbsp olive oil + extra for drizzling
- 1 tbsp red wine vinegar

Directions:

1. Preheat the oven to 400ºF. Place the kohlrabi on a baking sheet, drizzle with olive oil and bake in the oven for 25 minutes. After cooking, remove, and set aside to cool.
2. In a bowl, mix the Dijon mustard, erythritol, salt, pepper, vinegar, and olive oil. Set aside.
3. Then, preheat a grill pan over high heat while you season the meat with salt and pepper. Place the steak in the pan and brown on both sides for 4 minutes each. Remove to rest on a chopping board for 4 more minutes before slicing thinly.
4. In a shallow salad bowl, add the green onions, tomatoes, green beans, kohlrabi, salad greens, and steak slices. Drizzle the dressing over and toss with two spoons. Serve the rump steak salad warm with chunks of low carb bread.

Nutrition Info:

- Per Servings 4g Carbs, 28g Protein, 19g Fat, 325 Calories

Asian-style Beef Steak

Servings: 6
Cooking Time: 25 Minutes
Ingredients:

- 1 onion, sliced into rings
- 4 beef steaks, cut into strips
- 2 tablespoons lemon juice, freshly squeezed
- 2 tbsp soy sauce
- 1 tsp pepper
- 3 tablespoons oil
- A dash of salt

Directions:

1. On high fire, place a nonstick pan and heat oil for 3 minutes.
2. Stir in half of the onion rings and beef steaks. Stir fry for 10 minutes.
3. Add remaining ingredients except for lemon juice and fry for another 5 minutes.
4. Serve and enjoy with lemon juice.

Nutrition Info:

- Per Servings 0.7g Carbs, 20.4g Protein, 29.6g Fat, 350 Calories

Garlic Crispy Pork Loin

Servings: 4
Cooking Time: 1h 5 Minutes
Ingredients:

- 1 quart cold water
- 3 cloves garlic, crushed
- 3 tablespoons. chopped fresh ginger
- 1 boneless pork loin roast
- 2 tablespoons. Dijon mustard

- Salt and freshly ground black pepper to taste
- 2 teaspoons. dried rosemary
- 1 tablespoon olive oil
- 2 tablespoons stevia
- 1/2 teaspoon red pepper flakes

Directions:

1. Mix water, salt, 1 tbsp. stevia, garlic, ginger, rosemary and red pepper flakes in a large bowl.
2. Place pork loin in brine mixture and refrigerate for 8 to 10 hours. Remove pork from brine, pat dry, and season all sides with salt and black pepper.
3. Preheat oven to 325 degrees F.
4. Heat olive oil in a skillet over high heat. Cook pork for about 10 minutes.
5. Transfer skillet to the oven and roast for about 40 minutes.
6. Mix 2 tablespoons stevia and Dijon mustard together in a small bowl.
7. Remove pork roast from the oven and spread stevia mixture on all sides. Cook for an additional 15 minutes at 145 degrees F. Serve and enjoy.

Nutrition Info:

- Per Servings 19.3g Carbs, 30.7g Protein, 18.9g Fat, 376 Calories

Beef Enchilada Stew

Servings: 4
Cooking Time: 40 Minutes
Ingredients:

- 1 cup Mexican cheese, shredded
- 1 can mild green chilies, drained
- 2 teaspoons garlic salt
- 1 10-ounce can La Victoria mild red enchilada sauce
- 2-lbs London broil beef, sliced into 2-inch cubes
- Pepper and salt to taste

Directions:

1. Add all ingredients in a pot on high fire and bring to a boil.
2. Once boiling, lower fire to a simmer and cook for 25 minutes.
3. Adjust seasoning to taste.
4. Serve and enjoy.

Nutrition Info:

- Per Servings 10.1g Carbs, 64.2g Protein, 47.4g Fat, 764 Calories

Grilled Lamb On Lemony Sauce

Servings: 4
Cooking Time: 25 Minutes
Ingredients:

- 8 lamb chops
- 2 tbsp favorite spice mix
- 1 tsp olive oil
- Sauce:
- ¼ cup olive oil
- 1 tsp red pepper flakes

- 2 tbsp lemon juice
- 2 tbsp fresh mint
- 3 garlic cloves, pressed
- 2 tbsp lemon zest
- ¼ cup parsley
- ½ tsp smoked paprika

Directions:

1. Rub the lamb with the oil and sprinkle with the seasoning. Preheat the grill to medium. Grill the lamb chops for about 3 minutes per side. Whisk together the sauce ingredients. Serve the lamb chops with the sauce.

Nutrition Info:

- Per Servings 1g Carbs, 29g Protein, 31g Fat, 392 Calories

Ribeye Steak With Shitake Mushrooms

Servings: 1
Cooking Time: 25 Minutes

Ingredients:

- 6 ounces ribeye steak
- 2 tbsp butter
- 1 tsp olive oil
- ½ cup shitake mushrooms, sliced
- Salt and ground pepper, to taste

Directions:

1. Heat the olive oil in a pan over medium heat. Rub the steak with salt and pepper and cook about 4 minutes per side; set aside. Melt the butter in the pan and cook the shitakes for 4 minutes. Pour the butter and mushrooms over the steak to serve.

Nutrition Info:

- Per Servings 3g Carbs, 33g Protein, 31g Fat, 478 Calories

Beef Bourguignon

Servings: 4
Cooking Time: 60 Minutes + Marinated Time

Ingredients:

- 3 tbsp coconut oil
- 1 tbsp dried parsley flakes
- 1 cup red wine
- 1 tsp dried thyme
- Salt and black pepper, to taste
- 1 bay leaf
- ⅓ cup coconut flour
- 2 lb beef, cubed
- 12 small white onions
- 4 pancetta slices, chopped
- 2 garlic cloves, minced
- ½ lb mushrooms, chopped

Directions:

1. In a bowl, combine the wine with bay leaf, olive oil, thyme, pepper, parsley, salt, and the beef cubes; set aside for 3 hours. Drain the meat, and reserve the marinade. Toss the flour over the meat to coat.

2. Heat a pan over medium-high heat, stir in the pancetta, and cook until slightly browned. Place in the onions and garlic, and cook for 3 minutes. Stir-fry in the meat and mushrooms for 4-5 minutes.

3. Pour in the marinade and 1 cup of water; cover and cook for 50 minutes. Season to taste and serve.

Nutrition Info:

- Per Servings 7g Carbs, 45g Protein, 26g Fat, 435 Calories

Garlic Beef & Egg Frittata

Servings: 4
Cooking Time: 30 Minutes

Ingredients:

- 3 eggs, beaten
- 3 cloves of garlic, minced
- 1 onion, chopped
- ½ pound lean ground beef
- 1 stalk green onion, sliced
- 2 tablespoons olive oil
- A dash of salt
- ¼ tsp pepper

Directions:

1. Place a small cast iron pan on medium fire and heat for 2 minutes.
2. Add beef and crumble. Cook for 5 minutes.
3. Add onion and garlic, continue cooking beef until browned, around 5 minutes more. Discard any fat.
4. Season with pepper and salt.
5. Spread beef in the pan and lower fire to low.
6. Meanwhile, whisk eggs in a bowl. Pour over meat, cover, and cook for 10 minutes on low.
7. Place pan in the oven and broil on low for 3 minutes. Let it set for 5 minutes.
8. Serve and enjoy topped with green onions.

Nutrition Info:

- Per Servings 3.8g Carbs, 22.7g Protein, 20.5g Fat, 294 Calories

Beef And Egg Rice Bowls

Servings: 4
Cooking Time: 22 Minutes

Ingredients:

- 2 cups cauli rice
- 3 cups frozen mixed vegetables
- 3 tbsp ghee
- 1 lb skirt steak
- Salt and black pepper to taste
- 4 fresh eggs
- Hot sauce (sugar-free) for topping

Directions:

1. Mix the cauli rice and mixed vegetables in a bowl, sprinkle with a little water, and steam in the microwave for 1 minute to be tender. Share into 4 serving bowls.

2. Melt the ghee in a skillet, season the beef with salt and pepper, and brown for 5 minutes on each side. Use a perforated spoon to ladle the meat onto the vegetables.

3. Wipe out the skillet and return to medium heat, crack in an egg, season with salt and pepper and cook until the egg white has set, but the yolk is still runny 3 minutes. Remove egg onto the vegetable bowl and fry the remaining 3 eggs. Add to the other bowls.

4. Drizzle the beef bowls with hot sauce and serve.

Nutrition Info:

- Per Servings 4g Carbs, 15g Protein, 26g Fat, 320 Calories

Slow-cooked Beef Moroccan Style

Servings: 8
Cooking Time: 8 Hours
Ingredients:

- ½ cup apricots
- ½ cup sliced yellow onions
- 2 pounds beef roast
- 4 tablespoons garam masala seasoning
- 1 teaspoon sea salt
- 2 cups water

Directions:

1. Place onions and apricots on the bottom of Instant Pot.

2. Rub salt and garam masala all over roast beef and place roast beef on top of onions and apricots.

3. Pour water.

4. Cover, press the slow cook button, adjust cooking time to 6 hours.

5. Once done cooking, remove roast beef and shred with 2 forks.

6. Return to pot, cover, press slow cook, and adjust the time to 2 hours.

7. Serve and enjoy.

Nutrition Info:

- Per Servings 3.0g Carbs, 31.9g Protein, 14.7g Fat, 275 Calories

Italian Shredded Beef

Servings: 6
Cooking Time: 42 Minutes
Ingredients:

- 3 pounds chuck roast, trimmed from excess fat and cut into chunks
- 1 packet Italian salad dressing mix
- 8 ounces pepperoncini pepper slices
- 1 can beef broth
- Salt and pepper to taste
- 1 cup water
- 1 tsp oil

Directions:

1. Place a heavy-bottomed pot on medium-high fire and heat for 2 minutes. Add oil and swirl to coat the bottom and sides of pot and heat for a minute.

2. Season roast with pepper and salt. Brown roast for 4 minutes per side. Transfer to a chopping board and chop into 4 equal pieces.

3. Add remaining ingredients to the pot along with sliced beef.

4. Cover and simmer for 30 minutes or until beef is fork-tender. Stir the bottom of the pot now and then. Turn off the fire.

5. With two forks, shred beef.

6. Turn on fire to high and boil uncovered until sauce is rendered, around 5 minutes.

Nutrition Info:

- Per Servings 6.6g Carbs, 61.5g Protein, 20.5g Fat, 455 Calories

Jalapeno Beef Pot Roasted

Servings: 4
Cooking Time: 1 Hour 25 Minutes
Ingredients:

- 3½ pounds beef roast
- 4 ounces mushrooms, sliced
- 12 ounces beef stock
- 1 ounce onion soup mix
- ½ cup Italian dressing
- 2 jalapeños, shredded

Directions:

1. Using a bowl, combine the stock with the Italian dressing and onion soup mixture. Place the beef roast in a pan, stir in the stock mixture, mushrooms, and jalapeños; cover with aluminum foil.

2. Set in the oven at 300ºF, and bake for 1 hour. Take out the foil and continue baking for 15 minutes. Allow the roast to cool, slice, and serve alongside a topping of the gravy.

Nutrition Info:

- Per Servings 3.2g Carbs, 87g Protein, 46g Fat, 745 Calories

Beef And Butternut Squash Stew

Servings: 4
Cooking Time: 40 Minutes
Ingredients:

- 3 tsp olive oil
- 1 pound ground beef
- 1 cup beef stock
- 14 ounces canned tomatoes with juice
- 1 tbsp stevia
- 1 pound butternut squash, chopped
- 1 tbsp Worcestershire sauce
- 2 bay leaves
- Salt and ground black pepper, to taste
- 3 tbsp fresh parsley, chopped
- 1 onion, chopped
- 1 tsp dried sage
- 1 tbsp garlic, minced

Directions:

1. Set a pan over medium heat and heat olive oil, stir in the onion, garlic, and beef, and cook for 10 minutes. Add in butternut squash, Worcestershire sauce, bay leaves, stevia, beef stock, canned tomatoes, and sage, and bring to a boil. Reduce heat, and simmer for 20 minutes.
2. Adjust the seasonings. Split into bowls and enjoy.
Nutrition Info:
- Per Servings 7.3g Carbs, 32g Protein, 17g Fat, 343 Calories

Juicy Pork Medallions

Servings: 4
Cooking Time: 55 Minutes
Ingredients:
- 2 onions, chopped
- 6 bacon slices, chopped
- ½ cup vegetable stock
- Salt and black pepper, to taste
- 1 pound pork tenderloin, cut into medallions

Directions:
1. Set a pan over medium heat, stir in the bacon, cook until crispy, and remove to a plate. Add onions, some pepper, and salt, and cook for 5 minutes; set to the same plate with bacon.
2. Add the pork medallions to the pan, season with pepper and salt, brown for 3 minutes on each side, turn, reduce heat to medium, and cook for 7 minutes. Stir in the stock, and cook for 2 minutes. Return the bacon and onions to the pan and cook for 1 minute.
Nutrition Info:
- Per Servings 6g Carbs, 36g Protein, 18g Fat, 325 Calories

Herb Pork Chops With Raspberry Sauce

Servings: 4
Cooking Time: 17 Minutes
Ingredients:
- 1 tbsp olive oil + extra for brushing
- 2 lb pork chops
- Pink salt and black pepper to taste
- 2 cups raspberries
- ¼ cup water
- 1 ½ tbsp Italian Herb mix
- 3 tbsp balsamic vinegar
- 2 tsp sugar-free Worcestershire sauce

Directions:
1. Heat oil in a skillet over medium heat, season the pork with salt and black pepper and cook for 5 minutes on each side. Put on serving plates and reserve the pork drippings.
2. Mash the raspberries with a fork in a bowl until jam-like. Pour into a saucepan, add the water, and herb mix. Bring to boil on low heat for 4 minutes. Stir in pork drippings, vinegar, and Worcestershire sauce. Simmer for 1 minute. Spoon sauce over the pork chops and serve with braised rapini.
Nutrition Info:

- Per Servings 1.1g Carbs, 26.3g Protein, 32.5g Fat, 413 Calories

Adobo Beef Fajitas

Servings: 4
Cooking Time: 35 Minutes
Ingredients:
- 2 lb skirt steak, cut in halves
- 2 tbsp Adobo seasoning
- Pink salt to taste
- 2 tbsp olive oil
- 2 large white onion, chopped
- 1 cup sliced mixed bell peppers, chopped
- 12 low carb tortillas

Directions:
1. Season the steak with adobo and marinate in the fridge for one hour.
2. Preheat grill to 425°F and cook steak for 6 minutes on each side, flipping once until lightly browned. Remove from heat and wrap in foil and let sit for 10 minutes. This allows the meat to cook in its heat for a few more minutes before slicing.
3. Heat the olive oil in a skillet over medium heat and sauté the onion and bell peppers for 5 minutes or until soft. Cut steak against the grain into strips and share on the tortillas. Top with the veggies and serve with guacamole.
Nutrition Info:
- Per Servings 5g Carbs, 18g Protein, 25g Fat, 348 Calories

Keto Beefy Burritos

Servings: 6
Cooking Time: 25 Minutes
Ingredients:
- 1-pound lean ground beef
- 6 large kale leaves
- 1/4 cup onion
- 1/4 cup low-sodium tomato puree
- 1/4 teaspoon ground cumin
- What you'll need from the store cupboard:
- 1/4 teaspoon black pepper
- ½ tsp salt

Directions:
1. In a medium skillet, brown ground beef for 15 minutes; drain oil on paper towels.
2. Spray skillet with non-stick cooking spray; add onion to cook for 3-5 minutes, until vegetables are softened.
3. Add beef, tomato puree, black pepper, and cumin to onion/pepper mixture.
4. Mix well and cook for 3 to 5 minutes on low heat.
5. Divide the beef mixture among kale leaves.
6. Roll the kale leaves over burrito style, making sure that both ends are folded first, so the mixture does not fall out. Secure with a toothpick.
Nutrition Info:

- Per Servings 6.0g Carbs, 25.0g Protein, 32.0g Fat, 412 Calories

Roasted Pork Loin With Sauce

Servings: 8
Cooking Time: 3 H
Ingredients:

- 1 teaspoon. rubbed sage
- 1 clove garlic, crushed
- 1 boneless pork loin
- 1 tablespoon almond flour
- 1/4 cup. water
- 1/2 teaspoon salt
- 1/4 cup vinegar
- 2 tablespoons soy sauce, low-carb
- 1/4 teaspoon pepper

Directions:

1. Preheat oven to 325 degrees F.
2. In a bowl, combine sage, salt, pepper, and garlic. Rub thoroughly all over pork and place it in an uncovered roasting pan on the middle oven rack.
3. Bake in the preheated oven approximately 3 hours at least 145 degrees F.
4. Meanwhile, place flour, vinegar, water, and soy sauce in a small saucepan. Heat, stirring occasionally, until mixture thicken slightly.
5. Brush roast with glaze 3 or 4 times during the last 1/2 hour of cooking. Pour remaining glaze over roast, and serve.

Nutrition Info:

- Per Servings 13.9g Carbs, 45.8g Protein, 24.6g Fat, 472 Calories

Beef Cheeseburger Casserole

Servings: 6
Cooking Time: 30 Minutes
Ingredients:

- 2 lb ground beef
- Pink salt and black pepper to taste
- 1 cup cauli rice
- 2 cups chopped cabbage
- 14 oz can diced tomatoes
- ¼ cup water
- 1 cup shredded colby jack cheese

Directions:

1. Preheat oven to 370ºF and grease a baking dish with cooking spray. Put beef in a pot and season with salt and black pepper and cook over medium heat for 6 minutes until no longer pink. Drain the grease. Add cauli rice, cabbage, tomatoes, and water. Stir and bring to boil covered for 5 minutes to thicken the sauce. Adjust taste with salt and black pepper.
2. Spoon the beef mixture into the baking dish and spread evenly. Sprinkle with cheese and bake in the oven for 15 minutes until cheese has melted and it's golden brown. Remove and cool for 4 minutes and serve with low carb crusted bread.

Nutrition Info:

- Per Servings 5g Carbs, 20g Protein, 25g Fat, 385 Calories

Cherry-balsamic Sauced Beef

Servings: 4
Cooking Time: 40 Minutes
Ingredients:

- 2-lbs London broil beef, sliced into 2-inch cubes
- 1/3 cup balsamic vinegar
- ½ cup dried cherries
- ½ teaspoon pepper
- 1 teaspoon salt
- 1 tablespoon canola oil
- ½ cup water

Directions:

1. Add all ingredients in a pot on high fire and bring to a boil.
2. Once boiling, lower fire to a simmer and cook for 35 minutes.
3. Adjust seasoning to taste.
4. Serve and enjoy.

Nutrition Info:

- Per Servings 4.6g Carbs, 82.2g Protein, 17.2g Fat, 525 Calories

Spicy Pork Stew With Spinach

Servings: 4
Cooking Time: 40 Minutes
Ingredients:

- 1 lb. pork butt, cut into chunks
- 1 onion, chopped
- 4 cloves of garlic, minced
- 1 cup coconut milk, freshly squeezed
- 1 cup spinach leaves, washed and rinsed
- Salt and pepper to taste
- 1 cup water

Directions:

1. In a heavy-bottomed pot, add all ingredients, except for coconut milk and spinach. Mix well.
2. Cover and cook on medium-high fire until boiling. Lower fire to a simmer and cook for 30 minutes undisturbed.
3. Add remaining ingredients and cook on high fire uncovered for 5 minutes. Adjust seasoning if needed.
4. Serve and enjoy.

Nutrition Info:

- Per Servings 7.2g Carbs, 30.5g Protein, 34.4g Fat, 458 Calories

Soy-glazed Meatloaf

Servings: 6
Cooking Time: 60 Minutes
Ingredients:

- 1 cup white mushrooms, chopped
- 2 pounds ground beef
- 2 tbsp fresh parsley, chopped

- 2 garlic cloves, minced
- 1 onion, chopped
- 1 red bell pepper, seeded and chopped
- ½ cup almond flour
- ⅓ cup Parmesan cheese, grated
- 2 eggs
- Salt and black pepper, to taste
- 1 tsp balsamic vinegar
- 1 tbsp swerve
- 1 tbsp soy sauce
- 2 tbsp sugar-free ketchup
- 2 cups balsamic vinegar

Directions:

1. Using a bowl, combine the beef with salt, mushrooms, bell pepper, Parmesan cheese, 1 teaspoon vinegar, parsley, garlic, pepper, onion, almond flour, salt, and eggs. Set this into a loaf pan, and bake for 30 minutes in the oven at 370°F.

2. Meanwhile, heat a small pan over medium heat, add in the 2 cups vinegar, swerve, soy sauce, and ketchup, and cook for 20 minutes. Remove the meatloaf from the oven, spread the glaze over the meatloaf, and bake in the oven for 20 more minutes. Allow the meatloaf to cool, slice, and enjoy.

Nutrition Info:

- Per Servings 7.5g Carbs, 46g Protein, 21.4g Fat, 474 Calories

Slow Cooker Pork

Servings: 10
Cooking Time: 10 Hours

Ingredients:

- 3 lb. boneless pork loin roast
- ¼ cup Dijon mustard
- 1 tsp. dried thyme leaves
- 2 bay leaves
- 5 tablespoons olive oil
- Salt and pepper to taste
- 1 ½ cups water

Directions:

1. Place all ingredients in the slow cooker.
2. Season with salt and pepper and give a good stir.
3. Cover and cook on low for 10 hours.
4. Serve and enjoy.

Nutrition Info:

- Per Servings 0.4g Carbs, 30.7g Protein, 15.7g Fat, 245 Calories

Pork And Cabbage Soup

Servings: 10
Cooking Time: 50 Minutes

Ingredients:

- 3 lb. pork butt, cut into chunks
- 1 thumb-size ginger, sliced
- 1 head cabbage, cut into quarters
- 1 scallion, green part only

- 1 small onion, chopped
- Pepper and salt to taste
- 3 cups water

Directions:

1. Place all ingredients in a heavy-bottomed pot except for cabbage. Give a good stir and season with salt and pepper to taste.
2. Cover and bring to a boil. Once boiling, lower fire to a simmer and simmer for 30 minutes.
3. Add cabbage and simmer for another 10 minutes.
4. Adjust seasoning to taste.
5. Serve and enjoy.

Nutrition Info:

- Per Servings 4.6g Carbs, 35.2g Protein, 24.7g Fat, 383 Calories

Lettuce Taco Carnitas

Servings: 12
Cooking Time: 40 Minutes

Ingredients:

- 2 cups shredded Colby-Monterey jack cheese
- 1 can green chilies and diced tomatoes, undrained
- 1 envelope taco seasoning
- 1 boneless pork shoulder butt roast
- Lettuce leaves
- Pepper and salt to taste
- 1 cup water

Directions:

1. Add all ingredients in a pot, except for cheese and lettuce leaves, on high fire, and bring to a boil.
2. Once boiling, lower fire to a simmer and cook for 35 minutes.
3. Adjust seasoning to taste.
4. To serve, add a good amount of shredded pork into the center of one lettuce leaf. Top it with cheese, roll, and enjoy.

Nutrition Info:

- Per Servings 1.7g Carbs, 28.5g Protein, 10.4g Fat, 214 Calories

Old-style Beef Stew

Servings: 5
Cooking Time: 40 Minutes

Ingredients:

- 1 ½-pounds beef stew meat, cubed into 1-inch squares
- 16-ounce fresh cremini mushrooms
- 3 medium tomatoes, chopped
- 1 envelope reduced-sodium onion soup mix
- 5 tablespoons butter
- 1 cup water
- Pepper and salt to taste

Directions:

1. Add all ingredients in a pot on high fire and bring to a boil.
2. Once boiling, lower fire to a simmer and cook for 25 minutes.
3. Adjust seasoning to taste.

4. Serve and enjoy.
Nutrition Info:
- Per Servings 11.5g Carbs, 58g Protein, 27.8g Fat, 551 Calories

Oregano Pork Chops With Spicy Tomato Sauce

Servings: 4
Cooking Time: 50 Minutes
Ingredients:
- 4 pork chops
- 1 tbsp fresh oregano, chopped
- 2 garlic cloves, minced
- 1 tbsp canola oil
- 15 ounces canned diced tomatoes
- 1 tbsp tomato paste
- Salt and black pepper, to taste
- ¼ cup tomato juice
- 1 red chili, finely chopped

Directions:
1. Set a pan over medium-high heat and warm oil, place in the pork chops, season with pepper and salt, cook for 3 minutes, turn and cook for another 3 minutes; remove to a bowl. Add in the garlic, and cook for 30 seconds.
2. Stir in the tomato paste, tomatoes, tomato juice, and chili; bring to a boil, and reduce heat to medium-low. Place in the pork chops, cover pan and simmer everything for 30 minutes.
3. Remove the pork chops to plates and sprinkle with fresh oregano to serve.

Nutrition Info:
- Per Servings 3.6g Carbs, 39g Protein, 21g Fat, 410 Calories

Mushroom Pork Chops

Servings: 4
Cooking Time: 45 Minutes
Ingredients:
- 4 pork chops
- 3 cloves of garlic, chopped
- 1 onion, chopped
- 1 lb. fresh mushrooms, sliced
- 4 tbsp butter
- What you'll need from the store cupboard:
- Salt and pepper to taste
- 1 tbsp water
- 5 tbsp oil

Directions:
1. In a large saucepan, place on medium fire and heat oil for 3 minutes. Season pork chops with salt and pepper.
2. Cook for 4 minutes per side the porkchop, until lightly browned. Transfer to a plate and let it rest.
3. In the same pan, add butter. Increase fire to medium-high and sauté garlic. Stir in onions, water, and mushrooms.

Sauté until mushrooms are tender, around 7 minutes. Season with salt and pepper.
4. Serve pork chops topped with mushroom mixture.
Nutrition Info:
- Per Servings 7.7g Carbs, 46.8g Protein, 47.9g Fat, 649 Calories

Pork Chops And Peppers

Servings: 4
Cooking Time: 20 Minutes
Ingredients:
- 4 thick pork chops
- 1 onion, chopped
- 2 cloves of garlic, minced
- 2 red and yellow bell peppers, seeded and julienned
- Salt and pepper to taste
- 5 tablespoons oil

Directions:
1. In a large saucepan, place on medium fire and heat 1 tsp oil for 3 minutes.
2. Add pork chop and cook for 5 minutes per side. Season pork chops with salt and pepper.
3. Transfer pork chops to a plate and let it rest.
4. In the same pan, add remaining oil. Increase fire to medium-high and sauté garlic. Stir in onions and bell peppers. Sauté until tender and crisp around 5 minutes.
5. Serve pork chops topped with bell pepper mixture.

Nutrition Info:
- Per Servings 4.3g Carbs, 23.9g Protein, 16.3g Fat, 245 Calories

Cajun Pork

Servings: 8
Cooking Time: 40 Minutes
Ingredients:
- 5 lb. pork shoulder, cut into 4 to 6 chunks
- 4 tbsp organic Cajun spice mix
- 1 bay leaf
- 2 cups water
- Salt and pepper to taste

Directions:
1. In a heavy-bottomed pot, add all ingredients, including bone and mix well.
2. Cover and cook on medium-high fire until boiling. Lower fire to a simmer and cook for 30 minutes undisturbed.
3. Remove meat, transfer to a bowl, and shred with two forks. Return to pot, bring to a boil, and boil uncovered for 10 minutes until sauce is rendered.
4. Discard bay leaf, serve and enjoy.

Nutrition Info:
- Per Servings 2.6g Carbs, 71.5g Protein, 50.2g Fat, 768 Calories

Pork Pie With Cauliflower

Servings: 8
Cooking Time: 1 Hour And 30 Minutes
Ingredients:
- Crust:
- 1 egg
- ¼ cup butter
- 2 cups almond flour
- ¼ tsp xanthan gum
- ¼ cup shredded mozzarella
- A pinch of salt
- Filling:
- 2 pounds ground pork
- ½ cup water
- ⅓ cup pureed onion
- ¾ tsp allspice
- 1 cup cooked and mashed cauliflower
- 1 tbsp ground sage
- 2 tbsp butter

Directions:
1. Preheat your oven to 350°F.
2. Whisk together all crust ingredients in a bowl. Make two balls out of the mixture and refrigerate for 10 minutes. Combine the water, meat, and salt, in a pot over medium heat. Cook for about 15 minutes, place the meat along with the other ingredients in a bowl. Mix with your hands to combine.
3. Roll out the pie crusts and place one at the bottom of a greased pie pan. Spread the filling over the crust. Top with the other coat. Bake in the oven for 50 minutes then serve.

Nutrition Info:
- Per Servings 4g Carbs, 29g Protein, 41g Fat, 485 Calories

Lamb Stew With Veggies

Servings: 2
Cooking Time: 1 Hour 50 Minutes
Ingredients:
- 1 garlic clove, minced
- 1 parsnip, chopped
- 1 onion, chopped
- 1 tbsp olive oil
- 1 celery stalk, chopped
- 10 ounces lamb fillet, cut into pieces
- Salt and ground black pepper, to taste
- 1¼ cups vegetable stock
- 2 carrots, chopped
- ½ tbsp fresh rosemary, chopped
- 1 leek, chopped
- 1 tbsp mint sauce
- 1 tsp stevia
- 1 tbsp tomato puree
- ½ cauliflower, cut into florets
- ½ celeriac, chopped
- 2 tbsp butter

Directions:
1. Set the pot over medium heat and warm the oil, stir in the celery, onion, and garlic, and cook for 5 minutes. Stir in the lamb pieces, and cook for 3 minutes. Add in the stevia, carrot, parsnip, rosemary, mint sauce, stock, leek, tomato puree, boil the mixture, and cook for 1 hour and 30 minutes.
2. Meanwhile, heat a pot with water over medium heat, place in the celeriac, cover, and simmer for 10 minutes. Place in the cauliflower florets, cook for 15 minutes, drain everything, and combine with butter, pepper, and salt. Mash using a potato masher, and split the mash between 2 plates. Top with vegetable mixture and lamb and enjoy.

Nutrition Info:
- Per Servings 8.1g Carbs, 38g Protein, 42g Fat, 584 Calories

Smoked Pork Sausages With Mushrooms

Servings: 6
Cooking Time: 1 Hour 10 Minutes
Ingredients:
- 3 yellow bell peppers, seeded and chopped
- 2 pounds smoked sausage, sliced
- Salt and black pepper, to taste
- 2 pounds portobello mushrooms, sliced
- 2 sweet onions, chopped
- 1 tbsp swerve
- 2 tbsp olive oil
- Arugula to garnish

Directions:
1. In a baking dish, combine the sausage slices with swerve, oil, black pepper, onion, bell pepper, salt, and mushrooms. Toss well to ensure everything is coated, set in the oven at 320°F, and bake for 1 hour. To serve, divide the sausages between plates and scatter over the arugula.

Nutrition Info:
- Per Servings 7.3g Carbs, 29g Protein, 32g Fat, 525 Calories

Pork Osso Bucco

Servings: 6
Cooking Time: 1 Hour 55 Minutes
Ingredients:
- 4 tbsp butter, softened
- 6 pork shanks
- 2 tbsp olive oil
- 3 cloves garlic, minced
- 1 cup diced tomatoes
- Salt and black pepper to taste
- ½ cup chopped onions
- ½ cup chopped celery
- ½ cup chopped carrots
- 2 cups Cabernet Sauvignon
- 5 cups beef broth

- ½ cup chopped parsley + extra to garnish
- 2 tsp lemon zest

Directions:

1. Melt the butter in a large saucepan over medium heat. Season the pork with salt and pepper and brown it for 12 minutes; remove to a plate.
2. In the same pan, sauté 2 cloves of garlic and onions in the oil, for 3 minutes then return the pork shanks. Stir in the Cabernet, carrots, celery, tomatoes, and beef broth with a season of salt and pepper. Cover the pan and let it simmer on low heat for 1 ½ hours basting the pork every 15 minutes with the sauce.
3. In a bowl, mix the remaining garlic, parsley, and lemon zest to make a gremolata, and stir the mixture into the sauce when it is ready. Turn the heat off and dish the Osso Bucco. Garnish with parsley and serve with a creamy turnip mash.

Nutrition Info:

- Per Servings 6.1g Carbs, 34g Protein, 40g Fat, 590 Calories

Grilled Flank Steak With Lime Vinaigrette

Servings: 6
Cooking Time: 10 Minutes
Ingredients:

- 2 tablespoons lime juice, freshly squeezed
- ¼ cup chopped fresh cilantro
- 1 tablespoon ground cumin
- ¼ teaspoon red pepper flakes
- ¾ pound flank steak
- 2 tablespoons extra virgin olive oil
- ½ teaspoon ground black pepper
- ¼ tsp salt

Directions:

1. Heat the grill to low, medium heat
2. In a food processor, place all ingredients except for the cumin, red pepper flakes, and flank steak. Pulse until smooth. This will be the vinaigrette sauce. Set aside.
3. Season the flank steak with ground cumin and red pepper flakes and allow to marinate for at least 10 minutes.
4. Place the steak on the grill rack and cook for 5 minutes on each side. Cut into the center to check the doneness of the meat. You can also insert a meat thermometer to check the internal temperature.
5. Remove from the grill and allow to stand for 5 minutes.
6. Slice the steak to 2 inches long and toss the vinaigrette to flavor the meat.
7. Serve with salad if desired.

Nutrition Info:

- Per Servings 1.0g Carbs, 13.0g Protein, 1.0g Fat, 65 Calories

Bbq Pork Pizza With Goat Cheese

Servings: 4
Cooking Time: 30 Minutes
Ingredients:

- 1 low carb pizza bread
- Olive oil for brushing
- 1 cup grated manchego cheese
- 2 cups leftover pulled pork
- ½ cup sugar-free BBQ sauce
- 1 cup crumbled goat cheese

Directions:

1. Preheat oven to 400ºF and put pizza bread on a pizza pan. Brush with olive oil and sprinkle the manchego cheese all over. Mix the pork with BBQ sauce and spread over the cheese. Drop goat cheese on top and bake for 25 minutes until the cheese has melted and golden brown on top. Slice the pizza with a cutter and serve warm.

Nutrition Info:

- Per Servings 6g Carbs, 5g Protein, 24g Fat, 344 Calories

Herby Beef & Veggie Stew

Servings: 4
Cooking Time: 30 Minutes
Ingredients:

- 1 pound ground beef
- 2 tbsp olive oil
- 1 onion, chopped
- 2 garlic cloves, minced
- 14 ounces canned diced tomatoes
- 1 tbsp dried rosemary
- 1 tbsp dried sage
- 1 tbsp dried oregano
- 1 tbsp dried basil
- 1 tbsp dried marjoram
- Salt and black pepper, to taste
- 2 carrots, sliced
- 2 celery stalks, chopped
- 1 cup vegetable broth

Directions:

1. Set a pan over medium heat, add in the olive oil, onion, celery, and garlic, and sauté for 5 minutes. Place in the beef, and cook for 6 minutes. Stir in the tomatoes, carrots, broth, black pepper, oregano, marjoram, basil, rosemary, salt, and sage, and simmer for 15 minutes. Serve and enjoy!

Nutrition Info:

- Per Servings 5.2g Carbs, 30g Protein, 13g Fat, 253 Calories

Beef And Ale Pot Roast

Servings: 6
Cooking Time: 2 Hours 20 Minutes
Ingredients:

- 1 ½ lb brisket
- 1 tbsp olive oil
- 8 baby carrots, peeled
- 2 medium red onions, quartered
- 4 stalks celery, cut into chunks
- Salt and black pepper to taste

- 2 bay leaves
- 1 ½ cups low carb beer (ale)

Directions:

1. Preheat the oven to 370ºF. Heat the olive oil in a large skillet, while heating, season the brisket with salt and pepper. Brown the meat on both sides for 8 minutes. After, transfer to a deep casserole dish.

2. In the dish, arrange the carrots, onions, celery, and bay leaves around the brisket and pour the beer all over it. Cover the pot and cook the ingredients in the oven for 2 hours.

3. When ready, remove the casserole. Transfer the beef to a chopping board and cut it into thick slices. Serve the beef and vegetables with a drizzle of the sauce and with steamed turnips.

Nutrition Info:

- Per Servings 6g Carbs, 26g Protein, 34g Fat, 513 Calories

Spiced Pork Roast With Collard Greens

Servings: 4
Cooking Time: 40 Minutes
Ingredients:

- 2 tbsp olive oil
- Salt and black pepper, to taste
- 1 ½ pounds pork loin
- A pinch of dry mustard
- 1 tsp hot red pepper flakes
- ½ tsp ginger, minced
- 1 cup collard greens, chopped
- 2 garlic cloves, minced
- ½ lemon sliced
- ¼ cup water

Directions:

1. Using a bowl, combine the ginger with salt, mustard, and pepper. Add in the meat, toss to coat. Heat the oil in a saucepan over medium-high heat, brown the pork on all sides, for 10 minutes.

2. Transfer to the oven and roast for 1 hour at 390 F. To the saucepan, add collard greens, lemon slices, garlic, and water; cook for 10 minutes. Serve on a platter, sprinkle pan juices on top and enjoy.

Nutrition Info:

- Per Servings 3g Carbs, 45g Protein, 23g Fat, 430 Calories

Pork Sausage Bake

Servings: 4
Cooking Time: 50 Minutes
Ingredients:

- 12 pork sausages
- 5 large tomatoes, cut in rings
- 1 red bell pepper, seeded and sliced
- 1 yellow bell pepper, seeded and sliced
- 1 green bell pepper, seeded and sliced
- 1 sprig thyme, chopped

- 1 sprig rosemary, chopped
- 4 cloves garlic, minced
- 2 bay leaves
- 1 tbsp olive oil
- 2 tbsp balsamic vinegar

Directions:

1. Preheat the oven to 350ºF.

2. In the cast iron pan, add the tomatoes, bell peppers, thyme, rosemary, garlic, bay leaves, sausages, olive oil, and balsamic vinegar. Toss everything and arrange the sausages on top of the veggies.

3. Put the pan in the oven and bake for 20 minutes. After, remove the pan shake it a bit and turn the sausages over with a spoon. Continue cooking them for 25 minutes or until the sausages have browned to your desired color. Serve with the veggie and cooking sauce with cauli rice.

Nutrition Info:

- Per Servings 4.4g Carbs, 15.1g Protein, 41.6g Fat, 465 Calories

Russian Beef Gratin

Servings: 5
Cooking Time: 45 Minutes
Ingredients:

- 2 tsp onion flakes
- 2 pounds ground beef
- 2 garlic cloves, minced
- Salt and ground black pepper, to taste
- 1 cup mozzarella cheese, shredded
- 2 cups fontina cheese, shredded
- 1 cup Russian dressing
- 2 tbsp sesame seeds, toasted
- 20 dill pickle slices
- 1 iceberg lettuce head, torn

Directions:

1. Set a pan over medium heat, place in the beef, garlic, salt, onion flakes, and pepper, and cook for 5 minutes. Remove and set to a baking dish, stir in half of the Russian dressing, mozzarella cheese, and spread 1 cup of the fontina cheese.

2. Lay the pickle slices on top, spread over the remaining fontina cheese and sesame seeds, place in the oven at 350ºF, and bake for 20 minutes. Split the lettuce on serving plates, apply a topping of beef gratin, and the remaining Russian dressing.

Nutrition Info:

- Per Servings 5g Carbs, 41g Protein, 48g Fat, 584 Calories

Lamb Shashlyk

Servings: 4
Cooking Time: 20 Minutes
Ingredients:
- 1 pound ground lamb
- ¼ tsp cinnamon
- 1 egg
- 1 grated onion
- Salt and ground black pepper, to taste

Directions:
1. Place all ingredients in a bowl. Mix with your hands to combine well. Divide the meat into 4 pieces. Shape all meat portions around previously-soaked skewers. Preheat your grill to medium and grill the kebabs for about 5 minutes per side.

Nutrition Info:
- Per Servings 3.2g Carbs, 27g Protein, 37g Fat, 467 Calories

Homemade Classic Beef Burgers

Servings: 4
Cooking Time: 15 Minutes
Ingredients:
- 1 pound ground beef
- ½ tsp onion powder
- ½ tsp garlic powder
- 2 tbsp ghee
- 1 tsp Dijon mustard
- 4 low carb buns, halved
- ¼ cup mayonnaise
- 1 tsp sriracha
- 4 tbsp cabbage slaw

Directions:
1. Mix together the beef, onion, garlic powder, mustard, salt, and black pepper; create 4 burgers. Melt the ghee in a skillet and cook the burgers for about 3 minutes per side. Serve in buns topped with mayo, sriracha, and slaw.

Nutrition Info:
- Per Servings 7.9g Carbs, 39g Protein, 55g Fat, 664 Calories

Caribbean Beef

Servings: 8
Cooking Time: 1 Hour 10 Minutes
Ingredients:
- 2 onions, chopped
- 2 tbsp avocado oil
- 2 pounds beef stew meat, cubed
- 2 red bell peppers, seeded and chopped
- 1 habanero pepper, chopped
- 4 green chilies, chopped
- 14.5 ounces canned diced tomatoes
- 2 tbsp fresh cilantro, chopped
- 4 garlic cloves, minced
- ½ cup vegetable broth

- Salt and black pepper, to taste
- 1 ½ tsp cumin
- ½ cup black olives, chopped
- 1 tsp dried oregano

Directions:
1. Set a pan over medium-high heat and warm avocado oil. Brown the beef on all sides; remove and set aside. Stir-fry in the red bell peppers, green chilies, oregano, garlic, habanero pepper, onions, and cumin, for about 5-6 minutes. Pour in the tomatoes and broth, and cook for 1 hour. Stir in the olives, adjust the seasonings and serve in bowls sprinkled with fresh cilantro.

Nutrition Info:
- Per Servings 8g Carbs, 25g Protein, 14g Fat, 305 Calories

Beef Zucchini Boats

Servings: 4
Cooking Time: 45 Minutes
Ingredients:
- 2 garlic cloves, minced
- 1 tsp cumin
- 1 tbsp olive oil
- 1 pound ground beef
- ½ cup onion, chopped
- 1 tsp smoked paprika
- Salt and ground black pepper, to taste
- 4 zucchinis
- ¼ cup fresh cilantro, chopped
- ½ cup Monterey Jack cheese, shredded
- 1½ cups enchilada sauce
- 1 avocado, chopped, for serving
- Green onions, chopped, for serving
- Tomatoes, chopped, for serving

Directions:
1. Set a pan over high heat and warm the oil. Add the onions, and cook for 2 minutes. Stir in the beef, and brown for 4-5 minutes. Stir in the paprika, pepper, garlic, cumin, and salt; cook for 2 minutes.
2. Slice the zucchini in half lengthwise and scoop out the seeds. Set the zucchini in a greased baking pan, stuff each with the beef, scatter enchilada sauce on top, and spread with the Monterey cheese.
3. Bake in the oven at 350ºF for 20 minutes while covered. Uncover, spread with cilantro, and bake for 5 minutes. Top with tomatoes, green onions and avocado, place on serving plates and enjoy.

Nutrition Info:
- Per Servings 7.8g Carbs, 39g Protein, 33g Fat, 422 Calories

Italian Sausage Stew

Servings: 6
Cooking Time: 35 Minutes
Ingredients:

- 1 pound Italian sausage, sliced
- 1 red bell pepper, seeded and chopped
- 2 onions, chopped
- Salt and black pepper, to taste
- 1 cup fresh parsley, chopped
- 6 green onions, chopped
- ¼ cup avocado oil
- 1 cup beef stock
- 4 garlic cloves
- 24 ounces canned diced tomatoes
- 16 ounces okra, trimmed and sliced
- 6 ounces tomato sauce
- 2 tbsp coconut aminos
- 1 tbsp hot sauce

Directions:

1. Set a pot over medium-high heat and warm oil, place in the sausages, and cook for 2 minutes. Stir in the onion, green onions, garlic, pepper, bell pepper, and salt, and cook for 5 minutes.
2. Add in the hot sauce, stock, tomatoes, coconut aminos, okra, and tomato sauce, bring to a simmer and cook for 15 minutes. Adjust the seasoning with salt and pepper. Share into serving bowls and sprinkle with fresh parsley to serve.

Nutrition Info:

- Per Servings 7g Carbs, 16g Protein, 25g Fat, 314 Calories

Ground Beef And Cabbage Stir Fry

Servings: 5
Cooking Time:20 Minutes
Ingredients:

- 1 onion, chopped
- 3 cloves of garlic, minced
- 1 ½ pounds ground beef
- 1 tablespoon grated ginger
- ½ head cabbage, chopped
- 2 tablespoons oil
- Salt and pepper to taste
- 1 teaspoon chili flakes (optional)

Directions:

1. In a skillet, heat oil over medium flame.
2. Sauté the onion and garlic until fragrant.
3. Stir in the ground beef and season with salt and pepper to taste. Cook and crumble for 10 minutes.
4. Add grated ginger, chopped cabbage, and chili flakes. Cover and cook for 5 minutes.
5. Stir and continue cooking for another 3 minutes or until cabbage is translucent and wilted.
6. Serve and enjoy.

Nutrition Info:

- Per Servings 6.3g Carbs, 30.6g Protein, 23.7g Fat, 385 Calories

Sausage Links With Tomatoes & Pesto

Servings: 8
Cooking Time: 15 Minutes
Ingredients:

- 8 pork sausage links, sliced
- 1 lb mixed cherry tomatoes, cut in half
- 4 cups baby spinach
- 1 tbsp olive oil
- 1 pound Monterrey Jack cheese, cubed
- 2 tbsp lemon juice
- 1 cup basil pesto
- Salt and black pepper, to taste

Directions:

1. Set a pan over medium heat and warm oil, place in the sausage slices, and cook each side for 4 minutes. In a salad bowl, combine the spinach with Monterrey jack cheese, salt, pesto, pepper, cherry tomatoes, and lemon juice, and toss well to coat. Toss in the sausage pieces to coat and enjoy.

Nutrition Info:

- Per Servings 6.8g Carbs, 18g Protein, 26g Fat, 365 Calories

Beef Tripe In Vegetable Sauté

Servings: 6
Cooking Time: 27 Minutes + Cooling Time
Ingredients:

- 1 ½ lb beef tripe
- 4 cups buttermilk
- Pink salt to taste
- 2 tsp creole seasoning
- 3 tbsp olive oil
- 2 large onions, sliced
- 3 tomatoes, diced

Directions:

1. Put tripe in a bowl and cover with buttermilk. Refrigerate for 3 hours to extract bitterness and gamey taste. Remove from buttermilk, pat dry with paper towel, and season with salt and creole.
2. Heat 2 tablespoons of oil in a skillet over medium heat and brown the tripe on both sides for 6 minutes in total. Remove and set aside.
3. Add the remaining oil and sauté the onions for 3 minutes until soft. Include the tomatoes and cook for 10 minutes. Pour in a few tablespoons of water if necessary. Put the tripe in the sauce and cook for 3 minutes. Adjust taste with salt and serve with low carb rice.

Nutrition Info:

- Per Servings 1g Carbs, 22g Protein, 27g Fat, 342 Calories

Beef Cotija Cheeseburger

Servings: 4
Cooking Time: 15 Minutes
Ingredients:

- 1 lb ground beef
- 1 tsp dried parsley
- ½ tsp sugar-free Worcestershire sauce
- Salt and black pepper to taste
- 1 cup cotija cheese, shredded
- 4 low carb buns, halved

Directions:

1. Preheat a grill to 400ºF and grease the grate with cooking spray.
2. Mix the beef, parsley, Worcestershire sauce, salt, and black pepper with your hands until evenly combined. Make medium sized patties out of the mixture, about 4 patties. Cook on the grill for 7 minutes one side to be cooked through and no longer pink.
3. Flip the patties and top with cheese. Cook for another 7 minutes to be well done while the cheese melts onto the meat. Remove the patties and sandwich into two halves of a bun each. Serve with a tomato dipping sauce and zucchini fries.

Nutrition Info:

- Per Servings 2g Carbs, 21g Protein, 32g Fat, 386 Calories

Balsamic Grilled Pork Chops

Servings: 6
Cooking Time: 2 Hours 20 Minutes
Ingredients:

- 6 pork loin chops, boneless
- 2 tbsp erythritol
- ¼ cup balsamic vinegar
- 3 cloves garlic, minced
- ¼ cup olive oil
- ⅓ tsp salt
- Black pepper to taste

Directions:

1. Put the pork in a plastic bag. In a bowl, mix the erythritol, balsamic vinegar, garlic, olive oil, salt, pepper, and pour the sauce over the pork. Seal the bag, shake it, and place in the refrigerator.
2. Marinate the pork for 1 to 2 hours. Preheat the grill on medium-high heat, remove the pork when ready, and grill covered for 10 to 12 minutes on each side. Remove the pork chops, let them sit for 4 minutes, and serve with a syrupy parsnip sauté.

Nutrition Info:

- Per Servings 1.5g Carbs, 38.1g Protein, 26.8g Fat, 418 Calories

Chapter 4. Poultry Recipes

Chicken And Spinach Stir Fry

Servings: 4
Cooking Time: 10 Minutes
Ingredients:

- 2 cloves of garlic, minced
- 1 tablespoon fresh ginger, grated
- 1 ¼ pounds boneless chicken breasts, cut into strips
- 2 tablespoons yellow miso, diluted in water
- 2 cups baby spinach
- 2 tablespoons olive oil
- Pepper and salt to taste

Directions:

1. Heat oil in a skillet over medium-high heat and sauté the garlic for 30 seconds until fragrant.
2. Stir in the ginger and chicken breasts. Season lightly with pepper and salt.
3. Cook for 5 minutes while stirring constantly.
4. Stir in the diluted miso paste.
5. Continue cooking for 3 more minutes before adding spinach.
6. Cook for another minute or until the spinach leaves have wilted.

Nutrition Info:

- Per Servings 1.3g Carbs, 32.5g Protein, 10.5g Fat, 237 Calories

Herby Chicken Meatballs

Servings: 3
Cooking Time: 25 Minutes
Ingredients:

- 1 pound ground chicken
- Salt and black pepper, to taste
- 2 tbsp ranch dressing
- ½ cup almond flour
- ¼ cup mozzarella cheese, grated
- 1 tbsp dry Italian seasoning
- ¼ cup hot sauce + more for serving
- 1 egg

Directions:

1. Using a bowl, combine chicken meat, pepper, ranch dressing, Italian seasoning, flour, hot sauce, mozzarella cheese, salt, and the egg. Form 9 meatballs, arrange them on

a lined baking tray and cook for 16 minutes at 480ºF. Place the chicken meatballs in a bowl and serve along with hot sauce.

Nutrition Info:
- Per Servings 2.1g Carbs, 32g Protein, 31g Fat, 456 Calories

Stewed Italian Chicken

Servings: 4
Cooking Time: 25 Minutes
Ingredients:
- 3 ounces Italian dressing
- 4 boneless skinless chicken breasts thawed
- 5 tablespoons olive oil
- ½ cup water
- Salt and pepper to taste

Directions:
1. Add all ingredients in a pot on high fire and bring it to a boil.
2. Once boiling, lower fire to a simmer and cook for 20 minutes.
3. Adjust seasoning to taste.
4. Serve and enjoy.

Nutrition Info:
- Per Servings 3.6g Carbs, 53.6g Protein, 31.0g Fat, 545 Calories

Chicken & Squash Traybake

Servings: 4
Cooking Time: 60 Minutes
Ingredients:
- 2 lb chicken thighs
- 1 pound butternut squash, cubed
- ½ cup black olives, pitted
- ¼ cup olive oil
- 5 garlic cloves, sliced
- 1 tbsp dried oregano
- Salt and black pepper, to taste

Directions:
1. Set oven to 400ºF and grease a baking dish. Place in the chicken with the skin down. Set the garlic, olives and butternut squash around the chicken then drizzle with oil.
2. Spread pepper, salt, and oregano over the mixture then add into the oven. Cook for 45 minutes.

Nutrition Info:
- Per Servings 5.5g Carbs, 31g Protein, 15g Fat, 411 Calories

Pesto Chicken

Servings: 4
Cooking Time: 30 Minutes
Ingredients:
- 2 cups basil leaves
- ¼ cup + 1 tbsp extra virgin olive oil, divided
- 5 sun-dried tomatoes
- 4 chicken breasts

- 6 cloves garlic, smashed, peeled, and minced
- What you'll need from the store cupboard:
- Salt and pepper to taste
- Water

Directions:
1. Put in the food processor the basil leaves, ¼ cup olive oil, and tomatoes. Season with salt and pepper to taste. Add a cup of water if needed.
2. Season chicken breasts with pepper and salt generously.
3. On medium fire, heat a saucepan for 2 minutes. Add a tbsp of olive oil to the pan and swirl to coat bottom and sides. Heat oil for a minute.
4. Add chicken and sear for 5 minutes per side.
5. Add pesto sauce, cover, and cook on low fire for 15 minutes or until chicken is cooked thoroughly.
6. Serve and enjoy.

Nutrition Info:
- Per Servings 1.1g Carbs, 60.8g Protein, 32.7g Fat, 556 Calories

Fennel Shredded Chicken

Servings: 8
Cooking Time: 30 Minutes
Ingredients:
- 2 lb. chicken thighs, bone-in, and skin removed
- ¼ cup fennel bulb
- 4 cloves of garlic, minced
- 3 tbsp. lemon juice, freshly squeezed
- 1 tsp. cinnamon
- Salt and pepper to taste
- ½ cup water

Directions:
1. Place all ingredients in a heavy-bottomed pot and give a good stir.
2. Place on high fire and bring it to a boil for 5 minutes. Cover, lower fire to a simmer, and cook for 20 minutes.
3. Remove chicken and place in a bowl. Shred using two forks. Discard bones and return shredded chicken to the pot.
4. Boil for 5 minutes or until sauce is rendered.
5. Serve and enjoy.

Nutrition Info:
- Per Servings 1.9g Carbs, 18.7g Protein, 18.8g Fat, 257 Calories

Herbs And Lemony Roasted Chicken

Servings: 8
Cooking Time: 90 Minutes
Ingredients:
- 1 3-lb whole chicken
- 1 tbsp garlic powder
- 2 lemons
- 2 tsp Italian seasoning
- 5 tbsps butter
- 1 tsp ground black pepper
- 1 tsp salt

Directions:

1. In a small bowl, mix well black pepper, garlic powder, mustard powder, butter, and salt.
2. Rinse chicken well and slice off giblets.
3. In a greased 9 x 13 baking dish, place chicken and add 1 ½ tsp of seasoning made earlier inside the chicken and rub the remaining seasoning around the chicken.
4. Drizzle lemon juice all over the chicken.
5. Bake chicken in a preheated 350ºF oven until juices run clear, around 1 ½ hours. Occasionally, baste the chicken with its juices.

Nutrition Info:
- Per Servings 2.0g Carbs, 35.0g Protein, 19.0g Fat, 260 Calories

Chicken And Green Cabbage Casserole

Servings: 4
Cooking Time: 55 Minutes
Ingredients:
- 3 cups cheddar cheese, grated
- 10 ounces green cabbage, shredded
- 3 chicken breasts, skinless, boneless, cooked, cubed
- 1 cup mayonnaise
- 1 tbsp coconut oil, melted
- ⅓ cup chicken stock
- Salt and ground black pepper, to taste
- Juice of 1 lemon

Directions:
1. Apply oil to a baking dish, and set chicken pieces to the bottom. Spread green cabbage, followed by half of the cheese. Using a bowl, combine the mayonnaise with pepper, stock, lemon juice, and salt.
2. Pour this mixture over the chicken, spread the rest of the cheese, cover with aluminum foil, and bake for 30 minutes in the oven at 350ºF. Open the aluminum foil, and cook for 20 more minutes.

Nutrition Info:
- Per Servings 6g Carbs, 25g Protein, 15g Fat, 231 Calories

Chicken Pesto

Servings: 8
Cooking Time: 35 Minutes
Ingredients:
- 5 cloves of garlic
- 4 skinless, boneless chicken breast halves, cut into thin strips
- 3 tbsp grated Parmesan cheese
- ¼ cup pesto
- 1 ¼ cups heavy cream
- 10 tbsps olive oil
- Pepper to taste
- 1/8 tsp salt

Directions:
1. On medium fire, place a large saucepan and heat olive oil.

2. Add garlic and chicken, sauté for 7 minutes, or until chicken strips are nearly cooked.
3. Lower fire and add Parmesan cheese, pesto, cream, pepper, and salt.
4. Continue cooking for 5-10 minutes more or until chicken is fully cooked. Stir frequently.
5. Once penne is cooked, drain well and pour into a large saucepan, toss to coat, and serve.

Nutrition Info:
- Per Servings 3g Carbs, 30.0g Protein, 22.0g Fat, 330 Calories

Chicken Stroganoff

Servings: 4
Cooking Time: 4 Hours 15 Minutes
Ingredients:
- 2 garlic cloves, minced
- 8 oz mushrooms, chopped
- ¼ tsp celery seeds, ground
- 1 cup chicken stock
- 1 cup sour cream
- 1 cup leeks, chopped
- 1 pound chicken breasts
- 1½ tsp dried thyme
- 2 tbsp fresh parsley, chopped
- Salt and black pepper, to taste
- 4 zucchinis, spiralized

Directions:
1. Place the chicken in a slow cooker. Place in the salt, leeks, sour cream, half of the parsley, celery seeds, garlic, pepper, mushrooms, stock, and thyme. Cook on high for 4 hours while covered.
2. Uncover the pot, add more pepper and salt if desired, and the rest of the parsley. Heat a pan with water over medium heat, place in some salt, bring to a boil, stir in the zucchini pasta, cook for 1 minute, and drain. Place in serving bowls, top with the chicken mixture, and serve.

Nutrition Info:
- Per Servings 4g Carbs, 26g Protein, 22g Fat, 365 Calories

Turkey Enchilada Bowl

Servings: 4
Cooking Time: 30 Minutes
Ingredients:
- 2 tbsp coconut oil
- 1 lb boneless, skinless turkey thighs, cut into pieces
- ¾ cup red enchilada sauce (sugar-free)
- ¼ cup water
- ¼ cup chopped onion
- 3 oz canned diced green chilis
- 1 avocado, diced
- 1 cup shredded mozzarella cheese
- ¼ cup chopped pickled jalapeños
- ½ cup sour cream
- 1 tomato, diced

Directions:
1. Set a large pan over medium-high heat. Add coconut oil and warm. Place in the turkey and cook until browned on the outside. Stir in onion, chillis, water, and enchilada sauce, then close with a lid.
2. Allow simmering for 20 minutes until the turkey is cooked through. Spoon the turkey on a serving bowl and top with the sauce, cheese, sour cream, tomato, and avocado.
Nutrition Info:
*   Per Servings 5.9g Carbs, 38g Protein, 40.2g Fat, 568 Calories

Cheesy Turkey And Broccoli Traybake

Servings: 4
Cooking Time: 30 Minutes
Ingredients:
*   1 lb turkey breasts, cooked
*   2 tbsp olive oil
*   1 head broccoli, cut into florets
*   ½ cup sour cream
*   ½ cup heavy cream
*   1 cup Monterrey Jack cheese, grated
*   4 tbsp pork rinds, crushed
*   Salt and black pepper, to taste
*   ½ tsp paprika
*   1 tsp oregano
Directions:
1. Set oven to 450ºF and grease and line a baking tray. Boil water in a pan. Add in broccoli and cook for 8 minutes. Use two forks to shred the turkey.
2. Place the turkey into a large bowl together with sour cream, olive oil, and broccoli and stir to combine. Transfer the mixture to the baking tray, firmly press down. Sprinkle heavy cream over the dish, top with seasonings; and coat with grated cheese. Cover with the pork rinds.
3. Place in the oven and cook until bubbling for 20-25 minutes. Ladle to a serving plate and enjoy!
Nutrition Info:
*   Per Servings 2.6g Carbs, 29g Protein, 28g Fat, 365 Calories

Chicken Cauliflower Bake

Servings: 6
Cooking Time: 58 Minutes
Ingredients:
*   3 cups cubed leftover chicken
*   3 cups spinach
*   2 cauliflower heads, cut into florets
*   3 cups water
*   3 eggs, lightly beaten
*   2 cups grated sharp cheddar cheese
*   1 cup pork rinds, crushed
*   ½ cup unsweetened almond milk
*   3 tbsp olive oil
*   3 cloves garlic, minced
*   Salt and black pepper to taste

*   Cooking spray
Directions:
1. Preheat the oven to 350ºF and grease a baking dish with cooking spray. Set aside.
2. Then, pour the cauli florets and water in a pot; bring to boil over medium heat. Cover and steam the cauli florets for 8 minutes. After, drain them through a colander and set aside.
3. Also, combine the cheddar cheese and pork rinds in a large bowl and mix in the chicken. Set aside.
4. Next, heat the olive oil in a large skillet and cook the garlic and spinach until the spinach has wilted, about 5 minutes. Season with salt and pepper, and add the spinach mixture and cauli florets to the chicken bowl.
5. Top with the eggs and almond milk, mix and transfer everything to the baking dish. Layer the top of the ingredients and place the dish in the oven to bake for 30 minutes.
6. By this time the edges and top must have browned nicely, then remove the chicken from the oven, let rest for 5 minutes, and serve. Garnish with steamed and seasoned green beans.
Nutrition Info:
*   Per Servings 3g Carbs, 22g Protein, 27g Fat, 390 Calories

Duck & Vegetable Casserole

Servings: 2
Cooking Time: 20 Minutes
Ingredients:
*   2 duck breasts, skin on and sliced
*   2 zucchinis, sliced
*   1 tbsp coconut oil
*   1 green onion bunch, chopped
*   1 carrot, chopped
*   2 green bell peppers, seeded and chopped
*   Salt and ground black pepper, to taste
Directions:
1. Set a pan over medium-high heat and warm oil, stir in the green onions, and cook for 2 minutes. Place in the zucchini, bell peppers, pepper, salt, and carrot, and cook for 10 minutes.
2. Set another pan over medium-high heat, add in duck slices and cook each side for 3 minutes. Pour the mixture into the vegetable pan. Cook for 3 minutes. Set in bowls and enjoy.
Nutrition Info:
*   Per Servings 8g Carbs, 53g Protein, 21g Fat, 433 Calories

Chicken With Parmesan Topping

Servings: 4
Cooking Time: 45 Minutes
Ingredients:
*   4 chicken breast halves, skinless and boneless
*   Salt and black pepper, to taste
*   ¼ cup green chilies, chopped

- 5 bacon slices, chopped
- 8 ounces cream cheese
- ¼ cup onion, peeled and chopped
- ½ cup mayonnaise
- ½ cup Grana Padano cheese, grated
- 1 cup cheddar cheese, grated
- 2 ounces pork skins, crushed
- 4 tbsp melted butter
- ½ cup Parmesan cheese

Directions:

1. Lay the chicken breasts in a baking dish, season with pepper, and salt, place in the oven at 420°F and bake for 30 minutes. Set a pan over medium heat, add in the bacon, cook until crispy and remove to a plate. Stir in the onion, and cook for 3 minutes.

2. Remove from heat, add in bacon, cream cheese, ½ cup Grana Padano, mayonnaise, chilies, and cheddar cheese, and spread over the chicken. In a bowl, combine the pork skin with ½ cup Parmesan cheese, and butter. Spread over the chicken as well, place in an oven, and bake for 10 minutes.

Nutrition Info:

- Per Servings 5g Carbs, 25g Protein, 15g Fat, 361 Calories

Creamy Stewed Chicken

Servings: 6
Cooking Time: 30 Minutes
Ingredients:

- 10.5-ounce can cream of chicken soup
- 12-ounce package frozen broccoli
- 0.6-ounce package Italian dry mix dressing
- 8-ounces cream cheese
- 1 ½-pounds skinless, boneless chicken breasts
- 5 tablespoons olive oil
- ½ cup water
- Pepper and salt to taste

Directions:

1. Add all ingredients in a pot on high fire and bring to a boil.

2. Once boiling, lower fire to a simmer and cook for 25 minutes, stirring every now and then.

3. Adjust seasoning to taste.

4. Serve and enjoy.

Nutrition Info:

- Per Servings 7.0g Carbs, 31.0g Protein, 21.5g Fat, 350 Calories

Roasted Chicken With Tarragon

Servings: 4
Cooking Time: 50 Minutes
Ingredients:

- 2 lb chicken thighs
- 2 lb radishes, sliced
- 4 ¼ oz butter
- 1 tbsp tarragon
- Salt and black pepper, to taste

- 1 cup mayonnaise

Directions:

1. Set an oven to 400°F and grease a baking dish. Add in the chicken, radishes, tarragon, pepper, and salt. Place in butter then set into the oven and cook for 40 minutes. Kill the heat, set on a serving plate and enjoy alongside mayonnaise.

Nutrition Info:

- Per Servings 5.5g Carbs, 42g Protein, 23g Fat, 415 Calories

Chicken Goujons With Tomato Sauce

Servings: 8
Cooking Time: 50 Minutes
Ingredients:

- 1½ pounds chicken breasts, skinless, boneless, cubed
- Salt and ground black pepper, to taste
- 1 egg
- 1 cup almond flour
- ¼ cup Parmesan cheese, grated
- ½ tsp garlic powder
- 1½ tsp dried parsley
- ½ tsp dried basil
- 4 tbsp avocado oil
- 4 cups spaghetti squash, cooked
- 6 oz gruyere cheese, shredded
- 1½ cups tomato sauce
- Fresh basil, chopped, for serving

Directions:

1. Using a bowl, combine the almond flour with 1 teaspoon parsley, Parmesan cheese, pepper, garlic powder, and salt. In a separate bowl, combine the egg with pepper and salt. Dip the chicken in the egg, and then in almond flour mixture.

2. Set a pan over medium-high heat and warm 3 tablespoons avocado oil, add in the chicken, cook until golden, and remove to paper towels. Using a bowl, combine the spaghetti squash with salt, dried basil, rest of the parsley, 1 tablespoon avocado oil, and pepper.

3. Sprinkle this into a baking dish, top with the chicken pieces, followed by the marinara sauce. Scatter shredded gruyere cheese on top, and bake for 30 minutes at 360°F. Remove, and sprinkle with fresh basil before serving.

Nutrition Info:

- Per Servings 5g Carbs, 28g Protein, 36g Fat, 415 Calories

Pacific Chicken

Servings: 6
Cooking Time: 50 Minutes
Ingredients:

- 4 chicken breasts
- Salt and black pepper, to taste
- ½ cup mayonnaise
- 3 tbsp Dijon mustard
- 1 tsp xylitol

- ¾ cup pork rinds
- ¾ cup grated Grana-Padano cheese
- 2 tsp garlic powder
- 1 tsp onion powder
- ¼ tsp salt
- ¼ tsp black pepper
- 8 pieces ham, sliced
- 4 slices gruyere cheese

Directions:

1. Set an oven to 350ºF and grease a baking dish. Using a small bowl, place in the pork rinds and crush. Add chicken to a plate and season well.
2. In a separate bowl, mix mustard, mayonnaise, and xylitol. Take about ¼ of this mixture and spread over the chicken. Preserve the rest. Take ½ pork rinds, seasonings, most of Grana-Padano cheese, and place to the bottom of the baking dish. Add the chicken to the top.
3. Cover the chicken with the remaining Grana-Padano, pork rinds, and seasonings. Place in the oven for about 40 minutes until the chicken is cooked completely. Take out from the oven and top with gruyere cheese and ham. Place back in the oven and cook until golden brown.

Nutrition Info:

- Per Servings 2.6g Carbs, 33g Protein, 31g Fat, 465 Calories

Rotisserie Chicken With Garlic Paprika

Servings: 12
Cooking Time: 1 Hour And 40 Minutes
Ingredients:

- 1 whole chicken
- 1 tbsp. thyme
- 1 tbsp. paprika
- 6 cloves garlic
- 2 bay leaves
- 1 tsp salt
- ½ tbsp pepper

Directions:

1. In a small bowl, mix well thyme, paprika, salt, and pepper.
2. Rub and massage the entire chicken and inside the cavity with the spices.
3. Smash and peel 6 garlic cloves and mince. Rub all over chicken and inside of the chicken.
4. Smash remaining garlic and place in the chicken cavity along with bay leaves.
5. Place chicken on a wire rack placed on top of a baking pan. Tent with foil.
6. Pop in a preheated 350ºF oven and bake for 60 minutes.
7. Remove foil and continue baking for another 30 minutes.
8. Let chicken rest for 10 minutes before serving and enjoy.

Nutrition Info:

- Per Servings 1.4g Carbs, 21.3g Protein, 17.2g Fat, 249 Calories

Eggplant & Tomato Braised Chicken Thighs

Servings: 4
Cooking Time: 45 Minutes
Ingredients:

- 2 tbsp ghee
- 1 lb chicken thighs
- Pink salt and black pepper to taste
- 2 cloves garlic, minced
- 1 can whole tomatoes
- 1 eggplant, diced
- 10 fresh basil leaves, chopped + extra to garnish

Directions:

1. Melt ghee in a saucepan over medium heat, season the chicken with salt and black pepper, and fry for 4 minutes on each side until golden brown. Remove chicken onto a plate.
2. Sauté the garlic in the ghee for 2 minutes, pour in the tomatoes, and cook covered for 8 minutes.
3. Add in the eggplant and basil. Cook for 4 minutes. Season the sauce with salt and black pepper, stir and add the chicken. Coat with sauce and simmer for 3 minutes.
4. Serve chicken with sauce on a bed of squash pasta. Garnish with extra basil.

Nutrition Info:

- Per Servings 2g Carbs, 26g Protein, 39.5g Fat, 468 Calories

Avocado Cheese Pepper Chicken

Servings: 5
Cooking Time: 20 Minutes
Ingredients:

- ¼ tsp. cayenne pepper
- 1½ cup. cooked and shredded chicken
- 2 tbsps. cream cheese
- 2 tbsps. lemon juice
- 2 large avocados, diced
- Black pepper and salt to taste
- ¼ cup. mayonnaise
- 1 tsp. dried thyme
- ½ tsp. onion powder
- ½ tsp. garlic powder

Directions:

1. Remove the insides of your avocado halves and set them in a bowl.
2. Stir all ingredients to avocado flesh.
3. Fill avocados with chicken mix.
4. Serve and enjoy.

Nutrition Info:

- Per Servings 5g Carbs, 24g Protein, 40g Fat, 476 Calories

Chicken Breasts With Walnut Crust

Servings: 4
Cooking Time: 30 Minutes
Ingredients:
- 1 egg, whisked
- Salt and black pepper, to taste
- 3 tbsp coconut oil
- 1½ cups walnuts, ground
- 4 chicken breast halves, boneless and skinless

Directions:
1. Using a bowl, add in walnuts and the whisked egg in another. Season the chicken, dip in the egg and then in pecans. Warm oil in a pan over medium-high heat and brown the chicken.
2. Remove the chicken pieces to a baking sheet, set in the oven, and bake for 10 minutes at 350º F. Serve topped with lemon slices.

Nutrition Info:
- Per Servings 1.5g Carbs, 35g Protein, 18g Fat, 322 Calories

Marinara Chicken Sausage

Servings: 6
Cooking Time: 40 Minutes
Ingredients:
- 1-pound Italian chicken sausage
- 1 bell pepper, chopped
- 1 jar marinara sauce
- 1 cup mozzarella cheese, grated
- 4 tablespoons oil
- Salt and pepper to taste
- ¼ cup water

Directions:
1. Place a heavy-bottomed pot on medium-high fire and heat for 2 minutes. Add oil and swirl to coat the bottom and sides of pot and heat for a minute.
2. Sauté Italian chicken sausage for 5 minutes. Transfer to a chopping board and slice.
3. In the same pot, add marinara sauce, water, bell pepper, and sliced sausage. Cover and simmer for 30 minutes. Stir the bottom of the pot every now and then. Adjust seasoning to taste.
4. Top with marinara sauce.
5. Sprinkle top with pepper, serve, and enjoy.

Nutrition Info:
- Per Servings 4.4g Carbs, 33.9g Protein, 23.4g Fat, 402 Calories

Smoky Paprika Chicken

Servings: 8
Cooking Time: 10 Minutes
Ingredients:
- 2 lb. chicken breasts, sliced into strips
- 2 tbsp. smoked paprika
- 1 tsp Cajun seasoning
- 1 tbsp minced garlic
- 1 large onion, sliced thinly
- Salt and pepper to taste
- 1 tbsp. olive oil

Directions:
1. In a large bowl, marinate chicken strips in paprika, Cajun, pepper, salt, and minced garlic for at least 30 minutes.
2. On high fire, heat a saucepan for 2 minutes. Add oil to the pan and swirl to coat bottom and sides. Heat oil for a minute.
3. Stir fry chicken and onion for 7 minutes or until chicken is cooked.
4. Serve and enjoy.

Nutrition Info:
- Per Servings 1.5g Carbs, 34g Protein, 12.4g Fat, 217 Calories

Easy Chicken Chili

Servings: 4
Cooking Time: 30 Minutes
Ingredients:
- 4 chicken breasts, skinless, boneless, cubed
- 1 tbsp butter
- ½ onion, choppde
- 2 cups chicken broth
- 8 oz diced tomatoes
- 2 oz tomato puree
- 1 tbsp chili powder
- 1 tbsp cumin
- ½ tbsp garlic powder
- 1 serrano pepper, minced
- ½ cup shredded cheddar cheese
- Salt and black pepper to taste

Directions:
1. Set a large pan over medium-high heat and add the chicken. Cover with water and bring to a boil. Cook until no longer pink, for 10 minutes. Transfer the chicken to a flat surface to shred with forks.
2. In a large pot, pour in the butter and set over medium heat. Sauté onion until transparent for 5 minutes.
3. Stir in the chicken, tomatoes, cumin, serrano pepper, garlic powder, tomato puree, broth, and chili powder. Adjust the seasoning and let the mixture boil. Reduce heat to simmer for about 10 minutes.
4. Divide chili among bowls and top with shredded cheese to serve.

Nutrition Info:
- Per Servings 5.6g Carbs, 45g Protein, 21g Fat, 421 Calories

Turkey, Coconut And Kale Chili

Servings: 5
Cooking Time: 30 Minutes
Ingredients:

- 18 ounces turkey breasts, cubed
- 1 cup kale, chopped
- 20 ounces canned diced tomatoes
- 2 tbsp coconut oil
- 2 tbsp coconut cream
- 2 garlic cloves, peeled and minced
- 2 onions, and sliced
- 1 tbsp ground coriander
- 2 tbsp fresh ginger, grated
- 1 tbsp turmeric
- 1 tbsp cumin
- Salt and ground black pepper, to taste
- 2 tbsp chili powder

Directions:

1. Set a pan over medium-high heat and warm the coconut oil, stir in the turkey and onion, and cook for 5 minutes. Place in garlic and ginger, and cook for 1 minute. Stir in the tomatoes, pepper, turmeric, coriander, salt, cumin, and chili powder. Place in the coconut cream, and cook for 10 minutes.
2. Transfer to an immersion blender alongside kale; blend well. Allow simmering, cook for 15 minutes.

Nutrition Info:

- Per Servings 4.2g Carbs, 25g Protein, 15.2g Fat, 295 Calories

One-pot Chicken With Mushrooms And Spinach

Servings: 4
Cooking Time: 40 Minutes
Ingredients:

- 4 chicken thighs
- 2 cups mushrooms, sliced
- 1 cup spinach, chopped
- ¼ cup butter
- Salt and black pepper, to taste
- ½ tsp onion powder
- ½ tsp garlic powder
- ½ cup water
- 1 tsp Dijon mustard
- 1 tbsp fresh tarragon, chopped

Directions:

1. Set a pan over medium-high heat and warm half of the butter, place in the thighs, and sprinkle with onion powder, pepper, garlic powder, and salt. Cook each side for 3 minutes and set on a plate.
2. Place the remaining butter to the same pan and warm. Stir in mushrooms and cook for 5 minutes. Place in water and mustard, take the chicken pieces back to the pan, and cook for 15 minutes while covered. Stir in the tarragon and spinach, and cook for 5 minutes.

Nutrition Info:

- Per Servings 1g Carbs, 32g Protein, 23g Fat, 453 Calories

Poulet En Papiotte

Servings: 4
Cooking Time: 48 Minutes
Ingredients:

- 4 chicken breasts, skinless, scored
- 4 tbsp white wine
- 2 tbsp olive oil + extra for drizzling
- 4 tbsp butter
- 3 cups mixed mushrooms, teared up
- 3 medium celeriac, peeled, chopped
- 2 cups water
- 3 cloves garlic, minced
- 4 sprigs thyme, chopped
- 3 lemons, juiced
- Salt and black pepper to taste
- 2 tbsp Dijon mustard

Directions:

1. Preheat the oven to 450ºF.
2. Arrange the celeriac on a baking sheet, drizzle it with a little oil, and bake for 20 minutes; set aside.
3. In a bowl, evenly mix the chicken, roasted celeriac, mushrooms, garlic, thyme, lemon juice, salt, pepper, and mustard. Make 4 large cuts of foil, fold them in half, and then fold them in half again. Tightly fold the two open edges together to create a bag.
4. Now, share the chicken mixture into each bag, top with the white wine, olive oil, and a tablespoon each of butter on each. Seal the last open end securely making sure not to pierce the bag. Put the bag on a baking tray and bake the chicken in the middle of the oven for 25 minutes.

Nutrition Info:

- Per Servings 4.8g Carbs, 25g Protein, 16.5g Fat, 364 Calories

Tender Turkey Breast

Servings: 12
Cooking Time: 25 Minutes
Ingredients:

- 4 peeled garlic cloves
- 4 fresh rosemary sprigs
- 1 bone-in turkey breast
- 5 tablespoons olive oil
- ½ teaspoon coarsely ground pepper
- ¼ teaspoon salt
- ½ cup water

Directions:

1. Add all ingredients in a pot on high fire and bring it to a boil.
2. Once boiling, lower fire to a simmer and cook for 20 minutes.
3. Adjust seasoning to taste.
4. Serve and enjoy.

Nutrition Info:
- Per Servings 0.8g Carbs, 35.8g Protein, 22.7g Fat, 390 Calories

Yummy Chicken Queso

Servings: 4
Cooking Time: 25 Minutes
Ingredients:
- ½ teaspoon garlic salt
- 4-ounce can diced drained green chiles
- 10-ounce can mild rotel drained
- ¾ cup medium queso dip
- 4 boneless skinless boneless fresh or thawed chicken breasts
- 5 tablespoons olive oil
- 1 cup water

Directions:
1. Add all ingredients in a pot on high fire and bring it to a boil.
2. Once boiling, lower fire to a simmer and cook for 20 minutes. Stir frequently.
3. Adjust seasoning to taste.
4. Serve and enjoy.

Nutrition Info:
- Per Servings 7.2g Carbs, 56.6g Protein, 21.7g Fat, 500 Calories

Buttered Duck Breast

Servings: 1
Cooking Time: 30 Minutes
Ingredients:
- 1 medium duck breast, skin scored
- 1 tbsp heavy cream
- 2 tbsp butter
- Salt and black pepper, to taste
- 1 cup kale
- ¼ tsp fresh sage

Directions:
1. Set the pan over medium-high heat and warm half of the butter. Place in sage and heavy cream, and cook for 2 minutes. Set another pan over medium-high heat. Place in the remaining butter and duck breast as the skin side faces down, cook for 4 minutes, flip, and cook for 3 more minutes.
2. Place the kale to the pan containing the sauce, cook for 1 minute. Set the duck breast on a flat surface and slice. Arrange the duck slices on a platter and drizzle over the sauce.

Nutrition Info:
- Per Servings 2g Carbs, 35g Protein, 46g Fat, 547 Calories

Zesty Grilled Chicken

Servings: 8
Cooking Time: 35 Minutes
Ingredients:
- 2½ pounds chicken thighs and drumsticks
- 1 tbsp coconut aminos
- 1 tbsp apple cider vinegar
- A pinch of red pepper flakes
- Salt and black pepper, to taste
- ½ tsp ground ginger
- ⅓ cup butter
- 1 garlic clove, minced
- 1 tsp lime zest
- ½ cup warm water

Directions:
1. In a blender, combine the butter with water, salt, ginger, vinegar, garlic, pepper, lime zest, aminos, and pepper flakes. Pat the chicken pieces dry, lay on a pan, and top with the zesty marinade.
2. Toss to coat and refrigerate for 1 hour. Set the chicken pieces skin side down on a preheated grill over medium-high heat, cook for 10 minutes, turn, brush with some marinade, and cook for 10 minutes. Split among serving plates and enjoy.

Nutrition Info:
- Per Servings 3g Carbs, 42g Protein, 12g Fat, 375 Calories

Chicken Cacciatore

Servings: 6
Cooking Time: 35 Minutes
Ingredients:
- 6 chicken drumsticks, bone-in
- 1 bay leaf
- 4 roma tomatoes, chopped
- ½ cup black olives, pitted
- 3 cloves garlic, minced
- Salt and pepper to taste
- 1 cup water
- 1 tsp oil

Directions:
1. On high fire, heat a saucepan for 2 minutes. Add oil to the pan and swirl to coat bottom and sides. Heat oil for a minute.
2. Add garlic and sauté for a minute. Stir in tomatoes and bay leaf. Crumble and wilt tomatoes for 5 minutes.
3. Add chicken and continue sautéing for 7 minutes.
4. Deglaze the pot with ½ cup water.
5. Add remaining ingredients. Season generously with salt and pepper.
6. Lower fire to low, cover, and simmer for 20 minutes.
7. Serve and enjoy.

Nutrition Info:
- Per Servings 9.5g Carbs, 25.3g Protein, 13.2g Fat, 256 Calories

Easy Chicken Vindaloo

Servings: 5
Cooking Time: 30 Minutes
Ingredients:
- 1 lb. chicken thighs, skin and bones not removed
- 2 tbsp. garam masala
- 6 whole red dried chilies
- 1 onion, sliced
- 5 cloves of garlic, crushed
- Pepper and salt to taste
- 1 tsp oil
- 1 cup water

Directions:
1. On high fire, heat a saucepan for 2 minutes. Add oil to the pan and swirl to coat bottom and sides. Heat oil for a minute.
2. Add chicken with skin side touching pan and sear for 5 minutes. Turn chicken over and sear the other side for 3 minutes. Transfer chicken to a plate.
3. In the same pan, sauté garlic for a minute. Add onion and sauté for 3 minutes. Stir in garam masala and chilies.
4. Return chicken to the pot and mix well. Add water and season with pepper and salt.
5. Cover and lower fire to simmer and cook for 15 minutes.
6. Serve and enjoy.

Nutrition Info:
- Per Servings 1.4g Carbs, 15.2g Protein, 15.1g Fat, 206 Calories

Red Wine Chicken

Servings: 4
Cooking Time: 30 Minutes
Ingredients:
- 3 tbsp coconut oil
- 2 lb chicken breast halves, skinless and boneless
- 3 garlic cloves, minced
- Salt and black pepper, to taste
- 1 cup chicken stock
- 3 tbsp stevia
- ½ cup red wine
- 2 tomatoes, sliced
- 6 mozzarella slices
- Fresh basil, chopped, for serving

Directions:
1. Set a pan over medium-high heat and warm oil, add the chicken, season with pepper and salt, cook until brown. Stir in the stevia, garlic, stock, and red wine, and cook for 10 minutes.
2. Remove to a lined baking sheet and arrange mozzarella cheese slices on top. Broil in the oven over medium heat until cheese melts and lay tomato slices over chicken pieces.
3. Sprinkle with chopped basil to serve.

Nutrition Info:
- Per Servings 4g Carbs, 27g Protein, 12g Fat, 314 Calories

Greek Chicken Stew

Servings: 4
Cooking Time: 30 Minutes
Ingredients:
- ¼ cup feta cheese
- Sliced and pitted Kalamata olives
- 1 bottle ken's steak house Greek dressing with Feta cheese, olive oil, and black olives
- 4 boneless and skinless thawed chicken breasts
- 1 cup water

Directions:
1. Add all ingredients in a pot, except for feta, on high fire, and bring to a boil.
2. Once boiling, lower fire to a simmer and cook for 25 minutes.
3. Adjust seasoning to taste and stir in feta.
4. Serve and enjoy.

Nutrition Info:
- Per Servings 3.2g Carbs, 54.4g Protein, 65.1g Fat, 818 Calories

Chicken In Creamy Spinach Sauce

Servings: 4
Cooking Time: 20 Minutes
Ingredients:
- 1 pound chicken thighs
- 2 tbsp coconut oil
- 2 tbsp coconut flour
- 2 cups spinach, chopped
- 1 tsp oregano
- 1 cup heavy cream
- 1 cup chicken broth
- 2 tbsp butter

Directions:
1. Warm the coconut oil in a skillet and brown the chicken on all sides, about 6-8 minutes. Set aside.
2. Melt the butter and whisk in the flour over medium heat. Whisk in the heavy cream and chicken broth and bring to a boil. Stir in oregano. Add the spinach to the skillet and cook until wilted.
3. Add the thighs in the skillet and cook for an additional 5 minutes.

Nutrition Info:
- Per Servings 2.6g Carbs, 18g Protein, 38g Fat, 446 Calories

Quattro Formaggi Chicken

Servings: 8
Cooking Time: 40 Minutes
Ingredients:
- 3 pounds chicken breasts
- 2 ounces mozzarella cheese, cubed
- 2 ounces mascarpone cheese
- 4 ounces cheddar cheese, cubed
- 2 ounces provolone cheese, cubed

- 1 zucchini, shredded
- Salt and ground black pepper, to taste
- 1 tsp garlic, minced
- ½ cup pancetta, cooked and crumbled

Directions:

1. Sprinkle pepper and salt to the zucchini, squeeze well, and place to a bowl. Stir in the pancetta, mascarpone, cheddar cheese, provolone cheese, mozzarella, pepper, and garlic.

2. Cut slits into chicken breasts, apply pepper and salt, and stuff with the zucchini and cheese mixture. Set on a lined baking sheet, place in the oven at 400ºF, and bake for 45 minutes.

Nutrition Info:

- Per Servings 2g Carbs, 51g Protein, 37g Fat, 565 Calories

Chicken With Asparagus & Root Vegetables

Servings: 4
Cooking Time: 35 Minutes

Ingredients:

- 2 cups whipping cream
- 3 chicken breasts, boneless, skinless, chopped
- 3 tbsp butter
- ½ cup onion, chopped
- ¾ cup carrot, chopped
- 5 cups chicken stock
- Salt and black pepper, to taste
- 1 bay leaf
- 1 turnip, chopped
- 1 parsnip, chopped
- 17 ounces asparagus, trimmed
- 3 tsp fresh thyme, chopped

Directions:

1. Set a pan over medium heat and add whipping cream, allow simmering, and cook until it's reduced by half for about 7 minutes. Set another pan over medium heat and warm butter, sauté the onion for 3 minutes. Pour in the chicken stock, carrots, turnip, and parsnip, chicken, and bay leaf, bring to a boil, and simmer for 20 minutes.

2. Add in the asparagus and cook for 7 minutes. Discard the bay leaf, stir in the reduced whipping cream, adjust the seasoning and ladle the stew into serving bowls. Scatter with fresh thyme.

Nutrition Info:

- Per Servings 7.4g Carbs, 37g Protein, 31g Fat, 497 Calories

Turkey Burgers With Fried Brussels Sprouts

Servings: 4
Cooking Time: 30 Minutes

Ingredients:

- For the burgers

- 1 pound ground turkey
- 1 free-range egg
- ½ onion, chopped
- 1 tsp salt
- ½ tsp ground black pepper
- 1 tsp dried thyme
- 2 oz butter
- For the fried Brussels sprouts
- 1 ½ lb Brussels sprouts, halved
- 3 oz butter
- 1 tsp salt
- ½ tsp ground black pepper

Directions:

1. Combine the burger ingredients in a mixing bowl. Create patties from the mixture. Set a large pan over medium-high heat, warm butter, and fry the patties until cooked completely.

2. Place on a plate and cover with aluminium foil to keep warm. Fry brussels sprouts in butter, season to your preference, then set to a bowl. Plate the burgers and brussels sprouts and serve.

Nutrition Info:

- Per Servings 5.8g Carbs, 31g Protein, 25g Fat, 443 Calories

Stuffed Avocados With Chicken

Servings: 2
Cooking Time: 10 Minutes

Ingredients:

- 2 avocados, cut in half and pitted
- ¼ cup pesto
- 1 tsp dried thyme
- 2 tbsp cream cheese
- 1½ cups chicken, cooked and shredded
- Salt and ground black pepper, to taste
- ¼ tsp cayenne pepper
- ½ tsp onion powder
- ½ tsp garlic powder
- 1 tsp paprika
- Salt and black pepper, to taste
- 2 tbsp lemon juice

Directions:

1. Scoop the insides of the avocado halves, and place the flesh in a bowl. Add in the chicken. Stir in the remaining ingredients. Stuff the avocado cups with chicken mixture and enjoy.

Nutrition Info:

- Per Servings 5g Carbs, 24g Protein, 40g Fat, 511 Calories

Sweet Garlic Chicken Skewers

Servings: 4
Cooking Time: 17 Minutes + Time Refrigeration
Ingredients:
- For the Skewers
- 3 tbsp soy sauce
- 1 tbsp ginger-garlic paste
- 2 tbsp swerve brown sugar
- Chili pepper to taste
- 2 tbsp olive oil
- 3 chicken breasts, cut into cubes
- For the Dressing
- ½ cup tahini
- ½ tsp garlic powder
- Pink salt to taste
- ¼ cup warm water

Directions:
1. In a small bowl, whisk the soy sauce, ginger-garlic paste, brown sugar, chili pepper, and olive oil.
2. Put the chicken in a zipper bag, pour the marinade over, seal and shake for an even coat. Marinate in the fridge for 2 hours.
3. Preheat a grill to 400ºF and thread the chicken on skewers. Cook for 10 minutes in total with three to four turnings to be golden brown. Plate them. Mix the tahini, garlic powder, salt, and warm water in a bowl. Pour into serving jars.
4. Serve the chicken skewers and tahini dressing with cauli fried rice.

Nutrition Info:
- Per Servings 2g Carbs, 15g Protein, 17.4g Fat, 225 Calories

Chicken And Zucchini Bake

Servings: 4
Cooking Time: 45 Minutes
Ingredients:
- 1 zucchini, chopped
- Salt and black pepper, to taste
- 1 tsp garlic powder
- 1 tbsp avocado oil
- 2 chicken breasts, skinless, boneless, sliced
- 1 tomato, cored and chopped
- ½ tsp dried oregano
- ½ tsp dried basil
- ½ cup mozzarella cheese, shredded

Directions:
1. Apply pepper, garlic powder and salt to the chicken. Set a pan over medium heat and warm avocado oil, add in the chicken slices, cook until golden; remove to a baking dish. To the same pan add the zucchini, tomato, pepper, basil, oregano, and salt, cook for 2 minutes, and spread over chicken.
2. Bake in the oven at 330ºF for 20 minutes. Sprinkle the mozzarella over the chicken, return to the oven, and bake for

5 minutes until the cheese is melted and bubbling. Serve with green salad.
Nutrition Info:
- Per Servings 2g Carbs, 35g Protein, 11g Fat, 235 Calories

Easy Chicken Meatloaf

Servings: 8
Cooking Time: 50 Minutes
Ingredients:
- 1 cup sugar-free marinara sauce
- 2 lb ground chicken
- 2 tbsp fresh parsley, chopped
- 3 garlic cloves, minced
- 2 tsp onion powder
- 2 tsp Italian seasoning
- Salt and ground black pepper, to taste
- For the filling
- ½ cup ricotta cheese
- 1 cup Grana Padano cheese, grated
- 1 cup Colby cheese, shredded
- 2 tsp fresh chives, chopped
- 2 tbsp fresh parsley, chopped
- 1 garlic clove, minced

Directions:
1. Using a bowl, combine the chicken with half of the marinara sauce, pepper, onion powder, Italian seasoning, salt, and 2 garlic cloves. In a separate bowl, combine the ricotta cheese with half of the Grana Padano cheese, chives, pepper, 1 garlic clove, half of the Colby cheese, salt, and 2 tablespoons parsley. Place half of the chicken mixture into a loaf pan, and spread evenly.
2. Place in cheese filling and spread evenly. Top with the rest of the meat mixture and spread again. Set the meatloaf in the oven at 380ºF and bake for 25 minutes. Remove meatloaf from oven, spread the rest of the marinara sauce, Grana Padano cheese and Colby cheese, and bake for 18 minutes. Allow meatloaf cooling and serve in slices sprinkled with 2 tbsp of chopped parsley.

Nutrition Info:
- Per Servings 4g Carbs, 28g Protein, 14g Fat, 273 Calories

Chicken In White Wine Sauce

Servings: 4
Cooking Time: 50 Minutes
Ingredients:
- 8 chicken thighs
- Salt and black pepper, to taste
- 1 onion, peeled and chopped
- 1 tbsp coconut oil
- 4 pancetta strips, chopped
- 4 garlic cloves, minced
- 10 oz white mushrooms, halved
- 2 cups white wine
- 1 cup whipping cream

- ½ cup fresh parsley, chopped

Directions:

1. Set a pan over medium heat and warm oil, cook the pancetta until crispy, about 4-5 minutes and remove to paper towels. To the pancetta fat, add the chicken, sprinkle with pepper and salt, cook until brown, and remove to paper towels too.

2. In the same pan, sauté the onion and garlic for 4 minutes. Then, mix in the mushrooms and cook for another 5 minutes. Return the pancetta and browned chicken to the pan.

3. Stir in the wine and bring to a boil, reduce the heat, and simmer for 20 minutes. Pour in the whipping cream and warm without boiling. Split among serving bowls and enjoy. Scatter over the parsley and serve with steamed green beans.

Nutrition Info:

- Per Servings 4g Carbs, 24g Protein, 12g Fat, 345 Calories

Roasted Stuffed Chicken With Tomato Basil Sauce

Servings: 6
Cooking Time: 35 Minutes

Ingredients:

- 4 ounces cream cheese
- 3 ounces mozzarella slices
- 10 ounces spinach
- ⅓ cup shredded mozzarella
- 1 tbsp olive oil
- 1 cup tomato basil sauce
- 3 whole chicken breasts

Directions:

1. Preheat your oven to 400°F. Combine the cream cheese, shredded mozzarella, and spinach in the microwave.

2. Cut the chicken with the knife a couple of times horizontally. Stuff with the spinach mixture. Brush the top with olive oil. Place on a lined baking dish and bake in the oven for 25 minutes.

3. Pour the tomato basil sauce over and top with mozzarella slices. Return to the oven and cook for an additional 5 minutes.

Nutrition Info:

- Per Servings 2.5g Carbs, 37g Protein, 28g Fat, 338 Calories

Greek Chicken With Capers

Servings: 4
Cooking Time: 30 Minutes

Ingredients:

- ¼ cup olive oil
- 1 onion, chopped
- 4 chicken breasts, skinless and boneless
- 4 garlic cloves, minced
- Salt and ground black pepper, to taste
- ½ cup kalamata olives, pitted and chopped
- 1 tbsp capers
- 1 pound tomatoes, chopped

- ½ tsp red chili flakes

Directions:

1. Sprinkle pepper and salt on the chicken, and rub with half of the oil. Add the chicken to a pan set over high heat, cook for 2 minutes, flip to the other side, and cook for 2 more minutes. Set the chicken breasts in the oven at 450°F and bake for 8 minutes. Split the chicken into serving plates.

2. Set the same pan over medium heat and warm the remaining oil, place in the onion, olives, capers, garlic, and chili flakes, and cook for 1 minute. Stir in the tomatoes, pepper, and salt, and cook for 2 minutes. Sprinkle over the chicken breasts and enjoy.

Nutrition Info:

- Per Servings 2.2g Carbs, 25g Protein, 21g Fat, 387 Calories

Chicken With Anchovy Tapenade

Servings: 2
Cooking Time: 30 Minutes

Ingredients:

- 1 chicken breast, cut into 4 pieces
- 2 tbsp coconut oil
- 3 garlic cloves, and crushed
- For the tapenade
- 1 cup black olives, pitted
- 1 oz anchovy fillets, rinsed
- 1 garlic clove, crushed
- Salt and ground black pepper, to taste
- 2 tbsp olive oil
- ¼ cup fresh basil, chopped
- 1 tbsp lemon juice

Directions:

1. Using a food processor, combine the olives, salt, olive oil, basil, lemon juice, anchovy fillets, and pepper, blend well. Set a pan over medium-high heat and warm coconut oil, stir in the garlic, and cook for 2 minutes.

2. Place in the chicken pieces and cook each side for 4 minutes. Split the chicken among plates and apply a topping of the anchovy tapenade.

Nutrition Info:

- Per Servings 3g Carbs, 25g Protein, 13g Fat, 155 Calories

Chicken And Mushrooms

Servings: 8
Cooking Time: 15 Minutes

Ingredients:

- 1 large shallot, diced
- 8 chicken breasts, cubed
- 4 large cremini mushrooms, sliced
- ¼ cup yogurt
- 5 tablespoons olive oil
- ½ cup water
- Salt and pepper to taste

Directions:

1. Heat oil in a skillet over medium flame and sauté the shallot until fragrant.
2. Stir in the chicken breasts and continue cooking for 3 minutes while stirring constantly.
3. Add the mushrooms, water, and yogurt.
4. Season with salt and pepper to taste.
5. Close the lid and bring to a boil.
6. Reduce the heat to medium-low and allow simmering for 10 minutes.

Nutrition Info:
- Per Servings 1.5g Carbs, 55.8g Protein, 27.7g Fat, 512 Calories

Chicken Skewers With Celery Fries

Servings: 4
Cooking Time: 60 Minutes
Ingredients:
- 2 chicken breasts
- ½ tsp salt
- ¼ tsp ground black pepper
- 2 tbsp olive oil
- 1/4 chicken broth
- For the fries
- 1 lb celery root
- 2 tbsp olive oil
- ½ tsp salt
- ¼ tsp ground black pepper

Directions:
1. Set an oven to 400ºF. Grease and line a baking sheet. In a large bowl, mix oil, spices and the chicken; set in the fridge for 10 minutes while covered. Peel and chop celery root to form fry shapes and place into a separate bowl. Apply oil to coat and add pepper and salt for seasoning. Arrange to the baking tray in an even layer and bake for 10 minutes.
2. Take the chicken from the refrigerator and thread onto the skewers. Place over the celery, pour in the chicken broth, then set in the oven for 30 minutes. Serve with lemon wedges.

Nutrition Info:
- Per Servings 6g Carbs, 39g Protein, 43g Fat, 579 Calories

Spinach & Ricotta Stuffed Chicken Breasts

Servings: 3
Cooking Time: 25 Minutes
Ingredients:
- 1 cup spinach, cooked and chopped
- 3 chicken breasts
- Salt and ground black pepper, to taste
- 4 ounces cream cheese, softened
- 1/2 cup ricotta cheese, crumbled
- 1 garlic clove, peeled and minced
- 1 tbsp coconut oil

- ½ cup white wine

Directions:
1. Using a bowl, combine the ricotta cheese with cream cheese, salt, garlic, pepper, and spinach. Add the chicken breasts on a working surface, cut a pocket in each, stuff them with the spinach mixture, and add more pepper and salt.
2. Set a pan over medium-high heat and warm oil, add the stuffed chicken, cook each side for 5 minutes. Put in a baking tray, drizzle with white wine and 2 tablespoons of water and then place in the oven at 420ºF. Bake for 10 minutes, arrange on a serving plate and serve.

Nutrition Info:
- Per Servings 4g Carbs, 23g Protein, 12g Fat, 305 Calories

Lemon & Rosemary Chicken In A Skillet

Servings: 4
Cooking Time: 1 Hour And 20 Minutes
Ingredients:
- 8 chicken thighs
- 1 tsp salt
- 2 tbsp lemon juice
- 1 tsp lemon zest
- 2 tbsp olive oil
- 1 tbsp chopped rosemary
- ¼ tsp black pepper
- 1 garlic clove, minced

Directions:
1. Combine all ingredients in a bowl. Place in the fridge for one hour.
2. Heat a skillet over medium heat. Add the chicken along with the juices and cook until crispy, about 7 minutes per side.

Nutrition Info:
- Per Servings 2.5g Carbs, 31g Protein, 31g Fat, 477 Calories

Chicken Chipotle

Servings: 8
Cooking Time: 25 Minutes
Ingredients:
- 4 tablespoons McCormick grill mates' chipotle
- Roasted garlic seasoning
- 8 garlic cloves peeled and crushed
- 5-pounds whole chicken
- ½ cup water

Directions:
1. Add all ingredients in a pot on high fire and bring it to a boil.
2. Once boiling, lower fire to a simmer and cook for 25 minutes.
3. Adjust seasoning to taste.
4. Serve and enjoy.

Nutrition Info:

- Per Servings 5.7g Carbs, 52.0g Protein, 42.5g Fat, 613 Calories

Chicken Paella With Chorizo

Servings: 6
Cooking Time: 63 Minutes
Ingredients:
- 18 chicken drumsticks
- 12 oz chorizo, chopped
- 1 white onion, chopped
- 4 oz jarred piquillo peppers, finely diced
- 2 tbsp olive oil
- ½ cup chopped parsley
- 1 tsp smoked paprika
- 2 tbsp tomato puree
- ½ cup white wine
- 1 cup chicken broth
- 2 cups cauli rice
- 1 cup chopped green beans
- 1 lemon, cut in wedges
- Salt and pepper, to taste

Directions:
1. Preheat the oven to 350ºF.
2. Heat the olive oil in a cast iron pan over medium heat, meanwhile season the chicken with salt and pepper, and fry in the hot oil on both sides for 10 minutes to lightly brown. After, remove onto a plate with a perforated spoon.
3. Then, add the chorizo and onion to the hot oil, and sauté for 4 minutes. Include the tomato puree, piquillo peppers, and paprika, and let simmer for 2 minutes. Add the broth, and bring the ingredients to boil for 6 minutes until slightly reduced.
4. Stir in the cauli rice, white wine, green beans, half of the parsley, and lay the chicken on top. Transfer the pan to the oven and continue cooking for 20-25 minutes. Let the paella sit to cool for 10 minutes before serving garnished with the remaining parsley and lemon wedges.

Nutrition Info:
- Per Servings 3g Carbs, 22g Protein, 28g Fat, 440 Calories

Chicken, Broccoli & Cashew Stir-fry

Servings: 4
Cooking Time: 30 Minutes
Ingredients:
- 2 chicken breasts, cut into strips
- 3 tbsp olive oil
- 2 tbsp soy sauce
- 2 tsp white wine vinegar
- 1 tsp erythritol
- 2 tsp xanthan gum
- 1 lemon, juiced
- 1 cup unsalted cashew nuts
- 2 cups broccoli florets
- 1 white onion, thinly sliced

- Pepper to taste

Directions:
1. In a bowl, mix the soy sauce, vinegar, lemon juice, erythritol, and xanthan gum. Set aside.
2. Heat the oil in a wok and fry the cashew for 4 minutes until golden-brown. Remove the cashews into a paper towel lined plate and set aside. Sauté the onion in the same oil for 4 minutes until soft and browned; add to the cashew nuts.
3. Add the chicken to the wok and cook for 4 minutes; include the broccoli and pepper. Stir-fry and pour the soy sauce mixture in. Stir and cook the sauce for 4 minutes and pour in the cashews and onion. Stir once more, cook for 1 minute, and turn the heat off.
4. Serve the chicken stir-fry with some steamed cauli rice.

Nutrition Info:
- Per Servings 3.4g Carbs, 17.3g Protein, 10.1g Fat, 286 Calories

Coconut Aminos Chicken Bake

Servings: 4
Cooking Time: 20 Minutes
Ingredients:
- 3 green onions, chopped
- 4 chicken breasts
- 4 oz. cheddar cheese, shredded
- 4 bacon strips
- 1 oz. coconut aminos
- 2 tbsp. coconut oil

Directions:
1. Heat oil in a skillet over high heat. Add chicken breasts and cook for 7 minutes both sides.
2. In another pan over medium-high heat, sauté bacon and place to a plate lined with a paper towel and crumble it.
3. Lay the chicken in a baking dish, sprinkle with coconut aminos, bacon, shredded cheese and chopped green onions.
4. Place the baking dish in the broiler and cook on High for 5 minutes. Serve and enjoy.

Nutrition Info:
- Per Servings 2g Carbs, 18g Protein, 49g Fat, 570 Calories

Slow-cooked Mexican Turkey Soup

Servings: 4
Cooking Time: 4 Hours 15 Minutes
Ingredients:
- 1 ½ lb turkey breasts, skinless, boneless, cubed
- 4 cups chicken stock
- 1 chopped onion
- 1 cup canned chunky salsa
- 8 ounces cheddar cheese, into chunks
- ¼ tsp cayenne red pepper
- 4 oz canned diced green chilies
- 1 tsp fresh cilantro, chopped

Directions:
1. In a slow cooker, combine the turkey with salsa, onion, green chilies, cayenne pepper, chicken stock, and cheese,

and cook for 4 hours on high while covered. Open the slow cooker, sprinkle with fresh cilantro and ladle in bowls to serve.

Nutrition Info:
- Per Servings 6g Carbs, 38g Protein, 24g Fat, 387 Calories

Bacon Chicken Alfredo

Servings: 4
Cooking Time: 35 Minutes
Ingredients:
- 4-ounces mushrooms drained and sliced
- 1 cup shredded mozzarella cheese
- 1 jar Classico creamy alfredo sauce
- 6 slices chopped hickory bacon
- 4 boneless skinless chicken breasts thawed or fresh
- Pepper and salt to taste
- ½ cup water

Directions:
1. Add all ingredients in a pot on high fire and bring it to a boil.
2. Once boiling, lower fire to a simmer and cook for 30 minutes, stirring every now and then.
3. Adjust seasoning to taste.
4. Serve and enjoy.

Nutrition Info:
- Per Servings 7.7g Carbs, 75.8g Protein, 70.8g Fat, 976 Calories

Cilantro Chicken Breasts With Mayo-avocado Sauce

Servings: 4
Cooking Time: 22 Minutes
Ingredients:
- For the Sauce
- 1 avocado, pitted
- ½ cup mayonnaise
- Salt to taste
- For the Chicken
- 3 tbsp ghee
- 4 chicken breasts
- Pink salt and black pepper to taste
- 1 cup chopped cilantro leaves
- ½ cup chicken broth

Directions:
1. Spoon the avocado, mayonnaise, and salt into a small food processor and puree until smooth sauce is derived. Adjust taste with salt as desired.
2. Pour sauce into a jar and refrigerate while you make the chicken.
3. Melt ghee in a large skillet, season chicken with salt and black pepper and fry for 4 minutes on each side to golden brown. Remove chicken to a plate.
4. Pour the broth in the same skillet and add the cilantro. Bring to simmer covered for 3 minutes and add the chicken. Cover and cook on low heat for 5 minutes until liquid has

reduced and chicken is fragrant. Dish chicken only into serving plates and spoon the mayo-avocado sauce over.

Nutrition Info:
- Per Servings 4g Carbs, 24g Protein, 32g Fat, 398 Calories

Bacon And Chicken Cottage Pie

Servings: 4
Cooking Time: 55 Minutes
Ingredients:
- ½ cup onion, chopped
- 4 bacon slices
- 3 tbsp butter
- 1 carrot, chopped
- 3 garlic cloves, minced
- Salt and ground black pepper, to taste
- ¾ cup crème fraîche
- ½ cup chicken stock
- 12 ounces chicken breasts, cubed
- 2 tbsp Dijon mustard
- ¾ cup cheddar cheese, shredded
- For the dough
- ¾ cup almond flour
- 3 tbsp cream cheese
- 1½ cup mozzarella cheese, shredded
- 1 egg
- 1 tsp onion powder
- 1 tsp garlic powder
- 1 tsp Italian seasoning
- Salt and ground black pepper, to taste

Directions:
1. Set a pan over medium heat and warm butter and sauté the onion, garlic, pepper, bacon, salt, and carrot, for 5 minutes. Add in the chicken, and cook for 3 minutes. Stir in the crème fraîche, salt, mustard, pepper, and stock, cook for 7 minutes. Add in the cheddar and set aside.
2. Using a bowl, combine the mozzarella cheese with the cream cheese, and heat in a microwave for 1 minute. Stir in the garlic powder, salt, flour, pepper, Italian seasoning, onion powder, and egg. Knead the dough well, split into 4 pieces, and flatten each into a circle. Set the chicken mixture into 4 ramekins, top each with a dough circle, place in an oven at 370º F for 25 minutes.

Nutrition Info:
- Per Servings 8.2g Carbs, 41g Protein, 45g Fat, 571 Calories

Parmesan Wings With Yogurt Sauce

Servings: 6
Cooking Time: 25 Minutes
Ingredients:
- For the Dipping Sauce
- 1 cup plain yogurt
- 1 tsp fresh lemon juice
- Salt and black pepper to taste

- For the Wings
- 2 lb chicken wings
- Salt and black pepper to taste
- Cooking spray
- ½ cup melted butter
- ½ cup Hot sauce
- ¼ cup grated Parmesan cheese

Directions:

1. Mix the yogurt, lemon juice, salt, and black pepper in a bowl. Chill while making the chicken.

2. Preheat oven to 400ºF and season wings with salt and black pepper. Line them on a baking sheet and grease lightly with cooking spray. Bake for 20 minutes until golden brown. Mix butter, hot sauce, and parmesan in a bowl. Toss chicken in the sauce to evenly coat and plate. Serve with yogurt dipping sauce and celery strips.

Nutrition Info:

- Per Servings 4g Carbs, 24g Protein, 36.4g Fat, 452 Calories

Rosemary Grilled Chicken

Servings: 4
Cooking Time: 12 Minutes
Ingredients:

- 1 tablespoon fresh parsley, finely chopped
- 1 tablespoon fresh rosemary, finely chopped
- 4 tablespoons olive oil
- 4 pieces of 4-oz chicken breast, boneless and skinless
- 5 cloves garlic, minced
- Pepper and salt to taste

Directions:

1. In a shallow and large bowl, mix salt, parsley, rosemary, olive oil, and garlic. Place chicken breast and marinate in the bowl of herbs for at least an hour or more before grilling.

2. Grease grill, grate and preheat grill to medium-high fire. Once hot, grill chicken for 4 to 5 minutes per side or until juices run a clear and internal temperature of chicken is 168oF.

Nutrition Info:

- Per Servings 1.0g Carbs, 34.0g Protein, 16.0g Fat, 238 Calories

Fried Chicken With Coconut Sauce

Servings: 6
Cooking Time: 35 Minutes
Ingredients:

- 1 tbsp coconut oil
- 3 ½ pounds chicken breasts
- 1 cup chicken stock
- 1¼ cups leeks, chopped
- 1 tbsp lime juice
- ¼ cup coconut cream
- 2 tsp paprika
- 1 tsp red pepper flakes
- 2 tbsp green onions, chopped

- Salt and ground black pepper, to taste

Directions:

1. Set a pan over medium-high heat and warm oil, place in the chicken, cook each side for 2 minutes, set to a plate, and set aside. Set heat to medium, place the leeks to the pan and cook for 4 minutes.

2. Stir in the pepper, stock, pepper flakes, salt, paprika, coconut cream, and lime juice. Take the chicken back to the pan, place in more pepper and salt, cook while covered for 15 minutes.

Nutrition Info:

- Per Servings 3.2g Carbs, 58g Protein, 35g Fat, 491 Calories

Lemon Threaded Chicken Skewers

Servings: 4
Cooking Time: 2 Hours 17 Minutes
Ingredients:

- 3 chicken breasts, cut into cubes
- 2 tbsp olive oil, divided
- 2/3 jar preserved lemon, flesh removed, drained
- 2 cloves garlic, minced
- ½ cup lemon juice
- Salt and black pepper to taste
- 1 tsp rosemary leaves to garnish
- 2 to 4 lemon wedges to garnish

Directions:

1. First, thread the chicken onto skewers and set aside.

2. In a wide bowl, mix half of the oil, garlic, salt, pepper, and lemon juice, and add the chicken skewers, and lemon rind. Cover the bowl and let the chicken marinate for at least 2 hours in the refrigerator.

3. When the marinating time is almost over, preheat a grill to 350ºF, and remove the chicken onto the grill. Cook for 6 minutes on each side.

4. Remove and serve warm garnished with rosemary leaves and lemons wedges.

Nutrition Info:

- Per Servings 3.5g Carbs, 34g Protein, 11g Fat, 350 Calories

Oregano & Chili Flattened Chicken

Servings: 6
Cooking Time: 5 Minutes
Ingredients:

- 6 chicken breasts
- 4 cloves garlic, minced
- ½ cup oregano leaves, chopped
- ½ cup lemon juice
- 2/3 cup olive oil
- ¼ cup erythritol
- Salt and black pepper to taste
- 3 small chilies, minced

Directions:

1. Preheat a grill to 350ºF.

2. In a bowl, mix the garlic, oregano, lemon Juice, olive oil, and erythritol. Set aside.

3. While the spices incorporate in flavor, cover the chicken with plastic wraps, and use the rolling pin to pound to ½ - inch thickness. Remove the wrap afterward, and brush the mixture on the chicken on both sides. Place on the grill, cover the lid and cook for 15 minutes.

4. Then, baste the chicken with more of the spice mixture, and continue cooking for 15 more minutes.

Nutrition Info:

- Per Servings 3g Carbs, 26g Protein, 9g Fat, 265 Calories

Thyme Chicken Thighs

Servings: 4
Cooking Time: 30 Minutes
Ingredients:

- ½ cup chicken stock
- 1 tbsp olive oil
- ½ cup chopped onion
- 4 chicken thighs
- ¼ cup heavy cream
- 2 tbsp Dijon mustard
- 1 tsp thyme
- 1 tsp garlic powder

Directions:

1. Heat the olive oil in a pan. Cook the chicken for about 4 minutes per side. Set aside. Sauté the onion in the same pan for 3 minutes, add the stock, and simmer for 5 minutes. Stir in mustard and heavy cream, along with thyme and garlic powder. Pour the sauce over the chicken and serve.

Nutrition Info:

- Per Servings 4g Carbs, 33g Protein, 42g Fat, 528 Calories

Cheddar Chicken Tenders

Servings: 4
Cooking Time: 40 Minutes
Ingredients:

- 2 eggs
- 3 tbsp butter, melted
- 3 cups coarsely crushed cheddar cheese
- ½ cup pork rinds, crushed
- 1 lb chicken tenders
- Pink salt to taste

Directions:

1. Preheat oven to 350ºF and line a baking sheet with parchment paper. Whisk the eggs with the butter in one bowl and mix the cheese and pork rinds in another bowl.

2. Season chicken with salt, dip in egg mixture, and coat generously in cheddar mixture. Place on baking sheet, cover with aluminium foil and bake for 25 minutes. Remove foil and bake further for 12 minutes to golden brown. Serve chicken with mustard dip.

Nutrition Info:

- Per Servings 1.3g Carbs, 42g Protein, 54g Fat, 507 Calories

Oven-baked Skillet Lemon Chicken

Servings: 4
Cooking Time: 60 Minutes
Ingredients:

- 6 small chicken thighs
- 1 medium onion
- 1 lemon
- ¼ cup lemon juice, freshly squeezed
- Salt and pepper to taste

Directions:

1. Place all ingredients in a Ziploc bag and allow to marinate for at least 6 hours in the fridge.

2. Preheat the oven to 350F.

3. Place the chicken–sauce and all–into a skillet.

4. Put the skillet in the oven and bake for 1 hour or until the chicken is tender.

Nutrition Info:

- Per Servings 6.2g Carbs, 48.2g Protein, 42.4g Fat, 610 Calories

Spicy Chicken Kabobs

Servings: 6
Cooking Time: 1 Hour And 20 Minutes
Ingredients:

- 2 pounds chicken breasts, cubed
- 1 tsp sesame oil
- 1 tbsp olive oil
- 1 cup red bell pepper pieces
- 2 tbsp five spice powder
- 2 tbsp granulated sweetener
- 1 tbsp fish sauce

Directions:

1. Combine the sauces and seasonings in a bowl. Add the chicken, and let marinate for 1 hour in the fridge. Preheat the grill. Take 12 skewers and thread the chicken and bell peppers. Grill for 3 minutes per side.

Nutrition Info:

- Per Servings 3.1g Carbs, 17.5g Protein, 13.5g Fat, 198 Calories

Chapter 5. Fish And Seafood Recipes

Sautéed Savory Shrimps

Servings: 8
Cooking Time: 15 Minutes
Ingredients:

- 2 pounds shrimp, peeled and deveined
- 4 cloves garlic, minced
- ½ cup chicken stock, low sodium
- 1 tablespoon lemon juice
- Salt and pepper
- 5 tablespoons oil

Directions:
1. Place a heavy-bottomed pot on medium-high fire and heat pot for 3 minutes.
2. Once hot, add oil and stir around to coat pot with oil.
3. Sauté the garlic and corn for 5 minutes.
4. Add remaining ingredients and mix well.
5. Cover and bring to a boil, lower fire to a simmer, and simmer for 5 minutes.
6. Serve and enjoy.

Nutrition Info:
- Per Servings 1.7g Carbs, 25.2g Protein, 9.8g Fat, 182.6 Calories

Trout And Fennel Parcels

Servings: 4
Cooking Time: 20 Minutes
Ingredients:

- ½ lb deboned trout, butterflied
- Salt and black pepper to season
- 3 tbsp olive oil + extra for tossing
- 4 sprigs rosemary
- 4 sprigs thyme
- 4 butter cubes
- 1 cup thinly sliced fennel
- 1 medium red onion, sliced
- 8 lemon slices
- 3 tsp capers to garnish

Directions:
1. Preheat the oven to 400ºF. Cut out parchment paper wide enough for each trout. In a bowl, toss the fennel and onion with a little bit of olive oil and share into the middle parts of the papers.
2. Place the fish on each veggie mound, top with a drizzle of olive oil each, salt and pepper, a sprig of rosemary and thyme, and 1 cube of butter. Also, lay the lemon slices on the fish. Wrap and close the fish packets securely, and place them on a baking sheet.
3. Bake in the oven for 15 minutes, and remove once ready. Plate them and garnish the fish with capers and serve with a squash mash.

Nutrition Info:

- Per Servings 2.8g Carbs, 17g Protein, 9.3g Fat, 234 Calories

Avocado And Salmon

Serves: 2
Cooking Time: 0 Minutes
Ingredients:

- 1 avocado, halved, pitted
- 2 oz flaked salmon, packed in water
- 1 tbsp mayonnaise
- 1 tbsp grated cheddar cheese
- Seasoning:
- 1/8 tsp salt
- 2 tbsp coconut oil

Directions:
1. Prepare the avocado and for this, cut avocado in half and then remove its seed.Drain the salmon, add it in a bowl along with remaining ingredients, stir well and then scoop into the hollow on an avocado half.Serve.

Nutrition Info:
- 3 g Carbs; 19 g Protein; 48 g Fats; 525 Calories

Steamed Chili-rubbed Tilapia

Servings: 4
Cooking Time: 15 Minutes
Ingredients:

- 1 lb. tilapia fillet, skin removed
- 2 tbsp. chili powder
- 3 cloves garlic, peeled and minced
- 2 tbsp. extra virgin olive oil
- 2 tbsp soy sauce

Directions:
1. Place a trivet in a large saucepan and pour a cup or two of water into the pan. Bring it to a boil.
2. Place tilapia in a heatproof dish that fits inside a saucepan. Drizzle soy sauce and oil on the filet. Season with chili powder and garlic.
3. Seal dish with foil. Place the dish on the trivet inside the saucepan. Cover and steam for 15 minutes.
4. Serve and enjoy.

Nutrition Info:
- Per Servings 2g Carbs, 26g Protein, 10g Fat, 211 Calories

Seared Scallops With Chorizo And Asiago Cheese

Servings: 4
Cooking Time: 15 Minutes
Ingredients:

- 2 tbsp ghee
- 16 fresh scallops
- 8 ounces chorizo, chopped
- 1 red bell pepper, seeds removed, sliced

- 1 cup red onions, finely chopped
- 1 cup asiago cheese, grated
- Salt and black pepper to taste

Directions:

1. Melt half of the ghee in a skillet over medium heat, and cook the onion and bell pepper for 5 minutes until tender. Add the chorizo and stir-fry for another 3 minutes. Remove and set aside.
2. Pat dry the scallops with paper towels, and season with salt and pepper. Add the remaining ghee to the skillet and sear the scallops for 2 minutes on each side to have a golden brown color. Add the chorizo mixture back and warm through. Transfer to serving platter and top with asiago cheese.

Nutrition Info:

- Per Servings 5g Carbs, 36g Protein, 32g Fat, 491 Calories

Salmon Panzanella

Servings: 4
Cooking Time: 22 Minutes

Ingredients:

- 1 lb skinned salmon, cut into 4 steaks each
- 1 cucumber, peeled, seeded, cubed
- Salt and black pepper to taste
- 8 black olives, pitted and chopped
- 1 tbsp capers, rinsed
- 2 large tomatoes, diced
- 3 tbsp red wine vinegar
- ¼ cup thinly sliced red onion
- 3 tbsp olive oil
- 2 slices day-old zero carb bread, cubed
- ¼ cup thinly sliced basil leaves

Directions:

1. Preheat a grill to 350ºF and prepare the salad. In a bowl, mix the cucumbers, olives, pepper, capers, tomatoes, wine vinegar, onion, olive oil, bread, and basil leaves. Let sit for the flavors to incorporate.
2. Season the salmon steaks with salt and pepper; grill them on both sides for 8 minutes in total. Serve the salmon steaks warm on a bed of the veggies' salad.

Nutrition Info:

- Per Servings 3.1g Carbs, 28.5g Protein, 21.7g Fat, 338 Calories

Boiled Garlic Clams

Servings: 6
Cooking Time: 10 Minutes

Ingredients:

- 3 tbsp butter
- 6 cloves of garlic
- 50 small clams in the shell, scrubbed
- ½ cup fresh parsley, chopped
- 4 tbsp. extra virgin olive oil
- 1 cup water
- Salt and pepper to taste

Directions:

1. Heat the olive oil and butter in a large pot placed on medium-high fire for a minute.
2. Stir in the garlic and cook until fragrant and slightly browned.
3. Stir in the clams, water, and parsley. Season with salt and pepper to taste.
4. Cover and cook for 5 minutes or until clams have opened.
5. Discard unopened clams and serve.

Nutrition Info:

- Per Servings 0.9g Carbs, 11.3g Protein, 12.8g Fat, 159 Calories

Lemon Marinated Salmon With Spices

Servings: 2
Cooking Time: 15 Minutes

Ingredients:

- 2 tablespoons. lemon juice
- 1 tablespoon. yellow miso paste
- 2 teaspoons. Dijon mustard
- 1 pinch cayenne pepper and sea salt to taste
- 2 center-cut salmon fillets, boned; skin on
- 1 1/2 tablespoons mayonnaise
- 1 tablespoon ground black pepper

Directions:

1. In a bowl, combine lemon juice with black pepper. Stir in mayonnaise, miso paste, Dijon mustard, and cayenne pepper, mix well. Pour over salmon fillets, reserve about a tablespoon marinade. Cover and marinate the fish in the refrigerator for 30 minutes.
2. Preheat oven to 450 degrees F. Line a baking sheet with parchment paper.
3. Lay fillets on the prepared baking sheet. Rub the reserved lemon-pepper marinade on fillets. Then season with cayenne pepper and sea salt to taste.
4. Bake in the oven for 10 to 15 minutes until cooked through.

Nutrition Info:

- Per Servings 7.1g Carbs, 20g Protein, 28.1g Fat, 361 Calories

Halibut With Pesto

Servings: 4
Cooking Time: 15 Minutes

Ingredients:

- 4 halibut fillets
- 1 cup basil leaves
- 2 cloves of garlic, minced
- 1 tbsp. lemon juice, freshly squeezed
- 2 tbsp pine nuts
- 2 tbsp. oil, preferably extra virgin olive oil
- Salt and pepper to taste

Directions:

1. In a food processor, pulse the basil, olive oil, pine nuts, garlic, and lemon juice until coarse. Season with salt and pepper to taste.
2. Place a trivet in a large saucepan and pour a cup or two of water into the pan. Bring to a boil.
3. Place salmon in a heatproof dish that fits inside a saucepan. Season salmon with pepper and salt. Drizzle with pesto sauce.
4. Seal dish with foil. Place the dish on the trivet inside the saucepan. Cover and steam for 15 minutes.
5. Serve and enjoy.

Nutrition Info:
- Per Servings 0.8g Carbs, 75.8g Protein, 8.4g Fat, 401 Calories

Steamed Herbed Red Snapper

Servings: 4
Cooking Time: 15 Minutes
Ingredients:
- 4 red snapper fillets
- ¼ tsp. paprika
- 3 tbsp. lemon juice, freshly squeezed
- 1 ½ tsp chopped fresh herbs of your choice (rosemary, thyme, basil, or parsley)
- 6 tbsp olive oil
- Salt and pepper to taste

Directions:
1. In a small bowl, whisk well paprika, lemon juice, olive oil, and herbs. Season with pepper and salt.
2. Place a trivet in a large saucepan and pour a cup or two of water into the pan. Bring to a boil.
3. Place snapper in a heatproof dish that fits inside a saucepan. Season snapper with pepper and salt. Drizzle with lemon mixture.
4. Seal dish with foil. Place the dish on the trivet inside the saucepan. Cover and steam for 15 minutes.
5. Serve and enjoy.

Nutrition Info:
- Per Servings 2.1g Carbs, 45.6g Protein, 20.3g Fat, 374 Calories

Flounder With Dill And Capers

Servings: 4
Cooking Time: 15 Minutes
Ingredients:
- 4 flounder fillets
- 1 tbsp. chopped fresh dill
- 2 tbsp. capers, chopped
- 4 lemon wedges
- 6 tbsp olive oil
- Salt and pepper to taste

Directions:
1. Place a trivet in a large saucepan and pour a cup or two of water into the pan. Bring to a boil.
2. Place flounder in a heatproof dish that fits inside a saucepan. Season snapper with pepper and salt. Drizzle with

olive oil on all sides. Sprinkle dill and capers on top of the filet.
3. Seal dish with foil. Place the dish on the trivet inside the saucepan. Cover and steam for 15 minutes.
4. Serve and enjoy with lemon wedges.

Nutrition Info:
- Per Servings 8.6g Carbs, 20.3g Protein, 35.9g Fat, 447 Calories

Chili-lime Shrimps

Servings: 4
Cooking Time: 10 Minutes
Ingredients:
- 1 ½ lb. raw shrimp, peeled and deveined
- 1 tbsp. chili flakes
- 5 tbsp sweet chili sauce
- 2 tbsp. lime juice, freshly squeezed
- 1 tsp cayenne pepper
- Salt and pepper to taste
- 5 tbsp oil
- 3 tbsp water

Directions:
1. In a small bowl, whisk well chili flakes, sweet chili sauce, cayenne pepper, and water.
2. On medium-high fire, heat a nonstick saucepan for 2 minutes. Add oil to a pan and swirl to coat bottom and sides. Heat oil for a minute.
3. Stir fry shrimp, around 5 minutes. Season lightly with salt and pepper.
4. Stir in sweet chili mixture and toss well shrimp to coat.
5. Turn off fire, drizzle lime juice and toss well to coat.
6. Serve and enjoy.

Nutrition Info:
- Per Servings 1.7g Carbs, 34.9g Protein, 19.8g Fat, 306 Calories

Shrimp And Cauliflower Jambalaya

Servings: 4
Cooking Time: 15 Minutes
Ingredients:
- 2 cloves garlic, peeled and minced
- 1 head cauliflower, grated
- 1 cup chopped tomatoes
- 8 oz. raw shrimp, peeled and deveined
- 1 tbsp Cajun seasoning
- Salt and pepper
- 4 tbsp coconut oil
- 1 tbsp water

Directions:
1. On medium-high fire, heat a nonstick saucepan for 2 minutes. Add oil to a pan and swirl to coat bottom and sides. Heat oil for a minute.
2. Add garlic and sauté for a minute. Stir in tomatoes and stir fry for 5 minutes. Add water and deglaze the pan.
3. Add remaining ingredients. Season generously with pepper.

4. Increase fire to high and stir fry for 3 minutes.
5. Lower fire to low, cover, and cook for 5 minutes.
6. Serve and enjoy.
Nutrition Info:
- Per Servings 7.8g Carbs, 21.4g Protein, 22.25g Fat, 314 Calories

Dilled Salmon In Creamy Sauce

Servings: 2
Cooking Time: 20 Minutes
Ingredients:
- 2 salmon fillets
- ¾ tsp tarragon
- 1 tbsp duck fat
- ¾ tsp dill
- Sauce
- 2 tbsp butter
- ½ tsp dill
- ½ tsp tarragon
- ¼ cup heavy cream

Directions:
1. Season the salmon with dill and tarragon. Melt the duck fat in a pan over medium heat. Add salmon and cook for about 4 minutes on both sides. Set aside.
2. Melt the butter and add the dill and tarragon. Cook for 30 seconds to infuse the flavors. Whisk in the heavy cream and cook for one more minute. Serve the salmon topped with the sauce.

Nutrition Info:
- Per Servings 1.5g Carbs, 22g Protein, 40g Fat, 468 Calories

Pistachio-crusted Salmon

Servings: 4
Cooking Time: 35 Minutes
Ingredients:
- 4 salmon fillets
- ½ tsp pepper
- 1 tsp salt
- ¼ cup mayonnaise
- ½ cup chopped pistachios
- Sauce
- 1 chopped shallot
- 2 tsp lemon zest
- 1 tbsp olive oil
- A pinch of pepper
- 1 cup heavy cream

Directions:
1. Preheat the oven to 370ºF.
2. Brush the salmon with mayonnaise and season with salt and pepper. Coat with pistachios, place in a lined baking dish and bake for 15 minutes.
3. Heat the olive oil in a saucepan and sauté the shallot for 3 minutes. Stir in the rest of the sauce ingredients. Bring the mixture to a boil and cook until thickened. Serve the fish with the sauce.

Nutrition Info:
- Per Servings 6g Carbs, 34g Protein, 47g Fat, 563 Calories

Steamed Mustard Salmon

Servings: 4
Cooking Time: 15 Minutes
Ingredients:
- 2 tbsp Dijon mustard
- 1 whole lemon
- 2 cloves of garlic, minced
- 4 salmon fillets, skin removed
- 1 tbsp dill weed
- Salt and pepper to taste

Directions:
1. Slice lemon in half. Slice one lemon in circles and juice the other half in a small bowl.
2. Whisk in mustard, garlic, and dill weed in a bowl of lemon. Season with pepper and salt.
3. Place a trivet in a large saucepan and pour a cup or two of water into the pan. Bring to a boil.
4. Place lemon slices in a heatproof dish that fits inside a saucepan. Season salmon with pepper and salt. Slather mustard mixture on top of salmon.
5. Seal dish with foil. Place the dish on the trivet inside the saucepan. Cover and steam for 15 minutes.
6. Serve and enjoy.

Nutrition Info:
- Per Servings 2.2g Carbs, 65.3g Protein, 14.8g Fat, 402 Calories

Rosemary-lemon Shrimps

Servings: 4
Cooking Time: 8 Minutes
Ingredients:
- 5 tablespoons butter
- ½ cup lemon juice, freshly squeezed
- 1 ½ lb. shrimps, peeled and deveined
- ¼ cup coconut aminos
- 1 tsp rosemary
- Pepper to taste

Directions:
1. Place all ingredients in a large pan on a high fire.
2. Boil for 8 minutes or until shrimps are pink.
3. Serve and enjoy.

Nutrition Info:
- Per Servings 3.7g Carbs, 35.8g Protein, 17.9g Fat, 315 Calories

Alaskan Cod With Mustard Cream Sauce

Serves: 4
Cooking Time: 10 Minutes
Ingredients:

- 1 tablespoon coconut oil
- 4 Alaskan cod fillets
- Salt and freshly ground black pepper, to taste
- 6 leaves basil, chiffonade
- Mustard Cream Sauce:
- 1 teaspoon yellow mustard
- 1 teaspoon paprika
- 1/4 teaspoon ground bay leaf
- 3 tablespoons cream cheese
- 1/2 cup Greek-style yogurt
- 1 garlic clove, minced
- 1 teaspoon lemon zest
- 1 tablespoon fresh parsley, minced
- Sea salt and ground black pepper, to taste

Directions:

1. Heat coconut oil in a pan over medium heat. Sear the fish for 2 to 3 minutes per side. Season with salt and ground black pepper.
2. Mix all ingredients for the sauce until everything is well combined. Top the fish fillets with the sauce and serve garnished with fresh basil leaves. Bon appétit!

Nutrition Info:

- Per Serves 2.6g Carbs; 19.8g Protein; 8.2g Fat; 166 Calories;

Buttery Almond Lemon Tilapia

Servings: 4
Cooking Time: 10 Minutes
Ingredients:

- 4 tilapia fillets
- 1/4 cup butter, cubed
- 1/4 cup white wine or chicken broth
- 2 tablespoons lemon juice
- 1/4 cup sliced almonds
- 1/2 teaspoon salt
- 1/4 teaspoon pepper
- 1 tablespoon olive oil

Directions:

1. Sprinkle fillets with salt and pepper. In a large nonstick skillet, heat oil over medium heat.
2. Add fillets; cook until fish just begins to flake easily with a fork, 2-3 minutes on each side. Remove and keep warm.
3. Add butter, wine and lemon juice to the same pan; cook and stir until butter is melted.
4. Serve with fish; sprinkle with almonds.

Nutrition Info:

- Per Servings 2g Carbs, 22g Protein, 19g Fat, 269 Calories

Seasoned Salmon With Parmesan

Servings: 4
Cooking Time: 20 Mins
Ingredients:

- 2 lbs. salmon fillet
- 3 minced garlic cloves
- ¼ cup. chopped parsley
- ½ cup. grated parmesan cheese
- Salt and pepper to taste

Directions:

1. Preheat oven to 425 degrees F. Line a baking sheet with parchment paper.
2. Lay salmon fillets on the lined baking sheet, season with salt and pepper to taste.
3. Bake for 10 minutes. Remove from the oven and sprinkle with garlic, parmesan and parsley.
4. Place in the oven to cook for 5 more minutes. Transfer to plates before serving.

Nutrition Info:

- Per Servings 0.6g Carbs, 25g Protein, 12g Fat, 210 Calories

Steamed Greek Snapper

Servings: 12
Cooking Time: 15 Minutes
Ingredients:

- 6 tbsp. olive oil
- 1 clove of garlic, minced
- 2 tbsp. Greek yogurt
- 12 snapper fillets
- Salt and pepper to taste

Directions:

1. In a small bowl, combine the olive oil, garlic, and Greek yogurt. Season with salt and pepper to taste.
2. Place a trivet in a large saucepan and pour a cup or two of water into the pan. Bring to a boil.
3. Place snapper in a heatproof dish that fits inside a saucepan. If needed, cook in batches. Season snapper with pepper and salt and drizzle with olive oil. Slather with yogurt mixture.
4. Seal dish with foil. Place the dish on the trivet inside the saucepan. Cover and steam for 15 minutes.
5. Serve and enjoy.

Nutrition Info:

- Per Servings 0.4g Carbs, 44.8g Protein, 9.8g Fat, 280 Calories

Spicy Sea Bass With Hazelnuts

Servings: 2
Cooking Time: 30 Minutes
Ingredients:

- 2 sea bass fillets
- 2 tbsp butter
- ⅓ cup roasted hazelnuts
- A pinch of cayenne pepper

Directions:

1. Preheat your oven to 425 °F. Line a baking dish with waxed paper. Melt the butter and brush it over the fish. In a food processor, combine the rest of the ingredients. Coat the sea bass with the hazelnut mixture. Place in the oven and bake for about 15 minutes.

Nutrition Info:
- Per Servings 2.8g Carbs, 40g Protein, 31g Fat, 467 Calories

Simply Steamed Alaskan Cod

Servings: 2
Cooking Time: 15 Minutes
Ingredients:
- 1-lb fillet wild Alaskan Cod
- 1 cup cherry tomatoes, halved
- 1 tbsp balsamic vinegar
- 1 tbsp fresh basil chopped
- Salt and pepper to taste
- 5 tbsp olive oil

Directions:
1. In a heat-proof dish that fits inside the saucepan, add all ingredients except for basil. Mix well.
2. Place a large saucepan on the medium-high fire. Place a trivet inside the saucepan and fill pan halfway with water. Cover and bring to a boil.
3. Cover dish with foil and place on a trivet.
4. Cover pan and steam for 10 minutes. Let it rest in pan for another 5 minutes.
5. Serve and enjoy topped with fresh basil.

Nutrition Info:
- Per Servings 4.2g Carbs, 41.0g Protein, 36.6g Fat, 495.2 Calories

Baked Codfish With Lemon

Serves: 4
Cooking Time:25 Minutes
Ingredients:
- 4 fillets codfish
- 1 teaspoon salt
- 1 teaspoon pepper
- 2 tablespoons olive oil
- 2 teaspoons dried basil
- 2 tablespoons melted butter
- 1 teaspoon dried thyme
- 1/3 teaspoon onion powder
- 2 lemons, juiced
- lemon wedges, for garnish

Directions:
1. Preheat the oven to 400°F.
2. In a medium bowl combine the lemon juice, onion powder, olive oil, dried basil and thyme. Stir well. Season the fillets with salt and pepper.
3. Top each fillet into the mixture. Then place the fillets into a medium baking dish, greased with melted butter.
4. Bake the codfish fillets for 15-20 minutes. Serve with fresh lemon wedges. Enjoy!

Nutrition Info:
- Per serving: 3.9g Carbs; 21.2g Protein; 23.6g Fat; 308 Calories

Steamed Cod With Ginger

Servings: 4
Cooking Time: 15 Minutes
Ingredients:
- 4 cod fillets, skin removed
- 3 tbsp. lemon juice, freshly squeezed
- 2 tbsp. coconut aminos
- 2 tbsp. grated ginger
- 6 scallions, chopped
- 5 tbsp coconut oil
- Pepper and salt to taste

Directions:
1. Place a trivet in a large saucepan and pour a cup or two of water into the pan. Bring to a boil.
2. In a small bowl, whisk well lemon juice, coconut aminos, coconut oil, and grated ginger.
3. Place scallions in a heatproof dish that fits inside a saucepan. Season scallions mon with pepper and salt. Drizzle with ginger mixture. Sprinkle scallions on top.
4. Seal dish with foil. Place the dish on the trivet inside the saucepan. Cover and steam for 15 minutes.
5. Serve and enjoy.

Nutrition Info:
- Per Servings 10g Carbs, 28.3g Protein, 40g Fat, 514 Calories

Parmesan Fish Bake

Servings: 4
Cooking Time: 40 Minutes
Ingredients:
- Cooking spray
- 2 salmon fillets, cubed
- 3 white fish, cubed
- 1 broccoli, cut into florets
- 1 tbsp butter, melted
- Pink salt and black pepper to taste
- 1 cup crème fraiche
- ¼ cup grated Parmesan cheese
- Grated Parmesan cheese for topping

Directions:
1. Preheat oven to 400ºF and grease an 8 x 8 inches casserole dish with cooking spray. Toss the fish cubes and broccoli in butter and season with salt and pepper to taste. Spread in the greased dish.
2. Mix the crème fraiche with Parmesan cheese, pour and smear the cream on the fish, and sprinkle with some more Parmesan. Bake for 25 to 30 minutes until golden brown on top, take the dish out, sit for 5 minutes and spoon into plates. Serve with lemon-mustard asparagus.

Nutrition Info:
- Per Servings 4g Carbs, 28g Protein, 17g Fat, 354 Calories

Lemon Chili Halibut

Servings: 2
Cooking Time: 15 Minutes
Ingredients:
- 1-lb halibut fillets
- 1 lemon, sliced
- 1 tablespoon chili pepper flakes
- Pepper and salt to taste
- 4 tbsp olive oil

Directions:
1. In a heat-proof dish that fits inside saucepan, place fish. Top fish with chili flakes, lemon slices, salt, and pepper. Drizzle with olive oil. Cover dish with foil
2. Place a large saucepan on the medium-high fire. Place a trivet inside the saucepan and fill the pan halfway with water. Cover and bring to a boil.
3. Place dish on the trivet.
4. Cover pan and steam for 10 minutes. Let it rest in pan for another 5 minutes.
5. Serve and enjoy topped with pepper.

Nutrition Info:
- Per Servings 4.2g Carbs, 42.7g Protein, 58.4g Fat, 675 Calories

Coconut Curry Cod

Servings: 4
Cooking Time: 17 Minutes
Ingredients:
- 4 cod fillets
- 1 ½ cups coconut milk, freshly squeezed if possible
- 2 tsp. grated ginger
- 2 tsp. curry powder
- 1 sprig cilantro, chopped
- Salt and pepper to taste

Directions:
1. Add all ingredients in a nonstick saucepan. Cover and cook for 10 minutes on a high fire.
2. Lower fire to a simmer and simmer for 7 minutes.
3. Season with pepper and salt.
4. Serve and enjoy.

Nutrition Info:
- Per Servings 5.7g Carbs, 19.7g Protein, 22.1g Fat, 291 Calories

Chipotle Salmon Asparagus

Servings: 2
Cooking Time: 15 Minutes
Ingredients:
- 1-lb salmon fillet, skin on
- 2 teaspoon chipotle paste
- A handful of asparagus spears, trimmed
- 1 lemon, sliced thinly
- A pinch of rosemary
- Salt to taste
- 5 tbsp olive oil

Directions:
1. In a heat-proof dish that fits inside the saucepan, add asparagus spears on the bottom of the dish. Place fish, top with rosemary, and lemon slices. Season with chipotle paste and salt. Drizzle with olive oil. Cover dish with foil.
2. Place a large saucepan on the medium-high fire. Place a trivet inside the saucepan and fill the pan halfway with water. Cover and bring to a boil.
3. Place dish on the trivet.
4. Cover pan and steam for 10 minutes. Let it rest in pan for another 5 minutes.
5. Serve and enjoy topped with pepper.

Nutrition Info:
- Per Servings 2.8g Carbs, 35.0g Protein, 50.7g Fat, 651 Calories

Shrimp In Curry Sauce

Servings: 2
Cooking Time: 25 Minutes
Ingredients:
- ½ ounces grated Parmesan cheese
- 1 tbsp water
- 1 egg, beaten
- ¼ tsp curry powder
- 2 tsp almond flour
- 12 shrimp, shelled
- 3 tbsp coconut oil
- Sauce
- 2 tbsp curry leaves
- 2 tbsp butter
- ½ onion, diced
- ½ cup heavy cream
- ½ ounce cheddar

Directions:
1. Combine all dry ingredients for the batter. Melt the coconut oil in a skillet over medium heat. Dip the shrimp in the egg first, and then coat with the dry mixture. Fry until golden and crispy.
2. In another skillet, melt the butter. Add onion and cook for 3 minutes. Add curry leaves and cook for 30 seconds. Stir in heavy cream and cheddar and cook until thickened. Add the shrimp and coat well. Serve warm.

Nutrition Info:
- Per Servings 4.3g Carbs, 24.4g Protein, 41g Fat, 560 Calories

Halibut En Papillote

Servings: 4
Cooking Time: 15 Minutes
Ingredients:
- 4 halibut fillets
- ½ tbsp. grated ginger
- 1 cup chopped tomatoes
- 1 shallot, thinly sliced
- 1 lemon
- 5 tbsp olive oil

72

- Salt and pepper to taste

Directions:

1. Slice lemon in half. Slice one lemon in circles.

2. Juice the other half of the lemon in a small bowl. Mix in grated ginger and season with pepper and salt.

3. Place a trivet in a large saucepan and pour a cup or two of water into the pan. Bring to a boil.

4. Get 4 large foil and place one fillet in the middle of each foil. Season with fillet salt and pepper. Drizzle with olive oil. Add the grated ginger, tomatoes, and shallots equally. Fold the foil to create a pouch and crimp the edges.

5. Place the foil containing the fish on the trivet. Cover saucepan and steam for 15 minutes.

6. Serve and enjoy in pouches.

Nutrition Info:

- Per Servings 2.7g Carbs, 20.3g Protein, 32.3g Fat, 410 Calories

Bang Bang Shrimps

Serves: 2

Cooking Time: 6 Minutes

Ingredients:

- 4 oz shrimps¼ tsp paprika
- ¼ tsp apple cider vinegar
- 2 tbsp sweet chili sauce
- ¼ cup mayonnaise
- Seasoning:
- ¼ tsp salt
- 1/8 tsp ground black pepper
- 2 tsp avocado oil

Directions:

1. Take a medium skillet pan, place it over medium heat, add oil and wait until it gets hot.Season shrimps with salt, black pepper, and paprika until coated, add them to the pan, and cook for 2 to 3 minutes per side until pink and cooked.Take a medium bowl, place mayonnaise in it, and then whisk in vinegar and chili sauce until combined.Add shrimps into the mayonnaise mixture, toss until coated, and then serve.

Nutrition Info:

- 7.2 g Carbs; 13 g Protein; 23.1 g Fats; 290 Calories

Asian-style Steamed Mussels

Serves:6

Cooking Time： 25 Minutes

Ingredients:

- 5 tbsp sesame oil
- 1 onion, chopped
- 3 lb mussels, cleaned
- 2 garlic cloves, minced
- 12 oz coconut milk
- 16 oz white wine
- 1 lime, juiced
- 2 tsp red curry powder
- 2 tbsp cilantro, chopped

Directions:

1. Warm the sesame oil in a saucepan over medium heat and cook onion and garlic cloves for 3 minutes. Pour in wine, coconut milk, and curry powder and cook for 5 minutes. Add mussels, turn off the heat, cover the saucepan, and steam the mussels until the shells open up, 5 minutes. Discard any closed mussels. Top with cilantro and serve.

Nutrition Info:

- Per Serves 5.4g Carbs ; 28.2g Protein； 16g Fat ; 323 Calories

Angel Hair Shirataki With Creamy Shrimp

Serves:4

Cooking Time： 25 Minutes

Ingredients:

- 2 (8 oz) packs angel hair shirataki noodles
- 1 tbsp olive oil
- 1 lb shrimp, deveined
- 2 tbsp unsalted butter
- 6 garlic cloves, minced
- ½ cup dry white wine
- 1 ½ cups heavy cream
- ½ cup grated Asiago cheese
- 2 tbsp chopped fresh parsley

Directions:

1. Heat olive oil in a skillet, season the shrimp with salt and pepper, and cook on both sides, 2 minutes; set aside. Melt butter in the skillet and sauté garlic. Stir in wine and cook until reduced by half, scraping the bottom of the pan to deglaze. Stir in heavy cream. Let simmer for 1 minute and stir in Asiago cheese to melt. Return the shrimp to the sauce and sprinkle the parsley on top. Bring 2 cups of water to a boi. Strain shirataki pasta and rinse under hot running water. Allow proper draining and pour the shirataki pasta into the boiling water. Cook for 3 minutes and strain again. Place a dry skillet and stir-fry the pasta until dry, 1-2 minutes. Season with salt and plate. Top with the shrimp sauce and serve.

Nutrition Info:

- Per Serves 6.3g Carbs; 33g Protein ; 32g Fats; 493 Calories

Cod In Garlic Butter Sauce

Servings: 6

Cooking Time: 20 Minutes

Ingredients:

- 2 tsp olive oil
- 6 Alaska cod fillets
- Salt and black pepper to taste
- 4 tbsp salted butter
- 4 cloves garlic, minced
- ⅓ cup lemon juice
- 3 tbsp white wine
- 2 tbsp chopped chives

Directions:

1. Heat the oil in a skillet over medium heat and season the cod with salt and black pepper. Fry the fillets in the oil for 4 minutes on one side, flip and cook for 1 minute. Take out, plate, and set aside.

2. In another skillet over low heat, melt the butter and sauté the garlic for 3 minutes. Add the lemon juice, wine, and chives. Season with salt, black pepper, and cook for 3 minutes until the wine slightly reduces. Put the fish in the skillet, spoon sauce over, cook for 30 seconds and turn the heat off.

3. Divide fish into 6 plates, top with sauce, and serve with buttered green beans.

Nutrition Info:
- Per Servings 2.3g Carbs, 20g Protein, 17.3g Fat, 264 Calories

Asian Seafood Stir-fry

Serves: 4
Cooking Time: 15 Minutes
Ingredients:
- 4 teaspoons sesame oil
- 1/2 cup yellow onion, sliced
- 1 cup asparagus spears, sliced
- 1/2 cup celery, chopped
- 1/2 cup enoki mushrooms
- 1 pound bay scallops
- 1 tablespoon fresh parsley, chopped
- Kosher salt and ground black pepper, to taste
- 1/2 teaspoon red pepper flakes, crushed
- 1 tablespoon coconut aminos
- 2 tablespoons rice wine
- 1/2 cup dry roasted peanuts, roughly chopped

Directions:
1. Heat 1 teaspoon of the sesame oil in a wok over a medium-high flame. Now, fry the onion until crisp-tender and translucent; reserve.

2. Heat another teaspoon of the sesame oil and fry the asparagus and celery for about 3 minutes until crisp-tender; reserve.

3. Then, heat another teaspoon of the sesame oil and cook the mushrooms for 2 minutes more or until they start to soften; reserve.

4. Lastly, heat the remaining teaspoon of sesame oil and cook the bay scallops just until they are opaque.

5. Return all reserved vegetables to the wok. Add in the remaining ingredients and toss to combine. Serve warm and enjoy!

Nutrition Info:
- Per Serves 5.9g Carbs; 27g Protein; 12.5g Fat; 236 Calories

Five-spice Steamed Tilapia

Servings: 4
Cooking Time: 15 Minutes
Ingredients:
- 1 lb. Tilapia fillets,

- 1 tsp. Chinese five-spice powder
- 3 tablespoons coconut oil
- 3 scallions, sliced thinly
- Salt and pepper to taste

Directions:
1. Place a trivet in a large saucepan and pour a cup of water into the pan. Bring to a boil.

2. Place tilapia in a heatproof dish that fits inside a saucepan. Drizzle oil on tilapia. Season with salt, pepper, and Chinese five-spice powder. Garnish with scallions.

3. Seal dish with foil. Place the dish on the trivet inside the saucepan. Cover and steam for 15 minutes.

4. Serve and enjoy.

Nutrition Info:
- Per Servings 0.9g Carbs, 24g Protein, 12.3g Fat, 201 Calories

Creamy Hoki With Almond Bread Crust

Servings: 4
Cooking Time: 50 Minutes
Ingredients:
- 1 cup flaked smoked hoki, bones removed
- 1 cup cubed hoki fillets, cubed
- 4 eggs
- 1 cup water
- 3 tbsp almond flour
- 1 medium white onion, sliced
- 2 cups sour cream
- 1 tbsp chopped parsley
- 1 cup pork rinds, crushed
- 1 cup grated cheddar cheese
- Salt and black pepper to taste
- Cooking spray

Directions:
1. Preheat the oven to 360ºF and lightly grease a baking dish with cooking spray.

2. Then, boil the eggs in water in a pot over medium heat to be well done for 12 minutes, run the eggs under cold water and peel the shells. After, place on a cutting board and chop them.

3. Melt the butter in a saucepan over medium heat and sauté the onion for about 4 minutes. Turn the heat off and stir the almond flour into it to form a roux. Turn the heat back on and cook the roux to be golden brown and stir in the cream until the mixture is smooth. Season with salt and pepper, and stir in the parsley.

4. Spread the smoked and cubed fish in the baking dish, sprinkle the eggs on top, and spoon the sauce over. In a bowl mix the pork rinds with the cheddar cheese, and sprinkle it over the sauce.

5. Bake the casserole in the oven for 20 minutes until the top is golden and the sauce and cheese are bubbly. Remove the bake after and serve with a steamed green vegetable mix.

Nutrition Info:

- Per Servings 3.5g Carbs, 28.5g Protein, 27g Fat, 386 Calories

Chili-garlic Salmon

Servings: 4
Cooking Time: 15 Minutes
Ingredients:
- 5 tbsp. sweet chili sauce
- ¼ cup coconut aminos
- 4 salmon fillets
- 3 tbsp. green onions, chopped
- 3 cloves garlic, peeled and minced
- Pepper to taste

Directions:
1. Place a trivet in a large saucepan and pour a cup or two of water into the pan. Bring to a boil.
2. In a small bowl, whisk well sweet chili sauce, garlic, and coconut aminos.
3. Place salmon in a heatproof dish that fits inside a saucepan. Season salmon with pepper. Drizzle with sweet chili sauce mixture. Sprinkle green onions on top of the filet.
4. Seal dish with foil. Place the dish on the trivet inside the saucepan. Cover and steam for 15 minutes.
5. Serve and enjoy.

Nutrition Info:
- Per Servings 0.9g Carbs, 65.4g Protein, 14.4g Fat, 409 Calories

Baked Salmon With Pistachio Crust

Serves:4
Cooking Time: 35 Minutes
Ingredients:
- 4 salmon fillets
- ¼ cup mayonnaise
- ½ cup ground pistachios
- 1 chopped shallot
- 2 tsp lemon zest
- 1 tbsp olive oil
- A pinch of pepper
- 1 cup heavy cream

Directions:
1. Preheat oven to 375 °F. Brush salmon with mayo and season with salt and pepper. Coat with pistachios. Place in a lined baking dish and bake for 15 minutes. Heat the olive oil in a saucepan and sauté shallot for 3 minutes. Stir in heavy cream and lemon zest. Bring to a boil and cook until thickened. Serve salmon with the sauce.

Nutrition Info:
- Per Serves 6g Carbs; 34g Protein; 47g Fat ; 563 Calories

Thyme-sesame Crusted Halibut

Servings: 2
Cooking Time: 15 Minutes
Ingredients:
- 8 oz. halibut, cut into 2 portions
- 1 tbsp. lemon juice, freshly squeezed
- 1 tsp. dried thyme leaves
- 1 tbsp. sesame seeds, toasted
- Salt and pepper to taste

Directions:
1. Place a trivet in a large saucepan and pour a cup or two of water into the pan. Bring it to a boil.
2. Place halibut in a heatproof dish that fits inside a saucepan. Season with lemon juice, salt, and pepper. Sprinkle with dried thyme leaves and sesame seeds.
3. Seal dish with foil. Place the dish on the trivet inside the saucepan. Cover and steam for 15 minutes.
4. Serve and enjoy.

Nutrition Info:
- Per Servings 4.2g Carbs, 17.5g Protein, 17.7g Fat, 246 Calories

Cilantro Shrimp

Servings: 4
Cooking Time: 10 Minutes
Ingredients:
- 1/2 cup reduced-fat Asian sesame salad dressing
- 1-pound uncooked shrimp, peeled and deveined
- Lime wedges
- 1/4 cup chopped fresh cilantro
- 5 tablespoon olive oil
- Salt and pepper

Directions:
1. In a large nonstick skillet, heat 1 tablespoon dressing over medium heat. Add shrimp; cook and stir 1 minute.
2. Stir in remaining dressing; cook, uncovered, until shrimp turn pink, 1-2 minutes longer.
3. To serve, squeeze lime juice over the top; sprinkle with cilantro, pepper, and salt. If desired, serve with rice.

Nutrition Info:
- Per Servings 4.7g Carbs, 32g Protein, 39g Fat, 509 Calories

Avocado Tuna Boats

Serves: 2
Cooking Time: 10 Minutes
Ingredients:
- 4 oz tuna, packed in water, drained1 green onion sliced
- 1 avocado, halved, pitted
- 3 tbsp mayonnaise
- 1/3 tsp salt
- Seasoning:
- ¼ tsp ground black pepper
- ¼ tsp paprika

Directions:
1. Prepare the filling and for this, take a medium bowl, place tuna in it, add green onion, salt, black pepper, paprika and mayonnaise and then stir until well combined.Cut avocado in half lengthwise, then remove the pit and fill with prepared filling.Serve.

Nutrition Info:

- ; 7 g Carbs; 8 g Protein; 19 g Fats; 244 Calories

Coconut Crab Patties

Servings: 8
Cooking Time: 15 Minutes
Ingredients:
- 2 tbsp coconut oil
- 1 tbsp lemon juice
- 1 cup lump crab meat
- 2 tsp Dijon mustard
- 1 egg, beaten
- 1 ½ tbsp coconut flour

Directions:
1. In a bowl to the crabmeat add all the ingredients, except for the oil; mix well to combine. Make patties out of the mixture. Melt the coconut oil in a skillet over medium heat. Add the crab patties and cook for about 2-3 minutes per side.

Nutrition Info:
- Per Servings 3.6g Carbs, 15.3g Protein, 11.5g Fat, 215 Calories

Enchilada Sauce On Mahi Mahi

Servings: 2
Cooking Time: 15 Minutes
Ingredients:
- 2 Mahi fillets, fresh
- ¼ cup commercial enchilada sauce
- Pepper to taste

Directions:
1. In a heat-proof dish that fits inside saucepan, place fish and top with enchilada sauce.
2. Place a large saucepan on the medium-high fire. Place a trivet inside the saucepan and fill the pan halfway with water. Cover and bring to a boil.
3. Cover dish with foil and place on a trivet.
4. Cover pan and steam for 10 minutes. Let it rest in pan for another 5 minutes.
5. Serve and enjoy topped with pepper.

Nutrition Info:
- Per Servings 8.9g Carbs, 19.8g Protein, 15.9g Fat, 257 Calories

Cod With Balsamic Tomatoes

Servings: 4
Cooking Time: 30 Minutes
Ingredients:
- 4 center-cut bacon strips, chopped
- 4 cod fillets
- 2 cups grape tomatoes, halved
- 2 tablespoons balsamic vinegar
- 4 tablespoons olive oil
- 1/2 teaspoon salt
- 1/4 teaspoon pepper

Directions:
1. In a large skillet, heat olive oil and cook bacon over medium heat until crisp, stirring occasionally.

2. Remove with a slotted spoon; drain on paper towels.
3. Sprinkle fillets with salt and pepper. Add fillets to bacon drippings; cook over medium-high heat until fish just begins to flake easily with a fork, 4-6 minutes on each side. Remove and keep warm.
4. Add tomatoes to skillet; cook and stir until tomatoes are softened, 2-4 minutes. Stir in vinegar; reduce heat to medium-low. Cook until sauce is thickened, 1-2 minutes longer.
5. Serve cod with tomato mixture and bacon.

Nutrition Info:
- Per Servings 5g Carbs, 26g Protein, 30.4g Fat, 442 Calories

Sour Cream Salmon With Parmesan

Servings: 4
Cooking Time: 25 Minutes
Ingredients:
- 1 cup sour cream
- ½ tbsp minced dill
- ½ lemon, zested and juiced
- Pink salt and black pepper to season
- 4 salmon steaks
- ½ cup grated Parmesan cheese

Directions:
1. Preheat oven to 400ºF and line a baking sheet with parchment paper; set aside. In a bowl, mix the sour cream, dill, lemon zest, juice, salt and pepper, and set aside.
2. Season the fish with salt and black pepper, drizzle lemon juice on both sides of the fish and arrange them in the baking sheet. Spread the sour cream mixture on each fish and sprinkle with Parmesan.
3. Bake the fish for 15 minutes and after broil the top for 2 minutes with a close watch for a nice a brown color. Plate the fish and serve with buttery green beans.

Nutrition Info:
- Per Servings 1.2g Carbs, 16.2g Protein, 23.4g Fat, 288 Calories

Avocado Salad With Shrimp

Serves: 4
Cooking Time:10 Minutes
Ingredients:
- 2 tomatoes, sliced into cubes
- 2 medium avocados, cut into large pieces
- 3 tablespoons red onion, diced
- ½ large lettuce, chopped
- 2 lbs. shrimp, peeled and deveined
- For the Lime Vinaigrette Dressing
- 2 cloves garlic, minced
- 1 ½ teaspoon Dijon mustard
- 1/3 cup extra virgin olive oil
- salt and pepper to taste
- 1/3 cup lime juice

Directions:

1. Add the peeled and deveined shrimp and 2 quarts of water to a cooking pot and print to a boil, lower the heat and let them simmer for 1-2 minutes until the shrimp is pink. Set aside and let them cool.
2. Next add the chopped lettuce in a large bowl. Then add the avocado, tomatoes, shrimp and red onion.
3. In a small bowl whisk together the Dijon mustard, garlic, olive oil and lime juice. Mix well.
4. Pour the lime vinaigrette dressing over the salad and serve.

Nutrition Info:
- Per serving: 7g Carbs; 43.5g Protein; 17.6g Fat; 377 Calories;

Red Cabbage Tilapia Taco Bowl

Servings: 4
Cooking Time: 20 Minutes
Ingredients:
- 2 cups cauli rice
- Water for sprinkling
- 2 tsp ghee
- 4 tilapia fillets, cut into cubes
- ¼ tsp taco seasoning
- Pink salt and chili pepper to taste
- ¼ head red cabbage, shredded
- 1 ripe avocado, pitted and chopped

Directions:
1. Sprinkle cauli rice in a bowl with a little water and microwave for 3 minutes. Fluff after with a fork and set aside. Melt ghee in a skillet over medium heat, rub the tilapia with the taco seasoning, salt, and chili pepper, and fry until brown on all sides, for about 8 minutes in total.
2. Transfer to a plate and set aside. In 4 serving bowls, share the cauli rice, cabbage, fish, and avocado. Serve with chipotle lime sour cream dressing.

Nutrition Info:
- Per Servings 4g Carbs, 16.5g Protein, 23.4g Fat, 269 Calories

Golden Pompano In Microwave

Servings: 2
Cooking Time: 11 Minutes
Ingredients:
- ½-lb pompano
- 1 tbsp soy sauce, low sodium
- 1-inch thumb ginger, diced
- 1 lemon, halved
- 1 stalk green onions, chopped
- ¼ cup water
- 1 tsp pepper
- 4 tbsp olive oil

Directions:
1. In a microwavable casserole dish, mix well all ingredients except for pompano, green onions, and lemon.
2. Squeeze half of the lemon in dish and slice into thin circles the other half.

3. Place pompano in the dish and add lemon circles on top of the fish. Drizzle with pepper and olive oil.
4. Cover top of a casserole dish with a microwave-safe plate.
5. Microwave for 5 minutes.
6. Remove from microwave, turn over fish, sprinkle green onions, top with a microwavable plate.
7. Return to microwave and cook for another 3 minutes.
8. Let it rest for 3 minutes more.
9. Serve and enjoy.

Nutrition Info:
- Per Servings 6.3g Carbs, 22.2g Protein, 39.5g Fat, 464 Calories

Baked Cod And Tomato Capers Mix

Serves: 4
Cooking Time: 25 Minutes
Ingredients:
- 4 cod fillets, boneless
- 2 tablespoons avocado oil
- 1 cup tomato passata
- 2 tablespoons capers, drained
- 2 tablespoons parsley, choppedA pinch of salt and black pepper

Directions:
1. In a roasting pan, combine the cod with the oil and the other ingredients, toss gently, introduce in the oven at 370 °F and bake for 25 minutes.
2. Divide between plates and serve.

Nutrition Info:
- 0.7g carbs; 2g fat; 5g protein; 150 calories

Salmon With Pepita And Lime

Servings: 4
Cooking Time: 15 Minutes
Ingredients:
- 2 tbsp. Pepitas, ground
- ¼ tsp. chili powder
- 1 lb. salmon fillet, cut into 4 portions
- 2 tbsp. lime juice
- Salt and pepper to taste

Directions:
1. Place a trivet in a large saucepan and pour a cup of water into the pan. Bring it to a boil.
2. Place salmon in a heatproof dish that fits inside a saucepan. Drizzle lime juice on the fillet. Season with salt, pepper, and chili powder. Garnish with ground pepitas.
3. Seal dish with foil. Place the dish on the trivet inside the saucepan. Cover and steam for 15 minutes.
4. Serve and enjoy.

Nutrition Info:
- Per Servings 1g Carbs, 24g Protein, 9g Fat, 185 Calories

Blue Cheese Shrimps

Servings: 6
Cooking Time: 15 Minutes
Ingredients:
- 3 ounces cream cheese, softened
- 2/3 cup minced fresh parsley, divided
- 1/4 cup crumbled blue cheese
- 1/2 teaspoon Creole mustard
- 24 cooked jumbo shrimp, peeled and deveined
- Pepper and salt to taste
- 5 tablespoon olive oil

Directions:
1. In a small bowl, beat cream cheese until smooth. Beat in 1/3 cup parsley, blue cheese, and mustard. Season with pepper and salt as desired. Refrigerate at least 1 hour.
2. Make a deep slit along the back of each shrimp to within 1/4-1/2 inch of the bottom. Stuff with cream cheese mixture; press remaining parsley onto cream cheese mixture.
3. Drizzle with olive oil last.

Nutrition Info:
- Per Servings 1.7g Carbs, 6g Protein, 17.8g Fat, 180 Calories

Grilled Shrimp With Chimichurri Sauce

Servings: 4
Cooking Time: 55 Minutes
Ingredients:
- 1 pound shrimp, peeled and deveined
- 2 tbsp olive oil
- Juice of 1 lime
- Chimichurri
- ½ tsp salt
- ¼ cup olive oil
- 2 garlic cloves
- ¼ cup red onion, chopped
- ¼ cup red wine vinegar
- ½ tsp pepper
- 2 cups parsley
- ¼ tsp red pepper flakes

Directions:
1. Process the chimichurri ingredients in a blender until smooth; set aside. Combine shrimp, olive oil, and lime juice, in a bowl, and let marinate in the fridge for 30 minutes. Preheat your grill to medium. Add shrimp and cook about 2 minutes per side. Serve shrimp drizzled with the chimichurri sauce.

Nutrition Info:
- Per Servings 3.5g Carbs, 16g Protein, 20.3g Fat, 283 Calories

Baked Fish With Feta And Tomato

Serves: 2
Cooking Time: 15 Minutes
Ingredients:
- 2 pacific whitening fillets
- 1 scallion, chopped
- 1 Roma tomato, chopped
- 1 tsp fresh oregano
- 1-ounce feta cheese, crumbled
- Seasoning:
- 2 tbsp avocado oil
- 1/3 tsp salt
- 1/4 tsp ground black pepper
- ¼ crushed red pepper

Directions:
1. Turn on the oven, then set it to 400 °F and let it preheat.Take a medium skillet pan, place it over medium heat, add oil and when hot, add scallion and cook for 3 minutes.Add tomatoes, stir in ½ tsp oregano, 1/8 tsp salt, black pepper, red pepper, pour in ¼ cup water and bring it to simmer.Sprinkle remaining salt over fillets, add to the pan, drizzle with remaining oil, and then bake for 10 to 12 minutes until fillets are fork-tender.When done, top fish with remaining oregano and cheese and then serve.

Nutrition Info:
- 8 g Carbs; 26.7 g Protein; 29.5 g Fats; 427.5 Calories

Tilapia With Olives & Tomato Sauce

Servings: 4
Cooking Time: 30 Minutes
Ingredients:
- 4 tilapia fillets
- 2 garlic cloves, minced
- 2 tsp oregano
- 14 ounces diced tomatoes
- 1 tbsp olive oil
- ½ red onion, chopped
- 2 tbsp parsley
- ¼ cup kalamata olives

Directions:
1. Heat the olive oil in a skillet over medium heat and cook the onion for about 3 minutes. Add garlic and oregano and cook for 30 seconds. Stir in tomatoes and bring the mixture to a boil. Reduce the heat and simmer for 5 minutes. Add olives and tilapia, and cook for about 8 minutes. Serve the tilapia with tomato sauce.

Nutrition Info:
- Per Servings 6g Carbs, 23g Protein, 15g Fat, 282 Calories

Cedar Salmon With Green Onion

Servings: 5
Cooking Time: 20 Mins
Ingredients:
- 3 untreated cedar planks
- 1/4 cup. chopped green onions
- 1 tablespoon. grated fresh ginger root
- 1 teaspoon. minced garlic
- 2 salmon fillets, skin removed

- 1/3 cup. olive oil
- 1/3 cup. mayo
- 1 1/2 tablespoons. rice vinegar

Directions:
1. Soak cedar planks in warm water for 1 hour more.
2. Whisk olive oil, rice vinegar, mayo, green onions, ginger, and garlic in a bowl. Marinade salmon fillets to coat completely. Cover the bowl with plastic wrap and marinate for 15 to 60 minutes.
3. Preheat an outdoor grill over medium heat. Lay planks on the center of hot grate Place the salmon fillets onto the planks and remove the marinade. Cover the grill and cook until cooked through, about 20 minutes, or until salmon is done to your liking. Serve the salmon on a platter right off the planks.

Nutrition Info:
- Per Servings 10g Carbs, 18g Protein, 27g Fat, 355 Calories

Steamed Asparagus And Shrimps

Servings: 6
Cooking Time: 15 Minutes

Ingredients:
- 1-pound shrimps, peeled and deveined
- 1 bunch asparagus, trimmed
- ½ tablespoon Cajun seasoning
- 2 tablespoons butter
- 5 tablespoons oil
- Salt and pepper to taste

Directions:
1. In a heat-proof dish that fits inside the saucepan, add all ingredients. Mix well.
2. Place a large saucepan on the medium-high fire. Place a trivet inside the saucepan and fill the pan halfway with water. Cover and bring to a boil.
3. Cover dish with foil and place on a trivet.
4. Cover pan and steam for 10 minutes. Let it rest in pan for another 5 minutes.
5. Serve and enjoy.

Nutrition Info:
- Per Servings 1.1g Carbs, 15.5g Protein, 15.8g Fat, 204.8 Calories

Bacon Wrapped Mahi-mahi

Serves: 2
Cooking Time: 12 Minutes

Ingredients:
- 2 fillets of mahi-mahi
- 2 strips of bacon
- ½ of lime, zested
- 4 basil leaves
- ½ tsp salt
- Seasoning:
- ½ tsp ground black pepper
- 1 tbsp avocado oil

Directions:

1. Turn on the oven, then set it to 375 °F and let them preheat.Meanwhile, season fillets with salt and black pepper, top each fillet with 2 basil leaves, sprinkle with lime zest, wrap with a bacon strip and secure with a toothpick if needed.Take a medium skillet pan, place it over medium-high heat, add oil and when hot, place prepared fillets in it and cook for 2 minutes per side.Transfer pan into the oven and bake the fish for 5 to 7 minutes until thoroughly cooked.Serve.

Nutrition Info:
- 1.2 g Carbs; 27.1 g Protein; 11.3 g Fats; 217 Calories

Yummy Shrimp Fried Rice

Servings: 6
Cooking Time: 20 Minutes

Ingredients:
- 4 tablespoons butter, divided
- 4 large eggs, lightly beaten
- 3 cups shredded cauliflower
- 1-pound uncooked medium shrimp, peeled and deveined
- 1/2 teaspoon salt
- 1/4 teaspoon pepper

Directions:
1. In a large skillet, melt 1 tablespoon butter over medium-high heat.
2. Pour eggs into skillet. As eggs set, lift edges, letting uncooked portion flow underneath. Remove eggs and keep warm.
3. Melt remaining butter in the skillet. Add the cauliflower, and shrimp; cook and stir for 5 minutes or until shrimp turn pink.
4. Meanwhile, chop eggs into small pieces. Return eggs to the pan; sprinkle with salt and pepper. Cook until heated through, stirring occasionally. Sprinkle with bacon if desired.

Nutrition Info:
- Per Servings 3.3g Carbs, 13g Protein, 11g Fat, 172 Calories

Smoked Mackerel Patties

Servings: 6
Cooking Time: 30 Minutes

Ingredients:
- 1 turnip, peeled and diced
- 1 ½ cup water
- Pink salt and chili pepper to taste
- 3 tbsp olive oil + for rubbing
- 4 smoked mackerel steaks, bones removed, flaked
- 3 eggs, beaten
- 2 tbsp mayonnaise
- 1 tbsp pork rinds, crushed

Directions:
1. Bring the turnip to boil in salted water in a saucepan over medium heat for 8 minutes or until tender. Drain the turnip through a colander, transfer to a mixing bowl, and mash the lumps.

2. Add the mackerel, eggs, mayonnaise, pork rinds, salt, and chili pepper. With gloves on your hands, mix and make 6 compact patties.

3. Heat olive oil in a skillet over medium heat and fry the patties for 3 minutes on each side to be golden brown. Remove onto a wire rack to cool. Serve with sesame lime dipping sauce.

Nutrition Info:

- Per Servings 2.2g Carbs, 16g Protein, 27.1g Fat, 324 Calories

Tuna Steaks With Shirataki Noodles

Servings: 4
Cooking Time: 30 Minutes
Ingredients:

- 1 pack miracle noodle angel hair
- 3 cups water
- Cooking spray
- 1 red bell pepper, seeded and halved
- 4 tuna steaks
- Salt and black pepper to taste
- Olive oil for brushing
- 2 tbsp pickled ginger
- 2 tbsp chopped cilantro

Directions:

1. Cook the shirataki rice as per package instructions: In a colander, rinse the shirataki noodles with running cold water. Bring a pot of salted water to a boil; blanch the noodles for 2 minutes. Drain and transfer to a dry skillet over medium heat. Dry roast for a minute until opaque.

2. Grease a grill's grate with cooking spray and preheat on medium heat. Season the red bell pepper and tuna with salt and black pepper, brush with olive oil, and grill covered. Cook both for 3 minutes on each side. Transfer to a plate to cool. Dice bell pepper with a knife.

3. Assemble the noodles, tuna, and bell pepper in serving plate. Top with pickled ginger and garnish with cilantro. Serve with roasted sesame sauce (low-carb).

Nutrition Info:

- Per Servings 2g Carbs, 22g Protein, 18.2g Fat, 310 Calories

Salmon And Cauliflower Rice Pilaf

Servings: 4
Cooking Time: 25 Minutes
Ingredients:

- 1 cauliflower head, shredded
- ¼ cup dried vegetable soup mix
- 1 cup chicken broth
- 1 pinch saffron
- 1-lb wild salmon fillets
- 6 tbsp olive oil
- Pepper and salt to taste

Directions:

1. Place a heavy-bottomed pot on medium-high fire and add all ingredients and mix well.

2. Bring to a boil, lower fire to a simmer, and simmer for 10 minutes.

3. Turn off fire, shred salmon, adjust seasoning to taste.

4. Let it rest for 5 minutes.

5. Fluff again, serve, and enjoy.

Nutrition Info:

- Per Servings 4.7g Carbs, 31.8g Protein, 31.5g Fat, 429 Calories

Avocado & Cauliflower Salad With Prawns

Serves: 6
Cooking Time: 30 Minutes
Ingredients:

- 1 cauliflower head, florets only
- 1 lb medium-sized prawns
- ¼ cup + 1 tbsp olive oil
- 1 avocado, chopped
- 3 tbsp chopped dill
- ¼ cup lemon juice
- 2 tbsp lemon zest

Directions:

1. Heat 1 tbsp olive oil in a skillet and cook the prawns for 8-10 minutes. Microwave cauliflower for 5 minutes. Place prawns, cauliflower, and avocado in a large bowl. Whisk together the remaining olive oil, lemon zest, juice, dill, and some salt and pepper, in another bowl. Pour the dressing over, toss to combine and serve immediately.

Nutrition Info:

- Per Serves 5g Carbs ; 15g Protein ; 17g Fat; 214 Calories

Lemon Garlic Shrimp

Servings: 6
Cooking Time: 22 Minutes
Ingredients:

- ½ cup butter, divided
- 2 lb shrimp, peeled and deveined
- Pink salt and black pepper to taste
- ¼ tsp sweet paprika
- 1 tbsp minced garlic
- 3 tbsp water
- 1 lemon, zested and juiced
- 2 tbsp chopped parsley

Directions:

1. Melt half of the butter in a large skillet over medium heat, season the shrimp with salt, pepper, paprika, and add to the butter. Stir in the garlic and cook the shrimp for 4 minutes on both sides until pink. Remove to a bowl and set aside.

2. Put the remaining butter in the skillet; include the lemon zest, juice, and water. Cook until the butter has melted, about 1 minute. Add the shrimp, parsley, and adjust the taste with salt and black pepper. Cook for 2 minutes on low heat. Serve the shrimp and sauce with squash pasta.

Nutrition Info:
- Per Servings 2g Carbs, 13g Protein, 22g Fat, 258 Calories

Asian-style Fish Salad

Serves: 2
Cooking Time: 15 Minutes
Ingredients:
- Salad:
- 1/4 cup water
- 1/4 cup Sauvignon Blanc
- 1/2 pound salmon fillets
- 1 cup Chinese cabbage, sliced
- 1 tomato, sliced
- 2 radishes, sliced
- 1 bell pepper, sliced
- 1 medium-sized white onion, sliced
- Salad Dressing:
- 1/2 teaspoon fresh garlic, minced
- 1 fresh chili pepper, seeded and minced
- 1/2 teaspoon fresh ginger, peeled and grated
- 2 tablespoons fresh lime juice
- 1 tablespoon sesame oil
- 1 tablespoon tamari sauce
- 1 teaspoon xylitol
- 1 tablespoon fresh mint, roughly chopped
- Sea salt and freshly ground black pepper, to taste

Directions:
1. Place the water and Sauvignon Blanc in a sauté pan; bring to a simmer over moderate heat.
2. Place the salmon fillets, skin-side down in the pan and cover with the lid. Cook for 5 to 8 minutes or to your desired doneness; do not overcook the salmon; reserve.
3. Place the Chinese cabbage, tomato, radishes, bell pepper, and onion in a serving bowl.
4. Prepare the salad dressing by whisking all ingredients. Dress your salad, top with the salmon fillets and serve immediately!

Nutrition Info:
- Per Serves4.9g Carbs; 24.4g Protein; 15.1g Fat; 277 Calories

Sicilian-style Zoodle Spaghetti

Servings: 2
Cooking Time: 10 Minutes
Ingredients:
- 4 cups zoodles (spiralled zucchini)
- 2 ounces cubed bacon
- 4 ounces canned sardines, chopped
- ½ cup canned chopped tomatoes
- 1 tbsp capers
- 1 tbsp parsley
- 1 tsp minced garlic

Directions:

1. Pour some of the sardine oil in a pan. Add garlic and cook for 1 minute. Add the bacon and cook for 2 more minutes. Stir in the tomatoes and let simmer for 5 minutes. Add zoodles and sardines and cook for 3 minutes.

Nutrition Info:
- Per Servings 6g Carbs, 20g Protein, 31g Fat, 355 Calories

Baked Calamari And Shrimp

Serves: 1
Cooking Time: 20 Minutes
Ingredients:
- 8 ounces calamari, cut in medium rings
- 7 ounces shrimp, peeled and deveined
- 1 eggs
- 3 tablespoons coconut flour
- 1 tablespoon coconut oil
- 2 tablespoons avocado, chopped
- 1 teaspoon tomato paste
- 1 tablespoon mayonnaise
- A splash of Worcestershire sauce
- 1 teaspoon lemon juice
- 2 lemon slices
- Salt and black pepper to the taste
- ½ teaspoon turmeric

Directions:
1. In a bowl, whisk egg with coconut oil.
2. Add calamari rings and shrimp and toss to coat.
3. In another bowl, mix flour with salt, pepper and turmeric and stir.
4. Dredge calamari and shrimp in this mix, place everything on a lined baking sheet, introduce in the oven at 400 °F and bake for 10 minutes.
5. Flip calamari and shrimp and bake for 10 minutes more.
6. Meanwhile, in a bowl, mix avocado with mayo and tomato paste and mash using a fork.
7. Add Worcestershire sauce, lemon juice, salt and pepper and stir well.
8. Divide baked calamari and shrimp on plates and serve with the sauce and lemon juice on the side.
9. Enjoy!

Nutrition Info:
- 10 carbs; 34 protein; 23 fat; 368 calories

Sushi Shrimp Rolls

Servings: 5
Cooking Time: 10 Minutes
Ingredients:
- 2 cups cooked and chopped shrimp
- 1 tbsp sriracha sauce
- ¼ cucumber, julienned
- 5 hand roll nori sheets
- ¼ cup mayonnaise

Directions:
1. Combine shrimp, mayonnaise, and sriracha in a bowl. Lay out a single nori sheet on a flat surface and spread about 1/5 of the shrimp mixture. Roll the nori sheet as desired. Repeat with the other ingredients. Serve with sugar-free soy sauce.

Nutrition Info:
- Per Servings 1g Carbs, 18.7g Protein, 10g Fat, 216 Calories

Lemon-rosemary Shrimps

Servings: 4
Cooking Time: 12 Minutes
Ingredients:
- ½ cup lemon juice, freshly squeezed
- 1 ½ lb. shrimps, peeled and deveined
- 2 tbsp fresh rosemary
- ¼ cup coconut aminos
- 2 tbsp butter
- Pepper to taste
- 4 tbsp olive oil

Directions:
1. Place a nonstick saucepan on medium-high fire and heat oil and butter for 2 minutes.
2. Stir in shrimps and coconut aminos. Season with pepper Sauté for 5 minutes.
3. Add remaining ingredients and cook for another 5 minutes while stirring frequently.
4. Serve and enjoy.

Nutrition Info:
- Per Servings 3.7g Carbs, 35.8g Protein, 22.4g Fat, 359 Calories

Chapter 6. Sauces And Dressing Recipes

Simple Tomato Sauce

Servings: 4
Cooking Time: 20 Minutes
Ingredients:
- 1 can whole peeled tomatoes
- 3 garlic cloves, smashed
- 5 tablespoons olive oil
- Kosher salt
- 2 tablespoons unsalted butter
- Salt

Directions:
1. Purée tomatoes in a food processor until they're as smooth or chunky as you like.
2. Transfer tomatoes to a large Dutch oven or other heavy pot. (Or, use an immersion blender and blend directly in the pot.)
3. Add garlic, oil, and a 5-finger pinch of salt.
4. Bring to a boil and cook, occasionally stirring, until sauce is reduced by about one-third, about 20 minutes. Stir in butter.

Nutrition Info:
- Per Servings 7.6g Carbs, 1.9g Protein, 21.3g Fat, 219 Calories

Tzatziki

Servings: 4
Cooking Time: 10 Minutes, Plus At Least 30 Minutes To Chill
Ingredients:
- ½ large English cucumber, unpeeled
- 1½ cups Greek yogurt (I use Fage)
- 2 tablespoons olive oil
- Large pinch pink Himalayan salt
- Large pinch freshly ground black pepper
- Juice of ½ lemon
- 2 garlic cloves, finely minced
- 1 tablespoon fresh dill

Directions:
1. Halve the cucumber lengthwise, and use a spoon to scoop out and discard the seeds.
2. Grate the cucumber with a zester or grater onto a large plate lined with a few layers of paper towels. Close the paper towels around the grated cucumber, and squeeze as much water out of it as you can. (This can take a while and can require multiple paper towels. You can also allow it to drain overnight in a strainer or wrapped in a few layers of cheesecloth in the fridge if you have the time.)

3. In a food processor (or blender), blend the yogurt, olive oil, pink Himalayan salt, pepper, lemon juice, and garlic until fully combined.
4. Transfer the mixture to a medium bowl, and mix in the fresh dill and grated cucumber.
5. I like to chill this sauce for at least 30 minutes before serving. Keep in a sealed glass container in the refrigerator for up to 1 week.
Nutrition Info:
- Per Servings 5g Carbs, 8g Protein, 11g Fat, 149 Calories

Chunky Blue Cheese Dressing

Servings: 4
Cooking Time: 5 Minutes
Ingredients:
- ½ cup sour cream
- ½ cup mayonnaise
- Juice of ½ lemon
- ½ teaspoon Worcestershire sauce
- Pink Himalayan salt
- Freshly ground black pepper
- 2 ounces crumbled blue cheese

Directions:
1. In a medium bowl, whisk the sour cream, mayonnaise, lemon juice, and Worcestershire sauce. Season with pink Himalayan salt and pepper, and whisk again until fully combined.
2. Fold in the crumbled blue cheese until well combined.
3. Keep in a sealed glass container in the refrigerator for up to 1 week.
Nutrition Info:
- Per Servings 3g Carbs, 7g Protein, 32g Fat, 306 Calories

Lemon Tahini Sauce

Servings: 2
Cooking Time: 5 Minutes
Ingredients:
- 1/2 cup packed fresh herbs, such as parsley, basil, mint, cilantro, dill, or chives
- 1/4 cup tahini
- Juice of 1 lemon
- 1/2 teaspoon kosher salt
- 1 tablespoon water

Directions:
1. Place all the ingredients in the bowl of a food processor fitted with the blade attachment or a blender. Process continuously until the herbs are finely minced, and the sauce is well-blended, 3 to 4 minutes.
2. Serve immediately or store in a covered container in the refrigerator until ready to serve.
Nutrition Info:
- Per Servings 4.3g Carbs, 2.8g Protein, 8.1g Fat, 94 Calories

Celery-onion Vinaigrette

Servings: 4
Cooking Time: 0 Minutes
Ingredients:
- 1 tbsp finely chopped celery
- 1 tbsp finely chopped red onion
- 4 garlic cloves, minced
- ½ cup red wine vinegar
- 1 tbsp extra virgin olive oil

Directions:
1. Prepare the dressing by mixing pepper, celery, onion, olive oil, garlic, and vinegar in a small bowl. Whisk well to combine.
2. Let it sit for at least 30 minutes to let flavors blend.
3. Serve and enjoy with your favorite salad greens.
Nutrition Info:
- Per Servings 1.4g Carbs, 0.2g Protein, 3.4g Fat, 41 Calories

Caesar Salad Dressing

Servings: 6
Cooking Time: 10 Minutes
Ingredients:
- ½ cup olive oil
- 1 tablespoon Dijon mustard
- ½ cup parmesan cheese, grated
- 2/3-ounce anchovies, chopped
- ½ lemon juice, freshly squeezed
- Salt and pepper to taste

Directions:
1. Add all ingredients to a pot and bring to a simmer. Stir frequently.
2. Simmer for 10 minutes.
3. Adjust seasoning to taste.
Nutrition Info:
- Per Servings 1.5g Carbs, 3.4g Protein, 20.7g Fat, 203 Calories

Sriracha Mayo

Servings: 4
Cooking Time: 5 Minutes
Ingredients:
- ½ cup mayonnaise
- 2 tablespoons Sriracha sauce
- ½ teaspoon garlic powder
- ½ teaspoon onion powder
- ¼ teaspoon paprika

Directions:
1. In a small bowl, whisk together the mayonnaise, Sriracha, garlic powder, onion powder, and paprika until well mixed.
2. Pour into an airtight glass container, and keep in the refrigerator for up to 1 week.
Nutrition Info:
- Per Servings Calories: 2g Carbs, 1g Protein, 22g Fat, 201 Calories

Dijon Vinaigrette

Servings: 4
Cooking Time: 5 Minutes
Ingredients:
- 2 tablespoons Dijon mustard
- Juice of ½ lemon
- 1 garlic clove, finely minced
- 1½ tablespoons red wine vinegar
- Pink Himalayan salt
- Freshly ground black pepper
- 3 tablespoons olive oil

Directions:
1. In a small bowl, whisk the mustard, lemon juice, garlic, and red wine vinegar until well combined. Season with pink Himalayan salt and pepper, and whisk again.
2. Slowly add the olive oil, a little bit at a time, whisking constantly.
3. Keep in a sealed glass container in the refrigerator for up to 1 week.

Nutrition Info:
- Per Servings 1g Carbs, 1g Protein, 11g Fat, 99 Calories

Caesar Dressing

Servings: 4
Cooking Time: 5 Minutes
Ingredients:
- ½ cup mayonnaise
- 1 tablespoon Dijon mustard
- Juice of ½ lemon
- ½ teaspoon Worcestershire sauce
- Pinch pink Himalayan salt
- Pinch freshly ground black pepper
- ¼ cup grated Parmesan cheese

Directions:
1. In a medium bowl, whisk together the mayonnaise, mustard, lemon juice, Worcestershire sauce, pink Himalayan salt, and pepper until fully combined.
2. Add the Parmesan cheese, and whisk until creamy and well blended.
3. Keep in a sealed glass container in the refrigerator for up to 1 week.

Nutrition Info:
- Per Servings Calories: 2g Carbs, 2g Protein, 23g Fat, 222 Calories

Garlic Aioli

Servings: 4
Cooking Time: 5 Minutes, Plus 30 Minutes To Chill
Ingredients:
- ½ cup mayonnaise
- 2 garlic cloves, minced
- Juice of 1 lemon
- 1 tablespoon chopped fresh flat-leaf Italian parsley
- 1 teaspoon chopped chives
- Pink Himalayan salt

- Freshly ground black pepper

Directions:
1. In a food processor (or blender), combine the mayonnaise, garlic, lemon juice, parsley, and chives, and season with pink Himalayan salt and pepper. Blend until fully combined.
2. Pour into a sealed glass container and chill in the refrigerator for at least 30 minutes before serving. (This sauce will keep in the fridge for up to 1 week.)

Nutrition Info:
- Per Servings Calories: 3g Carbs, 1g Protein, 22g Fat, 204 Calories

Avocado-lime Crema

Servings: 4
Cooking Time: 5 Minutes
Ingredients:
- ½ cup sour cream
- ½ avocado
- 1 garlic clove, finely minced
- ¼ cup fresh cilantro leaves
- Juice of ½ lime
- Pinch pink Himalayan salt
- Pinch freshly ground black pepper

Directions:
1. In a food processor (or blender), mix the sour cream, avocado, garlic, cilantro, lime juice, pink Himalayan salt, and pepper until smooth and fully combined.
2. Spoon the sauce into an airtight glass jar and keep in the refrigerator for up to 3 days.

Nutrition Info:
- Per Servings Calories: 2g Carbs, 1g Protein, 8g Fat, 87 Calories

Vegetarian Fish Sauce

Servings: 16
Cooking Time: 20 Minutes
Ingredients:
- 1/4 cup dried shiitake mushrooms
- 1-2 tbsp tamari (for a depth of flavor)
- 3 tbsp coconut aminos
- 1 ¼ cup water
- 2 tsp sea salt

Directions:
1. To a small saucepan, add water, coconut aminos, dried shiitake mushrooms, and sea salt. Bring to a boil, then cover, reduce heat, and simmer for 15-20 minutes.
2. Remove from heat and let cool slightly. Pour liquid through a fine-mesh strainer into a bowl, pressing on the mushroom mixture with a spoon to squeeze out any remaining liquid.
3. To the bowl, add tamari. Taste and adjust as needed, adding more sea salt for saltiness.
4. Store in a sealed container in the refrigerator for up to 1 month and shake well before use. Or pour into an ice cube

tray, freeze, and store in a freezer-safe container for up to 2 months.

Nutrition Info:
- Per Servings 5g Carbs, 0.3g Protein, 2g Fat, 39.1 Calories

Roasted Garlic Lemon Dip

Servings: 3
Cooking Time: 30 Minutes

Ingredients:
- 3 medium lemons
- 3 cloves garlic, peeled and smashed
- 5 tablespoons olive oil, divided
- 1/2 teaspoon kosher salt
- Pepper to taste
- Salt
- Pepper

Directions:
1. Arrange a rack in the middle of the oven and heat to 400°F.
2. Cut the lemons in half crosswise and remove the seeds. Place the lemons cut-side up in a small baking dish. Add the garlic and drizzle with 2 tablespoons of the oil.
3. Roast until the lemons are tender and lightly browned, about 30 minutes. Remove the baking dish to a wire rack.
4. When the lemons are cool enough to handle, squeeze the juice into the baking dish. Discard the lemon pieces and any remaining seeds. Pour the contents of the baking dish, including the garlic, into a blender or mini food processor. Add the remaining 3 tablespoons oil and salt. Process until the garlic is completely puréed, and the sauce is emulsified and slightly thickened. Serve warm or at room temperature.

Nutrition Info:
- Per Servings 4.8g Carbs, 0.6g Protein, 17g Fat, 165 Calories

Buttery Dijon Sauce

Servings: 2
Cooking Time: 0 Minutes

Ingredients:
- 3 parts brown butter
- 1-part vinegar or citrus juice or a combo
- 1-part strong Dijon mustard
- A small handful of flat-leaf parsley (optional)
- 3/4 teaspoon freshly ground pepper
- 1 teaspoon salt

Directions:
1. Add everything to a food processor and blitz until just smooth.
2. You can also mix this up with an immersion blender. Use immediately or store in the refrigerator for up to one day. Blend again before use.

Nutrition Info:
- Per Servings 0.7g Carbs, 0.4g Protein, 34.4g Fat, 306 Calories

Feta Avocado Dip

Servings: 4
Cooking Time: 0 Minutes

Ingredients:
- 2 avocadoes (mashed)
- ½ cup feta cheese (crumbled)
- 1 plum tomatoes (diced)
- 1 teaspoon garlic (minced)
- ½ lemon (juiced)
- Salt
- Pepper
- 4 tablespoons olive oil

Directions:
1. Fold ingredients together. Do not stir too much to leave chunks of feta and avocado.
2. Serve and enjoy.

Nutrition Info:
- Per Servings 8.1g Carbs, 5g Protein, 19g Fat, 220 Calories

Green Jalapeno Sauce

Servings: 1
Cooking Time: 0 Minutes

Ingredients:
- ½ avocado
- 1 large jalapeno
- 1 cup fresh cilantro
- 2 tablespoons extra virgin olive oil
- 3 tablespoons water
- Water
- ½ teaspoon salt

Directions:
1. Add all ingredients in a blender.
2. Blend until smooth and creamy.
3. Serve and enjoy.

Nutrition Info:
- Per Servings 10g Carbs, 2.4g Protein, 42g Fat, 407 Calories

Alfredo Sauce

Servings: 2
Cooking Time: 10 Minutes
Ingredients:

- 4 tablespoons butter
- 2 ounces cream cheese
- 1 cup heavy (whipping) cream
- ½ cup grated Parmesan cheese
- 1 garlic clove, finely minced
- 1 teaspoon dried Italian seasoning
- Pink Himalayan salt
- Freshly ground black pepper

Directions:

1. In a heavy medium saucepan over medium heat, combine the butter, cream cheese, and heavy cream. Whisk slowly and constantly until the butter and cream cheese melt.
2. Add the Parmesan, garlic, and Italian seasoning. Continue to whisk until everything is well blended. Turn the heat to medium-low and simmer, stirring occasionally, for 5 to 8 minutes to allow the sauce to blend and thicken.
3. Season with pink Himalayan salt and pepper, and stir to combine.
4. Toss with your favorite hot, precooked, keto-friendly noodles and serve.
5. Keep this sauce in a sealed glass container in the refrigerator for up to 4 days.

Nutrition Info:

- Per Servings 2g Carbs, 5g Protein, 30g Fat, 294 Calories

Keto Ranch Dip

Servings: 8
Cooking Time: 10 Minutes
Ingredients:

- 1 cup egg white, beaten
- 1 lemon juice, freshly squeezed
- Salt and pepper to taste
- 1 teaspoon mustard paste
- 1 cup olive oil
- Salt and pepper to taste

Directions:

1. Add all ingredients to a pot and bring to a simmer. Stir frequently.

2. Simmer for 10 minutes.
3. Adjust seasoning to taste.

Nutrition Info:

- Per Servings 1.2g Carbs, 3.4g Protein, 27.1g Fat, 258 Calories

Cheesy Avocado Dip

Servings:
Cooking Time: 20 Minutes
Ingredients:

- 1/2 medium ripe avocado, peeled and pitted
- 2 crumbled blue cheese
- 1 freshly squeezed lemon juice
- 1/2 kosher salt
- 1/2 cup water

Directions:

1. Scoop the flesh of the avocado into the bowl of a food processor fitted with the blade attachment or blender.
2. Add the blue cheese, lemon juice, and salt. Blend until smooth and creamy, 30 to 40 seconds.
3. With the motor running, add the water and blend until the sauce is thinned and well-combined.

Nutrition Info:

- Per Servings 2.9g Carbs, 3.5g Protein, 7.2g Fat, 86 Calories

Fat-burning Dressing

Servings: 6
Cooking Time: 3 Minutes
Ingredients:

- 2 tablespoons coconut oil
- ¼ cup olive oil
- 2 cloves of garlic, minced
- 2 tablespoons freshly chopped herbs of your choice
- ¼ cup mayonnaise
- Salt and pepper to taste

Directions:

1. Heat the coconut oil and olive oil and sauté the garlic until fragrant in a saucepan.
2. Allow cooling slightly before adding the mayonnaise.
3. Season with salt and pepper to taste.

Nutrition Info:

- Per Servings 0.6g Carbs, 14.1g Protein, 22.5g Fat, 262 Calories

Chapter 7. Soups, Stew & Salads

Easy Tomato Salad

Servings: 4
Cooking Time: 0 Minutes
Ingredients:
- 1 ½ cups cherry tomatoes, sliced
- ¼ cup white wine vinegar
- 1/8 cup chives
- 3 tablespoons olive oil
- Salt and pepper to taste

Directions:
1. Put all ingredients in a bowl.
2. Toss to combine.
3. Serve immediately.

Nutrition Info:
- Per Servings 0.6g Carbs, 0.3g Protein, 10.1g Fat, 95 Calories

Asparagus Niçoise Salad

Servings: 4
Cooking Time: 0 Minutes
Ingredients:
- 1-pound fresh asparagus, trimmed and blanched
- 2 ½ ounces white tuna in oil
- ½ cup pitted Greek olives, halved
- ½ cup zesty Italian salad dressing
- Salt and pepper to taste
- 3 tablespoons olive oil

Directions:
1. Place all ingredients in a bowl.
2. Toss to mix all ingredients.
3. Serve.

Nutrition Info:
- Per Servings 10g Carbs, 8g Protein, 20g Fat, 239 Calories

Mushroom-broccoli Soup

Servings: 4
Cooking Time: 20 Minutes
Ingredients:
- 1 onion, diced
- 3 cloves of garlic, diced
- 2 cups mushrooms, chopped
- 2 heads of broccoli, cut into florets
- 1 cup full-fat milk
- 3 cups water
- Pepper and salt to taste

Directions:
1. Place a heavy-bottomed pot on medium-high fire and heat for 3 minutes.
2. Add onion, garlic, water, and broccoli. Season generously with pepper and salt.

3. Cover and bring to a boil. Once boiling, lower fire to a simmer and let it cook for 7 minutes.
4. With a handheld blender, puree mixture until smooth and creamy.
5. Stir in mushrooms and milk, cover, and simmer for another 8 minutes.
6. Serve and enjoy.

Nutrition Info:
- Per Servings 8.5g Carbs, 3.8g Protein, 1.0g Fat, 58.2 Calories

Creamy Soup With Greens

Servings: 6
Cooking Time: 20 Minutes
Ingredients:
- ½-pounds collard greens, torn to bite-sized pieces
- 5 cups chicken broth
- 2 cups broccoli florets
- 1 cup diced onion
- 3 tablespoon oil
- 4 tablespoons butter
- Salt and pepper to taste

Directions:
1. Add all ingredients to the pot and bring to a boil.
2. Lower fire to a simmer and simmer for 15 minutes while covered.
3. With an immersion blender, puree soup until creamy.
4. Adjust seasoning to taste.
5. Serve and enjoy.

Nutrition Info:
- Per Servings 6.5g Carbs, 50.6g Protein, 33.5g Fat, 548 Calories

Creamy Cauliflower Soup With Chorizo Sausage

Servings: 4
Cooking Time: 40 Minutes
Ingredients:
- 1 cauliflower head, chopped
- 1 turnip, chopped
- 3 tbsp butter
- 1 chorizo sausage, sliced
- 2 cups chicken broth
- 1 small onion, chopped
- 2 cups water
- Salt and black pepper, to taste

Directions:
1. Melt 2 tbsp. of the butter in a large pot over medium heat. Stir in onion and cook until soft and golden, about 3-4 minutes. Add cauliflower and turnip, and cook for another 5 minutes.
2. Pour the broth and water over. Bring to a boil, simmer covered, and cook for about 20 minutes until the vegetables

are tender. Remove from heat. Melt the remaining butter in a skillet. Add the chorizo sausage and cook for 5 minutes until crispy. Puree the soup with a hand blender until smooth. Taste and adjust the seasonings. Serve the soup in deep bowls topped with the chorizo sausage.

Nutrition Info:

- Per Servings 5.7g Carbs, 10g Protein, 19.1g Fat, 251 Calories

Mediterranean Salad

Servings: 4
Cooking Time: 10 Minutes
Ingredients:

- 3 tomatoes, sliced
- 1 large avocado, sliced
- 8 kalamata olives
- ¼ lb buffalo mozzarella cheese, sliced
- 2 tbsp pesto sauce
- 2 tbsp olive oil

Directions:

1. Arrange the tomato slices on a serving platter and place the avocado slices in the middle. Arrange the olives around the avocado slices and drop pieces of mozzarella on the platter. Drizzle the pesto sauce all over, and drizzle olive oil as well.

Nutrition Info:

- Per Servings 4.3g Carbs, 9g Protein, 25g Fat, 290 Calories

Bacon Tomato Salad

Servings: 6
Cooking Time: 0 Minutes
Ingredients:

- 6 ounces iceberg lettuce blend
- 2 cups grape tomatoes, halved
- ¾ cup coleslaw salad dressing
- ¾ cup cheddar cheese, shredded
- 12 bacon strips, cooked and crumbled
- Salt and pepper to taste

Directions:

1. Put the lettuce and tomatoes in a salad bowl.
2. Drizzle with the dressing and sprinkle with cheese. Season with salt and pepper to taste then mix.
3. Garnish with bacon bits on top.

Nutrition Info:

- Per Servings 8g Carbs, 10g Protein, 20g Fat, 268 Calories

Chicken Cabbage Soup

Servings: 6
Cooking Time: 30 Minutes
Ingredients:

- 1 can Italian-style tomatoes
- 3 cups chicken broth
- 1 chicken breast
- ½ head of cabbage, shredded

- 1 packet Italian seasoning mix
- Salt and pepper to taste
- 1 cup water
- 1 tsp oil

Directions:

1. Place a heavy-bottomed pot on medium fire and heat for a minute. Add oil and swirl to coat the bottom and sides of the pot.
2. Pan fry chicken breast for 4 minutes per side. Transfer to a chopping board and cut into ½-inch cubes.
3. Add all ingredients to the pot and stir well.
4. Cover and bring to a boil, lower fire to a simmer, and cook for 20 minutes.
5. Adjust seasoning to taste, serve, and enjoy.

Nutrition Info:

- Per Servings 5.6g Carbs, 34.1g Protein, 9.3g Fat, 248 Calories

Simplified French Onion Soup

Servings: 5
Cooking Time: 30 Minutes
Ingredients:

- 3 large onions, sliced
- 2 bay leaves
- 5 cups Beef Bone Broth
- 1 teaspoon dried thyme
- 1-oz Gruyere cheese, sliced into 5 equal pieces
- Pepper to taste
- 4 tablespoons oil

Directions:

1. Place a heavy-bottomed pot on medium-high fire and heat pot for 3 minutes.
2. Add oil and heat for 2 minutes. Stir in onions and sauté for 5 minutes.
3. Lower fire to medium-low, continue sautéing onions for 10 minutes until soft and browned, but not burned.
4. Add remaining ingredients and mix well.
5. Bring to a boil, lower fire to a simmer, cover and cook for 5 minutes.
6. Ladle into bowls, top with cheese.
7. Let it sit for 5 minutes.
8. Serve and enjoy.

Nutrition Info:

- Per Servings 9.9g Carbs, 4.3g Protein, 16.8g Fat, 208 Calories

Creamy Squash Bisque

Servings: 8
Cooking Time: 25 Minutes
Ingredients:

- ½ tablespoon turmeric powder
- ½ teaspoon cumin
- ½ cup onion, chopped
- 2 medium-sized kabocha squash, seeded and chopped
- 1 cup coconut milk
- 3 tablespoons oil

- 1 cup water
- Pepper and salt to taste

Directions:

1. Place a heavy-bottomed pot on medium-high fire and heat for 3 minutes.
2. Add oil to the pot and swirl to coat sides and bottom of the pot. Heat for 2 minutes.
3. Place squash in a single layer and season generously with pepper and salt.
4. Sprinkle turmeric, cumin, and onion. Add water.
5. Cover and bring to a boil. Once boiling, lower fire to a simmer and let it cook for 10 minutes.
6. With a handheld blender, puree squash. Stir in coconut milk and mix well. Cook until heated through, around 5 minutes.
7. Serve and enjoy.

Nutrition Info:

- Per Servings 10.9g Carbs, 3.1g Protein, 18.1g Fat, 218 Calories

Spinach Fruit Salad With Seeds

Servings: 4
Cooking Time: 1 Hour 10 Minutes

Ingredients:

- 2 tablespoons sesame seeds
- 1 tablespoon poppy seeds
- 1 tablespoon minced onion
- 10 ounces fresh spinach - rinsed, dried and torn into bite-size pieces
- 1 quart strawberries - cleaned, hulled and sliced
- 1/2 cup stevia
- 1/2 cup olive oil
- 1/4 cup distilled white vinegar
- 1/4 teaspoon Worcestershire sauce
- 1/4 teaspoon paprika

Directions:

1. Mix together the spinach and strawberry in a large bowl, stir in the sesame seeds, poppy seeds, stevia, olive oil, vinegar, paprika, Worcestershire sauce and onion in a medium bowl. Cover and cool for 1 hour.
2. Pour dressing over salad to combine well. Serve immediately or refrigerate for 15 minutes.

Nutrition Info:

- Per Servings 8.6g Carbs, 6g Protein, 18g Fat, 220 Calories

Brazilian Moqueca (shrimp Stew)

Servings: 6
Cooking Time: 25 Minutes

Ingredients:

- 1 cup coconut milk
- 2 tbsp lime juice
- ¼ cup diced roasted peppers
- 1 ½ pounds shrimp, peeled and deveined
- ¼ cup olive oil
- 1 garlic clove, minced

- 14 ounces diced tomatoes
- 2 tbsp sriracha sauce
- 1 chopped onion
- ¼ cup chopped cilantro
- Fresh dill, chopped to garnish
- Salt and black pepper, to taste

Directions:

1. Heat the olive oil in a pot over medium heat. Add onion and cook for 3 minutes or until translucent. Add the garlic and cook for another minute, until soft. Add tomatoes, shrimp, and cilantro. Cook until the shrimp becomes opaque, about 3-4 minutes.
2. Stir in sriracha sauce and coconut milk, and cook for 2 minutes. Do not bring to a boil. Stir in the lime juice and season with salt and pepper. Spoon the stew in bowls, garnish with fresh dill to serve.

Nutrition Info:

- Per Servings 5g Carbs, 23.1g Protein, 21g Fat, 324 Calories

Chicken Creamy Soup

Servings: 4
Cooking Time: 15 Minutes

Ingredients:

- 2 cups cooked and shredded chicken
- 3 tbsp butter, melted
- 4 cups chicken broth
- 4 tbsp chopped cilantro
- ⅓ cup buffalo sauce
- ½ cup cream cheese
- Salt and black pepper, to taste

Directions:

1. Blend the butter, buffalo sauce, and cream cheese, in a food processor, until smooth. Transfer to a pot, add the chicken broth and heat until hot but do not bring to a boil. Stir in chicken, salt, black pepper and cook until heated through. When ready, remove to soup bowls and serve garnished with cilantro.

Nutrition Info:

- Per Servings 5g Carbs, 26.5g Protein, 29.5g Fat, 406 Calories

Bacon Chowder

Servings: 6
Cooking Time: 15 Minutes

Ingredients:

- 1-pound bacon strips, chopped
- 1/4 cup chopped onion
- 1 can evaporated milk
- 1 sprig parsley, chopped
- 5 tablespoons butter
- 1/4 teaspoon salt
- 1/4 teaspoon pepper

Directions:

1. In a large skillet, cook bacon over medium heat until crisp, stirring occasionally. Remove with a slotted spoon;

drain on paper towels. Discard drippings, reserving 1-1/2 teaspoons in the pan. Add onion to drippings; cook and stir over medium-high heat until tender.

2. Meanwhile, place all ingredients Bring to a boil over high heat. Reduce heat to medium; cook, uncovered, 10-15 minutes or until tender. Reserve 1 cup potato water.

3. Add milk, salt and pepper to the saucepan; heat through. Stir in bacon and onion.

Nutrition Info:

- Per Servings 5.4g Carbs, 10g Protein, 31.9g Fat, 322 Calories

Spicy Chicken Bean Soup

Servings: 8
Cooking Time:1h 20 Mins
Ingredients:

- 8 skinless, boneless chicken breast halves
- 5 cubes chicken bouillon
- 2 cans peeled and diced tomatoes
- 1 container sour cream
- 1 cups frozen cut green beans
- 3 tablespoons. olive oil
- Salt and black pepper to taste
- 1 onion, chopped
- 3 cloves garlic, chopped
- 1 cups frozen cut green beans

Directions:

1. Heat olive oil in a large pot over medium heat, add onion, garlic and cook until tender. Stir in water, chicken, salt, pepper, bouillon cubes and bring to boil, simmer for 1 hour on Low. Remove chicken from the pot, reserve 5 cups broth and slice.

2. Stir in the remaining ingredients in the pot and simmer 30 minutes. Serve and enjoy.

Nutrition Info:

- Per Servings 7.6g Carbs, 26.5g Protein, 15.3g Fat, 275.1 Calories

Clam Chowder

Servings: 5
Cooking Time: 10 Minutes
Ingredients:

- 1 can condensed cream of celery soup, undiluted
- 2 cups half-and-half cream
- 2 cans minced/chopped clams, drained
- 1/4 teaspoon ground nutmeg
- 5 tablespoons butter
- Pepper to taste

Directions:

1. In a large saucepan, combine all ingredients. Cook and stir over medium heat until heated through.

Nutrition Info:

- Per Servings 3.8g Carbs, 10g Protein, 14g Fat, 251 Calories

Bacon And Pea Salad

Servings: 6
Cooking Time: 5 Minutes
Ingredients:

- 4 bacon strips
- 2 cups fresh peas
- ½ cup shredded cheddar cheese
- ½ cup ranch salad dressing
- 1/3 cup chopped red onions
- Salt and pepper to taste
- 3 tablespoons olive oil

Directions:

1. Heat skillet over medium flame and fry the bacon until crispy or until the fat has rendered. Transfer into a plate lined with a paper towel and crumble.

2. In a bowl, combine the rest of the ingredients and toss to coat.

3. Add in the bacon bits last.

Nutrition Info:

- Per Servings 2.9g Carbs, 3.5g Protein, 20.4g Fat, 205 Calories

Cobb Egg Salad In Lettuce Cups

Servings: 4
Cooking Time: 20 Minutes
Ingredients:

- 2 chicken breasts, cut into pieces
- 1 tbsp olive oil
- Salt and black pepper to season
- 6 large eggs
- 1 ½ cups water
- 2 tomatoes, seeded, chopped
- 6 tbsp Greek yogurt
- 1 head green lettuce, firm leaves removed for cups

Directions:

1. Preheat oven to 400ºF. Put the chicken pieces in a bowl, drizzle with olive oil, and sprinkle with salt and black pepper. Mix the ingredients until the chicken is well coated with the seasoning.

2. Put the chicken on a prepared baking sheet and spread out evenly. Slide the baking sheet in the oven and bake the chicken until cooked through and golden brown for 8 minutes, turning once.

3. Bring the eggs to boil in salted water in a pot over medium heat for 6 minutes. Run the eggs in cold water, peel, and chop into small pieces. Transfer to a salad bowl.

4. Remove the chicken from the oven when ready and add to the salad bowl. Include the tomatoes and Greek yogurt; mix evenly with a spoon. Layer two lettuce leaves each as cups and fill with two tablespoons of egg salad each. Serve with chilled blueberry juice.

Nutrition Info:

- Per Servings 4g Carbs, 21g Protein, 24.5g Fat, 325 Calories

Power Green Soup

Servings: 6
Cooking Time: 30 Minutes
Ingredients:
- 1 broccoli head, chopped
- 1 cup spinach
- 1 onion, chopped
- 2 garlic cloves, minced
- ½ cup watercress
- 5 cups veggie stock
- 1 cup coconut milk
- 1 tsp salt
- 1 tbsp ghee
- 1 bay leaf
- Salt and black pepper, to taste

Directions:
1. Melt the ghee in a large pot over medium heat. Add onion and cook for 3 minutes. Add garlic and cook for another minute. Add broccoli and cook for an additional 5 minutes.
2. Pour the stock over and add the bay leaf. Close the lid, bring to a boil, and reduce the heat. Simmer for about 3 minutes.
3. In the end, add spinach and watercress, and cook for 3 more minutes. Stir in the coconut cream, salt and pepper. Discard the bay leaf, and blend the soup with a hand blender.

Nutrition Info:
- Per Servings 5.8g Carbs, 4.9g Protein, 37.6g Fat, 392 Calories

Tuna Salad With Lettuce & Olives

Servings: 2
Cooking Time: 5 Minutes
Ingredients:
- 1 cup canned tuna, drained
- 1 tsp onion flakes
- 3 tbsp mayonnaise
- 1 cup shredded romaine lettuce
- 1 tbsp lime juice
- Sea salt, to taste
- 6 black olives, pitted and sliced

Directions:
1. Combine the tuna, mayonnaise, lime juice, and salt in a small bowl; mix to combine well. In a salad platter, arrange the shredded lettuce and onion flakes. Spread the tuna mixture over; top with black olives to serve.

Nutrition Info:
- Per Servings 2g Carbs, 18.5g Protein, 20g Fat, 248 Calories

Strawberry Salad With Spinach, Cheese & Almonds

Servings: 2
Cooking Time: 20 Minutes
Ingredients:
- 4 cups spinach
- 4 strawberries, sliced
- ½ cup flaked almonds
- 1 ½ cup grated hard goat cheese
- 4 tbsp raspberry vinaigrette
- Salt and black pepper, to taste

Directions:
1. Preheat your oven to 400ºF. Arrange the grated goat cheese in two circles on two pieces of parchment paper. Place in the oven and bake for 10 minutes.
2. Find two same bowls, place them upside down, and carefully put the parchment paper on top to give the cheese a bowl-like shape. Let cool that way for 15 minutes. Divide spinach among the bowls stir in salt, pepper and drizzle with vinaigrette. Top with almonds and strawberries.

Nutrition Info:
- Per Servings 5.3g Carbs, 33g Protein, 34.2g Fat, 445 Calories

Green Minestrone Soup

Servings: 4
Cooking Time: 25 Minutes
Ingredients:
- 2 tbsp ghee
- 2 tbsp onion garlic puree
- 2 heads broccoli, cut in florets
- 2 stalks celery, chopped
- 5 cups vegetable broth
- 1 cup baby spinach
- Salt and black pepper to taste

Directions:
1. Melt the ghee in a saucepan over medium heat and sauté the garlic for 3 minutes until softened. Mix in the broccoli and celery, and cook for 4 minutes until slightly tender. Pour in the broth, bring to a boil, then reduce the heat to medium-low and simmer covered for about 5 minutes.
2. Drop in the spinach to wilt, adjust the seasonings, and cook for 4 minutes. Ladle soup into serving bowls. Serve with a sprinkle of grated Gruyere cheese and freshly baked low carb carrot bread.

Nutrition Info:
- Per Servings 2g Carbs, 8g Protein, 20.3g Fat, 227 Calories

Green Salad With Bacon And Blue Cheese

Servings: 4
Cooking Time: 15 Minutes
Ingredients:
- 2 pack mixed salad greens
- 8 strips bacon
- 1 ½ cups crumbled blue cheese
- 1 tbsp white wine vinegar
- 3 tbsp extra virgin olive oil
- Salt and black pepper to taste

Directions:

1. Pour the salad greens in a salad bowl; set aside. Fry bacon strips in a skillet over medium heat for 6 minutes, until browned and crispy. Chop the bacon and scatter over the salad. Add in half of the cheese, toss and set aside.

2. In a small bowl, whisk the white wine vinegar, olive oil, salt, and black pepper until dressing is well combined. Drizzle half of the dressing over the salad, toss, and top with remaining cheese. Divide salad into four plates and serve with crusted chicken fries along with remaining dressing.

Nutrition Info:

- Per Servings 2g Carbs, 4g Protein, 20g Fat, 205 Calories

Thyme & Wild Mushroom Soup

Servings: 4
Cooking Time: 25 Minutes
Ingredients:

- ¼ cup butter
- ½ cup crème fraiche
- 12 oz wild mushrooms, chopped
- 2 tsp thyme leaves
- 2 garlic cloves, minced
- 4 cups chicken broth
- Salt and black pepper, to taste

Directions:

1. Melt the butter in a large pot over medium heat. Add garlic and cook for one minute until tender. Add mushrooms, salt and pepper, and cook for 10 minutes. Pour the broth over and bring to a boil.

2. Reduce the heat and simmer for 10 minutes. Puree the soup with a hand blender until smooth. Stir in crème Fraiche. Garnish with thyme leaves before serving.

Nutrition Info:

- Per Servings 5.8g Carbs, 6.1g Protein, 25g Fat, 281 Calories

Rustic Beef Soup

Servings: 4
Cooking Time: 20 Minutes
Ingredients:

- 3 cups beef broth
- 2 cups frozen mixed vegetables
- 1 teaspoon ground mustard
- Beef roast
- 1 teaspoon water
- Pinch of salt

Directions:

1. In a large saucepan, combine all the ingredients.
2. Bring to a boil.
3. Reduce heat; simmer, uncovered, for 15-20 minutes or until barley is tender.

Nutrition Info:

- Per Servings 8g Carbs, 51g Protein, 24g Fat, 450 Calories

Creamy Cauliflower Soup With Bacon Chips

Servings: 4
Cooking Time: 25 Minutes
Ingredients:

- 2 tbsp ghee
- 1 onion, chopped
- 2 head cauliflower, cut into florets
- 2 cups water
- Salt and black pepper to taste
- 3 cups almond milk
- 1 cup shredded white cheddar cheese
- 3 bacon strips

Directions:

1. Melt the ghee in a saucepan over medium heat and sauté the onion for 3 minutes until fragrant.

2. Include the cauli florets, sauté for 3 minutes to slightly soften, add the water, and season with salt and black pepper. Bring to a boil, and then reduce the heat to low. Cover and cook for 10 minutes.

3. Puree cauliflower with an immersion blender until the ingredients are evenly combined and stir in the almond milk and cheese until the cheese melts. Adjust taste with salt and black pepper.

4. In a non-stick skillet over high heat, fry the bacon, until crispy. Divide soup between serving bowls, top with crispy bacon, and serve hot.

Nutrition Info:

- Per Servings 6g Carbs, 8g Protein, 37g Fat, 402 Calories

Homemade Cold Gazpacho Soup

Servings: 6
Cooking Time: 15 Minutes
Ingredients:

- 2 small green peppers, roasted
- 2 large red peppers, roasted
- 2 medium avocados, flesh scoped out
- 2 garlic cloves
- 2 spring onions, chopped
- 1 cucumber, chopped
- 1 cup olive oil
- 2 tbsp lemon juice
- 4 tomatoes, chopped
- 7 ounces goat cheese
- 1 small red onion, chopped
- 2 tbsp apple cider vinegar
- Salt to taste

Directions:

1. Place the peppers, tomatoes, avocados, red onion, garlic, lemon juice, olive oil, vinegar, and salt, in a food processor. Pulse until your desired consistency is reached. Taste and adjust the seasoning.

2. Transfer the mixture to a pot. Stir in cucumber and spring onions. Cover and chill in the fridge at least 2 hours.

Divide the soup between 6 bowls. Serve very cold, generously topped with goat cheese and an extra drizzle of olive oil.
Nutrition Info:
- Per Servings 6.5g Carbs, 7.5g Protein, 45.8g Fat, 528 Calories

Coconut Cauliflower Soup

Servings: 10
Cooking Time: 26 Minutes
Ingredients:
- 1 medium onion, finely chopped
- 3 tablespoons yellow curry paste
- 2 medium heads cauliflower, broken into florets
- 1 carton vegetable broth
- 1 cup coconut milk
- 2 tablespoons olive oil

Directions:
1. In a large saucepan, heat oil over medium heat. Add onion; cook and stir until softened, 2-3 minutes.
2. Add curry paste; cook until fragrant, 1-2 minutes.
3. Add cauliflower and broth. Increase heat to high; bring to a boil. Reduce heat to medium-low; cook, covered, about 20 minutes.
4. Stir in coconut milk; cook an additional minute.
5. Remove from heat; cool slightly.
6. Puree in batches in a blender or food processor.
7. If desired, top with minced fresh cilantro.

Nutrition Info:
- Per Servings 10g Carbs, 3g Protein, 8g Fat, 111 Calories

Pork Burger Salad With Yellow Cheddar

Servings: 4
Cooking Time: 25 Minutes
Ingredients:
- 1 lb ground pork
- Salt and black pepper to season
- 1 tbsp olive oil
- 2 hearts romaine lettuce, torn into pieces
- 2 firm tomatoes, sliced
- ¼ red onion, sliced
- 3 oz yellow cheddar cheese, shredded

Directions:
1. Season the pork with salt and black pepper, mix and make medium-sized patties out of them.
2. Heat the oil in a skillet over medium heat and fry the patties on both sides for 10 minutes until browned and cook within. Transfer to a wire rack to drain oil. When cooled, cut into quarters.
3. Mix the lettuce, tomatoes, and red onion in a salad bowl, season with a little oil, salt, and pepper. Toss and add the pork on top.
4. Melt the cheese in the microwave for about 90 seconds. Drizzle the cheese over the salad and serve.

Nutrition Info:
- Per Servings 2g Carbs, 22g Protein, 23g Fat, 310 Calories

Fruit Salad With Poppy Seeds

Servings: 5
Cooking Time: 25 Mins
Ingredients:
- 1 tablespoon poppy seeds
- 1 head romaine lettuce, torn into bite-size pieces
- 4 ounces shredded Swiss cheese
- 1 avocado- peeled, cored and diced
- 2 teaspoons diced onion
- 1/2 cup lemon juice
- 1/2 cup stevia
- 1/2 teaspoon salt
- 2/3 cup olive oil
- 1 teaspoon Dijon style prepared mustard

Directions:
1. Combine stevia, lemon juice, onion, mustard, and salt in a blender. Process until well blended.
2. Add oil until mixture is thick and smooth. Add poppy seeds, stir just a few seconds or more to mix.
3. In a large serving bowl, toss together the remaining ingredients.
4. Pour dressing over salad just before serving, and toss to coat.

Nutrition Info:
- Per Servings 6g Carbs, 4.9g Protein, 20.6g Fat, 277 Calories

Insalata Caprese

Servings: 8
Cooking Time: 0 Minutes
Ingredients:
- 2 ½ pounds tomatoes, cut into 1-in pieces
- 8 ounces mozzarella cheese pearls
- ½ cup ripe olives, pitted
- ¼ cup fresh basil, sliced thinly
- Balsamic vinegar (optional)
- Salt and pepper to taste
- 3 tablespoons olive oil

Directions:
1. Place all ingredients in a bowl.
2. Season with salt and pepper to taste. Drizzle with balsamic vinegar if available.
3. Toss to coat.
4. Serve immediately.

Nutrition Info:
- Per Servings 7g Carbs, 6g Protein, 12g Fat, 160 Calories

Mexican Soup

Servings: 4
Cooking Time: 25 Minutes
Ingredients:
- 1-pound boneless skinless chicken thighs, cut into 3/4-inch pieces
- 1 tablespoon reduced-sodium taco seasoning
- 1 cup salsa
- 1 carton reduced-sodium chicken broth
- 4 tablespoons olive oil

Directions:
1. In a large saucepan, heat oil over medium-high heat. Add chicken; cook and stir 6-8 minutes or until no longer pink. Stir in taco seasoning.
2. Add remaining ingredients; bring to a boil. Reduce heat; simmer, uncovered, 5 minutes to allow flavors to blend. Skim fat before serving.

Nutrition Info:
- Per Servings 5.6g Carbs, 25g Protein, 16.5g Fat, 281 Calories

Warm Baby Artichoke Salad

Servings: 4
Cooking Time: 30 Minutes
Ingredients:
- 6 baby artichokes
- 6 cups water
- 1 tbsp lemon juice
- ¼ cup cherry peppers, halved
- ¼ cup pitted olives, sliced
- ¼ cup olive oil
- ¼ tsp lemon zest
- 2 tsp balsamic vinegar, sugar-free
- 1 tbsp chopped dill
- ½ tsp salt
- ¼ tsp black pepper
- 1 tbsp capers
- ¼ tsp caper brine

Directions:
1. Combine the water and salt in a pot over medium heat. Trim and halve the artichokes; add to the pot. Bring to a boil, lower the heat, and let simmer for 20 minutes until tender.
2. Combine the rest of the ingredients, except the olives in a bowl. Drain and place the artichokes in a serving plate. Pour the prepared mixture over; toss to combine well. Serve topped with the olives.

Nutrition Info:
- Per Servings 5g Carbs, 1g Protein, 13g Fat, 170 Calories

Bacon And Spinach Salad

Servings: 4
Cooking Time: 20 Minutes
Ingredients:
- 2 large avocados, 1 chopped and 1 sliced
- 1 spring onion, sliced
- 4 cooked bacon slices, crumbled
- 2 cups spinach
- 2 small lettuce heads, chopped
- 2 hard-boiled eggs, chopped
- Vinaigrette:
- 3 tbsp olive oil
- 1 tsp Dijon mustard
- 1 tbsp apple cider vinegar

Directions:
1. Combine the spinach, lettuce, eggs, chopped avocado, and spring onion, in a large bowl. Whisk together the vinaigrette ingredients in another bowl.
2. Pour the dressing over, toss to combine and top with the sliced avocado and bacon.

Nutrition Info:
- Per Servings 3.4g Carbs, 7g Protein, 33g Fat, 350 Calories

Crispy Bacon Salad With Mozzarella & Tomato

Servings: 2
Cooking Time: 10 Minutes
Ingredients:
- 1 large tomato, sliced
- 4 basil leaves
- 8 mozzarella cheese slices
- 2 tsp olive oil
- 6 bacon slices, chopped
- 1 tsp balsamic vinegar
- Sea salt, to taste

Directions:
1. Place the bacon in a skillet over medium heat and cook until crispy. Divide the tomato slices between two serving plates. Arrange the mozzarella slices over and top with the basil leaves. Add the crispy bacon on top, drizzle with olive oil and vinegar. Sprinkle with sea salt and serve.

Nutrition Info:
- Per Servings 1.5g Carbs, 21g Protein, 26g Fat, 279 Calories

Caesar Salad With Chicken And Parmesan

Servings: 4
Cooking Time: 1 Hour And 30 Minutes
Ingredients:
- 4 boneless, skinless chicken thighs
- ¼ cup lemon juice
- 2 garlic cloves, minced
- 4 tbsp olive oil
- ½ cup caesar salad dressing, sugar-free
- 12 bok choy leaves
- 3 Parmesan crisps
- Parmesan cheese, grated for garnishing

Directions:

1. Combine the chicken, lemon juice, 2 tbsp of olive oil, and garlic in a Ziploc bag. Seal the bag, shake to combine, and refrigerate for 1 hour. Preheat the grill to medium heat and grill the chicken for about 4 minutes per side.
2. Cut the bok choy leaves lengthwise, and brush it with the remaining olive oil. Grill the bok choy for about 3 minutes. Place on a serving bowl. Top with the chicken and drizzle the caesar salad dressing over. Top with parmesan crisps and sprinkle the grated parmesan cheese over.

Nutrition Info:
- Per Servings 5g Carbs, 33g Protein, 39g Fat, 529 Calories

Sour Cream And Cucumbers

Servings: 8
Cooking Time: 0 Minutes

Ingredients:
- ½ cup sour cream
- 3 tablespoons white vinegar
- 4 medium cucumbers, sliced thinly
- 1 small sweet onion, sliced thinly
- Salt and pepper to taste
- 3 tablespoons olive oil

Directions:
1. In a bowl, whisk the sour cream and vinegar. Season with salt and pepper to taste. Whisk until well-combined.
2. Add in the cucumber and the rest of the ingredients.
3. Toss to coat.
4. Allow chilling before serving.

Nutrition Info:
- Per Servings 4.8g Carbs, 0.9g Protein, 8.3g Fat, 96 Calories

Tuna Caprese Salad

Servings: 4
Cooking Time: 10 Minutes

Ingredients:
- 2 cans tuna chunks in water, drained
- 2 tomatoes, sliced
- 8 oz fresh mozzarella cheese, sliced
- 6 basil leaves
- ½ cup black olives, pitted and sliced
- 2 tbsp extra virgin olive oil
- ½ lemon, juiced

Directions:
1. Place the tuna in the center of a serving platter. Arrange the cheese and tomato slices around the tuna. Alternate a slice of tomato, cheese, and a basil leaf.
2. To finish, scatter the black olives over the top, drizzle with olive oil and lemon juice, and serve with grilled chicken breasts.

Nutrition Info:
- Per Servings 1g Carbs, 21g Protein, 31g Fat, 360 Calories

Green Mackerel Salad

Servings: 2
Cooking Time: 25 Minutes

Ingredients:
- 2 mackerel fillets
- 2 hard-boiled eggs, sliced
- 1 tbsp coconut oil
- 2 cups green beans
- 1 avocado, sliced
- 4 cups mixed salad greens
- 2 tbsp olive oil
- 2 tbsp lemon juice
- 1 tsp Dijon mustard
- Salt and black pepper, to taste

Directions:
1. Fill a saucepan with water and add the green beans and salt. Cook over medium heat for about 3 minutes. Drain and set aside.
2. Melt the coconut oil in a pan over medium heat. Add the mackerel fillets and cook for about 4 minutes per side, or until opaque and crispy. Divide the green beans between two salad bowls. Top with mackerel, egg, and avocado slices.
3. In a bowl, whisk together the lemon juice, olive oil, mustard, salt, and pepper, and drizzle over the salad.

Nutrition Info:
- Per Servings 7.6g Carbs, 27.3g Protein, 41.9g Fat, 525 Calories

Lobster Salad With Mayo Dressing

Servings: 4
Cooking Time: 1 Hour 10 Minutes

Ingredients:
- 1 small head cauliflower, cut into florets
- ⅓ cup diced celery
- ½ cup sliced black olives
- 2 cups cooked large shrimp
- 1 tbsp dill, chopped
- Dressing:
- ½ cup mayonnaise
- 1 tsp apple cider vinegar
- ¼ tsp celery seeds
- A pinch of black pepper
- 2 tbsp lemon juice
- 2 tsp swerve
- Salt to taste

Directions:
1. Combine the cauliflower, celery, shrimp, and dill in a large bowl. Whisk together the mayonnaise, vinegar, celery seeds, black pepper, sweetener, and lemon juice in another bowl. Season with salt to taste.
2. Pour the dressing over and gently toss to combine; refrigerate for 1 hour. Top with olives to serve.

Nutrition Info:
- Per Servings 2g Carbs, 12g Protein, 15g Fat, 182 Calories

Coconut, Green Beans, And Shrimp Curry Soup

Servings: 4
Cooking Time: 20 Minutes
Ingredients:
- 2 tbsp ghee
- 1 lb jumbo shrimp, peeled and deveined
- 2 tsp ginger-garlic puree
- 2 tbsp red curry paste
- 6 oz coconut milk
- Salt and chili pepper to taste
- 1 bunch green beans, halved

Directions:
1. Melt ghee in a medium saucepan over medium heat. Add the shrimp, season with salt and pepper, and cook until they are opaque, 2 to 3 minutes. Remove shrimp to a plate. Add the ginger-garlic puree and red curry paste to the ghee and sauté for 2 minutes until fragrant.
2. Stir in the coconut milk; add the shrimp, salt, chili pepper, and green beans. Cook for 4 minutes. Reduce the heat to a simmer and cook an additional 3 minutes, occasionally stirring. Adjust taste with salt, fetch soup into serving bowls, and serve with cauli rice.

Nutrition Info:
- Per Servings 2g Carbs, 9g Protein, 35.4g Fat, 375 Calories

Arugula Prawn Salad With Mayo Dressing

Servings: 4
Cooking Time: 15 Minutes
Ingredients:
- 4 cups baby arugula
- ½ cup garlic mayonnaise
- 3 tbsp olive oil
- 1 lb tiger prawns, peeled and deveined
- 1 tsp Dijon mustard
- Salt and chili pepper to season
- 2 tbsp lemon juice

Directions:
1. Add the mayonnaise, lemon juice and mustard in a small bowl. Mix until smooth and creamy. Heat 2 tbps of olive oil in a skillet over medium heat, add the prawns, season with salt, and chili pepper, and fry in the oil for 3 minutes on each side until prawns are pink. Set aside to a plate.
2. Place the arugula in a serving bowl and pour half of the dressing on the salad. Toss with 2 spoons until mixed, and add the remaining dressing. Divide salad into 4 plates and serve with prawns.

Nutrition Info:
- Per Servings 2g Carbs, 8g Protein, 20.3g Fat, 215 Calories

Creamy Cauliflower Soup

Servings: 4
Cooking Time: 20 Minutes
Ingredients:
- 1 cauliflower head, chopped
- ½ cup onions, chopped
- 4 cups chicken broth
- 1 tablespoon butter
- 1 cup heavy cream
- Pepper and salt to taste

Directions:
1. Place all ingredients in a pot on medium-high fire, except for the heavy cream.
2. Season with salt and pepper to taste.
3. Give a good stir to combine everything.
4. Cover and bring to a boil, and simmer for 15 minutes.
5. With an immersion blender, blend well until smooth and creamy.
6. Stir in heavy cream and continue simmering for another 5 minutes. Adjust seasoning if needed.
7. Serve and enjoy.

Nutrition Info:
- Per Servings 7.3g Carbs, 53.9g Protein, 30.8g Fat, 53? Calories

Garlic Chicken Salad

Servings: 4
Cooking Time: 15 Minutes
Ingredients:
- 2 chicken breasts, boneless, skinless, flattened
- Salt and black pepper to taste
- 2 tbsp garlic powder
- 1 tsp olive oil
- 1 ½ cups mixed salad greens
- 1 tbsp red wine vinegar
- 1 cup crumbled blue cheese

Directions:
1. Season the chicken with salt, black pepper, and garlic powder. Heat oil in a pan over high heat and fry the chicken for 4 minutes on both sides until golden brown. Remove chicken to a cutting board and let cool before slicing.
2. Toss salad greens with red wine vinegar and share the salads into 4 plates. Divide chicken slices on top and sprinkle with blue cheese. Serve salad with carrots fries.

Nutrition Info:
- Per Servings 4g Carbs, 14g Protein, 23g Fat, 286 Calories

Balsamic Cucumber Salad

Servings: 6
Cooking Time: 0 Minutes
Ingredients:
- 1 large English cucumber, halved and sliced
- 1 cup grape tomatoes, halved
- 1 medium red onion, sliced thinly
- ¼ cup balsamic vinaigrette
- ¾ cup feta cheese
- Salt and pepper to taste

- ¼ cup olive oil

Directions:
1. Place all ingredients in a bowl.
2. Toss to coat everything with the dressing.
3. Allow chilling before serving.

Nutrition Info:
- Per Servings 9g Carbs, 4.8g Protein, 16.7g Fat, 253 Calories

Salmon Salad With Walnuts

Servings: 2
Cooking Time: 10 Minutes

Ingredients:
- 2 salmon fillets
- 2 tablespoons balsamic vinaigrette, divided
- 1/8 teaspoon pepper
- 2 cups mixed salad greens
- 1/4 cup walnuts
- 2 tablespoons crumbled cheese
- Salt and pepper to taste
- 3 tablespoons olive oil

Directions:
1. Brush the salmon with half of the balsamic vinaigrette and sprinkle with pepper.
2. Grill the salmon over medium heat for 5 minutes on each side.
3. Crumble the salmon and place in a mixing bowl. Add the rest of the ingredients and season with salt and pepper to taste.

Nutrition Info:
- Per Servings 8g Carbs, 5g Protein, 30g Fat, 313 Calories

Shrimp With Avocado & Cauliflower Salad

Servings: 6
Cooking Time: 30 Minutes

Ingredients:
- 1 cauliflower head, florets only
- 1 pound medium shrimp
- ¼ cup + 1 tbsp olive oil
- 1 avocado, chopped
- 3 tbsp chopped dill
- ¼ cup lemon juice
- 2 tbsp lemon zest
- Salt and black pepper to taste

Directions:
1. Heat 1 tbsp olive oil in a skillet and cook the shrimp until opaque, about 8-10 minutes. Place the cauliflower florets in a microwave-safe bowl, and microwave for 5 minutes. Place the shrimp, cauliflower, and avocado in a large bowl.
2. Whisk together the remaining olive oil, lemon zest, juice, dill, and some salt and pepper, in another bowl. Pour the dressing over, toss to combine and serve immediately.

Nutrition Info:

- Per Servings 5g Carbs, 15g Protein, 17g Fat, 214 Calories

Brussels Sprouts Salad With Pecorino Romano

Servings: 6
Cooking Time: 35 Minutes

Ingredients:
- 2 lb Brussels sprouts, halved
- 3 tbsp olive oil
- Salt and black pepper to taste
- 2 ½ tbsp balsamic vinegar
- ¼ red cabbage, shredded
- 1 tbsp Dijon mustard
- 1 cup pecorino romano cheese, grated

Directions:
1. Preheat oven to 400ºF and line a baking sheet with foil. Toss the brussels sprouts with olive oil, a little salt, black pepper, and balsamic vinegar, in a bowl, and spread on the baking sheet in an even layer. Bake until tender on the inside and crispy on the outside, about 20 to 25 minutes.
2. Transfer to a salad bowl and add the red cabbage, Dijon mustard and half of the cheese. Mix until well combined. Sprinkle with the remaining cheese, share the salad onto serving plates, and serve with syrup-grilled salmon.

Nutrition Info:
- Per Servings 6g Carbs, 4g Protein, 18g Fat, 210 Calories

Celery Salad

Servings: 4
Cooking Time: 0 Minutes

Ingredients:
- 3 cups celery, thinly sliced
- ½ cup parmigiana cheese, shaved
- 1/3 cup toasted walnuts
- 4 tablespoons extra virgin olive oil
- 1 tablespoon red wine vinegar
- Salt and pepper to taste

Directions:
1. Place the celery, cheese, and walnuts in a bowl.
2. In a smaller bowl, combine the olive oil and vinegar. Season with salt and pepper to taste. Whisk to combine everything.
3. Drizzle over the celery, cheese, and walnuts. Toss to coat.

Nutrition Info:
- Per Servings 3.6g Carbs, 4.3g Protein, 14g Fat, 156 Calories

Traditional Greek Salad

Servings: 4
Cooking Time: 10 Minutes
Ingredients:
- 5 tomatoes, chopped
- 1 large cucumber, chopped
- 1 green bell pepper, chopped
- 1 small red onion, chopped
- 16 kalamata olives, chopped
- 4 tbsp capers
- 1 cup feta cheese, chopped
- 1 tsp oregano, dried
- 4 tbsp olive oil
- Salt to taste

Directions:
1. Place tomatoes, bell pepper, cucumber, onion, feta cheese and olives in a bowl; mix to combine well. Season with salt. Combine capers, olive oil, and oregano, in a small bowl. Drizzle with the dressing to serve.

Nutrition Info:
- Per Servings 8g Carbs, 9.3g Protein, 28g Fat, 323 Calories

Green Salad

Servings: 4
Cooking Time: 30 Minutes
Ingredients:
- 2 cups green beans, chopped
- 2 cups shredded spinach
- ½ cup parmesan cheese
- 3 cups basil leaves
- 3 cloves of garlic
- Salt to taste
- ¼ cup olive oil

Directions:
1. Heat a little olive oil in a skillet over medium heat and add the green beans and season with salt to taste. Sauté for 3 to 5 minutes.
2. Place the green beans in a bowl and add in the spinach.
3. In a food processor, combine half of the parmesan cheese, basil, and garlic. Add in the rest of the oil and season with salt and pepper to taste.
4. Pour into the green beans and toss to coat the ingredients.

Nutrition Info:
- Per Servings 6g Carbs, 5g Protein, 17g Fat, 196 Calories

Pesto Tomato Cucumber Salad

Servings: 8
Cooking Time: 0 Minutes
Ingredients:
- ½ cup Italian salad dressing
- ¼ cup prepared pesto
- 3 large tomatoes, sliced
- 2 medium cucumbers, halved and sliced
- 1 small red onion, sliced
- Salt and pepper to taste
- 3 tablespoons olive oil

Directions:
1. In a bowl, whisk the salad dressing and pesto. Season with salt and pepper to taste.
2. Toss gently to incorporate everything.
3. Refrigerate before serving.

Nutrition Info:
- Per Servings 3.7g Carbs, 1.8g Protein, 12g Fat, 128 Calories

Kale And Brussels Sprouts

Servings: 6
Cooking Time: 0 Minutes
Ingredients:
- 1 small bunch kale, thinly sliced
- ½ pound fresh Brussels sprouts, thinly sliced
- ½ cup pistachios, chopped coarsely
- ½ cup honey mustard salad dressing
- ¼ cup parmesan cheese, shredded
- Salt and pepper to taste

Directions:
1. Place all ingredients in a salad bowl.
2. Toss to coat everything.
3. Serve.

Nutrition Info:
- Per Servings 9g Carbs, 5g Protein, 15g Fat, 198 Calories

Tomato Hamburger Soup

Servings: 8
Cooking Time: 25 Minutes
Ingredients:
- 1-pound ground beef
- 1 can V-8 juice
- 2 packages frozen vegetable mix
- 1 can condensed mushroom soup
- 2 teaspoon dried onion powder
- 5 tablespoons olive oil
- Salt and pepper to taste
- 1 cup water

Directions:
1. Place a pot over medium flame and heat for 2 minutes. Add oil and heat for a minute.
2. Sauté the beef until lightly browned, around 7 minutes. Season with salt, pepper, and onion powder.
3. Add the mushroom soup and water.
4. Give a good stir to combine everything.
5. Cover and bring to a boil, lower fire to a simmer and cook for 10 minutes.
6. Stir in vegetables. Cook until heated through around 5 minutes. Adjust seasoning if needed.
7. Serve and enjoy.

Nutrition Info:

- Per Servings 10g Carbs, 18.1g Protein, 14.8g Fat, 227 Calories

Pumpkin & Meat Peanut Stew

Servings: 6
Cooking Time: 45 Minutes
Ingredients:
- 1 cup pumpkin puree
- 2 pounds chopped pork stew meat
- 1 tbsp peanut butter
- 4 tbsp chopped peanuts
- 1 garlic clove, minced
- ½ cup chopped onion
- ½ cup white wine
- 1 tbsp olive oil
- 1 tsp lemon juice
- ¼ cup granulated sweetener
- ¼ tsp cardamom
- ¼ tsp allspice
- 2 cups water
- 2 cups chicken stock

Directions:
1. Heat the olive oil in a large pot and sauté onion for 3 minutes, until translucent. Add garlic and cook for 30 more seconds. Add the pork and cook until browned, about 5-6 minutes, stirring occasionally. Pour in the wine and cook for one minute.
2. Add in the remaining ingredients, except for the lemon juice and peanuts. Bring the mixture to a boil, and cook for 5 minutes. Reduce the heat to low, cover the pot, and let cook for about 30 minutes. Adjust seasoning and stir in the lemon juice before serving.
3. Ladle into serving bowls and serve topped with peanuts.

Nutrition Info:
- Per Servings 4g Carbs, 27.5g Protein, 33g Fat, 451 Calories

Citrusy Brussels Sprouts Salad

Servings: 6
Cooking Time: 3 Minutes
Ingredients:
- 2 tablespoons olive oil
- ¾ pound Brussels sprouts
- 1 cup walnuts
- Juice from 1 lemon
- ½ cup grated parmesan cheese
- Salt and pepper to taste

Directions:
1. Heat oil in a skillet over medium flame and sauté the Brussels sprouts for 3 minutes until slightly wilted. Removed from heat and allow to cool.
2. In a bowl, toss together the cooled Brussels sprouts and the rest of the ingredients.
3. Toss to coat.

Nutrition Info:

- Per Servings 8g Carbs, 6g Protein, 23g Fat, 259 Calories

Pesto Arugula Salad

Servings: 4
Cooking Time: 10 Minutes
Ingredients:
- ¾ cup red peppers, seeded and chopped
- ¾ cup commercial basil pesto
- 1 small mozzarella cheese ball, diced
- 3 handfuls of arugulas, washed
- Salt and pepper to taste
- 5 tablespoons olive oil

Directions:
1. Mix all ingredients in a salad bowl and toss to coat.
2. Season with salt and pepper to taste.

Nutrition Info:
- Per Servings 2.8g Carbs, 6.7g Protein, 20g Fat, 214 Calories

Strawberry, Mozzarella Salad

Servings: 3
Cooking Time: 10 Minutes
Ingredients:
- 5 ounces organic salad greens of your choice
- 2 medium cucumber, spiralized
- 2 cups strawberries, hulled and chopped
- 8 ounces mini mozzarella cheese balls
- ½ cup balsamic vinegar
- 5 tablespoons olive oil
- Salt to taste

Directions:
1. Toss all ingredients in a salad bowl.
2. Allow chilling in the fridge for at least 10 minutes before serving.

Nutrition Info:
- Per Servings 10g Carbs, 7g Protein, 31g Fat, 351 Calories

Chicken Stock And Green Bean Soup

Servings: 6
Cooking Time:1h 30 Mins
Ingredients:
- 2 tablespoons butter
- 1/2 onion, diced
- 2 ribs celery, diced
- 1 cup green beans
- 6 bacon slices
- What you'll need from the store cupboard:
- 3 cloves garlic, sliced
- 1 quart chicken stock
- 2 1/2 cups water
- 1 bay leaf
- Salt and ground black pepper to taste

Directions:

1. In a large pot over medium-low heat, melt the butter. Add the onions, celery, and sliced garlic, cook for 5-8 minutes, or until onions are soft.
2. Stir in in bacon slices, bay leaf, and green beans. Add chicken stock and water, stirring until well combined, and simmer for 1 hour and 15 minutes, or green beans are soft. Sprinkle with salt and black pepper before serving.

Nutrition Info:
- Per Servings 7g Carbs, 15.1g Protein, 11.3g Fat, 208.6 Calories

Beef Reuben Soup

Servings: 6
Cooking Time: 20 Minutes
Ingredients:
- 1 onion, diced
- 6 cups beef stock
- 1 tsp caraway seeds
- 2 celery stalks, diced
- 2 garlic cloves, minced
- 2 cups heavy cream
- 1 cup sauerkraut
- 1 pound corned beef, chopped
- 3 tbsp butter
- 1 ½ cup swiss cheese
- Salt and black pepper, to taste

Directions:
1. Melt the butter in a large pot. Add onion and celery, and fry for 3 minutes until tender. Add garlic and cook for another minute.
2. Pour the beef stock over and stir in sauerkraut, salt, caraway seeds, and add a pinch of pepper. Bring to a boil. Reduce the heat to low, and add the corned beef. Cook for about 15 minutes, adjust the seasoning. Stir in heavy cream and cheese and cook for 1 minute.

Nutrition Info:
- Per Servings 8g Carbs, 23g Protein, 37g Fat, 450 Calories

Chapter 8. Vegan, Vegetable & Meatless Recipes

Vegetable Burritos

Servings: 4
Cooking Time: 10 Minutes
Ingredients:
- 2 large low carb tortillas
- 2 tsp olive oil
- 1 small onion, sliced
- 1 bell pepper, seeded and sliced
- 1 large ripe avocado, pitted and sliced
- 1 cup lemon cauli couscous
- Salt and black pepper to taste
- ⅓ cup sour cream
- 3 tbsp Mexican salsa

Directions:
1. Heat the olive oil in a skillet and sauté the onion and bell pepper until they start to brown on the edges, about 4 minutes. Turn the heat off and set the skillet aside.
2. Lay the tortillas on a flat surface and top each with halves of the onion and bell pepper mixture, avocado, cauli couscous, season with salt and pepper, sour cream, and Mexican salsa. Fold in the sides of each tortilla, and roll them in and over the filling to be completely enclosed.
3. Wrap with foil, cut in halves, and serve warm.

Nutrition Info:
- Per Servings 5.4g Carbs, 17.9g Protein, 23.2g Fat, 373 Calories

Zucchini Boats

Servings: 4
Cooking Time: 50 Minutes
Ingredients:
- 1 tbsp olive oil
- 12 ounces firm tofu, drained and crumbled
- 2 garlic cloves, pressed
- ½ cup onions, chopped
- 2 cups tomato paste
- ¼ tsp turmeric
- Sea salt and chili pepper, to taste
- 3 zucchinis, cut into halves, scoop out the insides
- 1 tbsp nutritional yeast
- ¼ cup almonds, chopped

Directions:
1. Set a pan over medium-high heat and warm oil; add in onion, garlic, and tofu and cook for 5 minutes.Place in scooped zucchini flesh, all seasonings and 1 cup of tomato paste; cook for 6 more minutes, until the tofu starts to brown.
2. Set oven to 360ºF. Grease a baking dish with a cooking spray. Plate the tofu mixture among the zucchini shells. Arrange the stuffed zucchini shells in the baking dish. Stir in the remaining 1 cup of tomato paste. Bake for about 30 minutes. Sprinkle with almonds and Nutritional yeast and continue baking for 5 to 6 more minutes.

Nutrition Info:
- Per Servings 9.8g Carbs, 7.5g Protein, 10g Fat, 148 Calories

Cauliflower Mash

Servings: 4
Cooking Time: 10 Minutes
Ingredients:
- 1 head of cauliflower
- ¼ tsp, garlic powder
- 1 handful of chives, chopped
- What you'll need from the store cupboard:
- ¼ tsp, salt
- ¼ tsp, ground black pepper

Directions:
1. Bring a pot of water to boil.
2. Chop cauliflower into florets. Place in a pot of boiling water and boil for 5 minutes.
3. Drain well.
4. Place florets in a blender. Add remaining ingredients except for chives and pulse to desired consistency.
5. Transfer to a bowl and toss in chives.
6. Serve and enjoy.

Nutrition Info:
- Per Servings 3.7g Carbs, 1.3g Protein, 0.2g Fat, 18 Calories

Butternut Squash And Cauliflower Stew

Servings: 4
Cooking Time:10 Minutes
Ingredients:
- 3 cloves of garlic, minced
- 1 cup cauliflower florets
- 1 ½ cups butternut squash, cubed
- 2 ½ cups heavy cream
- Pepper and salt to taste
- 3 tbsp coconut oil

Directions:
1. Heat the oil in a pan and saute the garlic until fragrant.
2. Stir in the rest of the ingredients and season with salt and pepper to taste.
3. Close the lid and bring to a boil for 10 minutes.
4. Serve and enjoy.

Nutrition Info:
- Per Servings 10g Carbs, 2g Protein, 38.1g Fat, 385 Calories

Cauliflower & Hazelnut Salad

Servings: 4
Cooking Time: 15 Minutes + Chilling Time
Ingredients:
- 1 head cauliflower, cut into florets
- 1 cup green onions, chopped
- 4 ounces bottled roasted peppers, chopped
- ¼ cup extra-virgin olive oil
- 1 tbsp wine vinegar
- 1 tsp yellow mustard
- Salt and black pepper, to taste
- ½ cup black olives, pitted and chopped
- ½ cup hazelnuts, chopped

Directions:
1. Place the cauliflower florets over low heat and steam for 5 minutes; let cool and set aside. Add roasted peppers and green onions in a salad bowl.
2. Using a mixing dish, combine salt, olive oil, mustard, pepper, and vinegar. Sprinkle the mixture over the veggies. Place in the reserved cauliflower and shake to mix well. Top with hazelnut and black olives and serve.

Nutrition Info:
- Per Servings 6.6g Carbs, 4.2g Protein, 18g Fat, 221 Calories

Chard Swiss Dip

Servings: 6
Cooking Time: 25 Minutes
Ingredients:
- 2 cups Swiss chard
- 1 cup tofu, pressed, drained, crumbled
- ½ cup almond milk
- 2 tsp nutritional yeast
- 2 garlic cloves, minced
- 2 tbsp olive oil
- Salt and pepper to taste
- ½ tsp paprika
- ½ tsp chopped fresh mint leaves

Directions:
1. Set oven to 400ºF. Spray a nonstick cooking spray on a casserole pan. Boil Swiss chard until wilted. Using a blender, puree the remaining ingredients. Season with salt and pepper. Stir in the Swiss chard to get a homogeneous mixture. Bake for 13 minutes. Serve alongside baked vegetables.

Nutrition Info:
- Per Servings 7.9g Carbs, 2.9g Protein, 7.3g Fat, 105 Calories

Vegetable Tempura

Servings: 4
Cooking Time: 17 Minutes
Ingredients:
- ½ cup coconut flour + extra for dredging
- Salt and black pepper to taste
- 3 egg yolks
- 2 red bell peppers, cut into strips
- 1 squash, peeled and cut into strips
- 1 broccoli, cut into florets
- 1 cup Chilled water
- Olive oil for frying
- Lemon wedges to serve
- Sugar-free soy sauce to serve

Directions:
1. In a deep frying pan or wok, heat the olive oil over medium heat. Beat the eggs lightly with ½ cup of coconut flour and water. The mixture should be lumpy. Dredge the

vegetables lightly in some flour, shake off the excess flour, dip it in the batter, and then into the hot oil.

2. Fry in batches for 1 minute each, not more, and remove with a perforated spoon onto a wire rack. Sprinkle with salt and pepper and serve with the lemon wedges and soy sauce.

Nutrition Info:

- Per Servings 0.9g Carbs, 3g Protein, 17g Fat, 218 Calories

Tasty Cauliflower Dip

Servings: 4
Cooking Time: 10 Minutes

Ingredients:

- ¾ pound cauliflower, cut into florets
- ¼ cup olive oil
- Salt and black pepper, to taste
- 1 garlic clove, smashed
- 1 tbsp sesame paste
- 1 tbsp fresh lime juice
- ½ tsp garam masala

Directions:

1. Steam cauliflower until tender for 7 minutes in. Transfer to a blender and pulse until you attain a rice-like consistency.

2. Place in Garam Masala, oil, black paper, fresh lime juice, garlic, salt, and sesame paste. Blend the mixture until well combined. Decorate with some additional olive oil and serve. Otherwise, refrigerate until ready to use.

Nutrition Info:

- Per Servings 4.7g Carbs, 3.7g Protein, 8.2g Fat, 100 Calories

Spaghetti Squash With Eggplant & Parmesan

Servings: 4
Cooking Time: 15 Minutes

Ingredients:

- 1 tbsp butter
- 1 cup cherry tomatoes
- 2 tbsp parsley
- 1 eggplant, cubed
- ¼ cup Parmesan cheese
- 3 tbsp scallions, chopped
- 1 cup snap peas
- 1 tsp lemon zest
- 2 cups cooked spaghetti squash

Directions:

1. Melt the butter in a saucepan and cook eggplant for 5 minutes until tender. Add the tomatoes and peas, and cook for 5 more minutes. Stir in parsley, zest, and scallions, and remove the pan from heat. Stir in spaghetti squash and parmesan.

Nutrition Info:

- Per Servings 6.8g Carbs, 6.9g Protein, 8.2g Fat, 139 Calories

Garlicky Bok Choy

Servings: 4
Cooking Time: 25 Minutes

Ingredients:

- 2 pounds bok choy, chopped
- 2 tbsp almond oil
- 1 tsp garlic, minced
- ½ tsp thyme
- ½ tsp red pepper flakes, crushed
- Salt and black pepper, to the taste

Directions:

1. Add Bok choy in a pot containing salted water and cook for 10 minutes over medium heat. Drain and set aside. Place a sauté pan over medium-high heat and warm the oil.

2. Add in garlic and cook until soft. Stir in the Bok choy, red pepper, black pepper, salt, and thyme and ensure they are heated through. Add more seasonings if needed and serve warm with cauli rice.

Nutrition Info:

- Per Servings 13.4g Carbs, 2.9g Protein, 7g Fat, 118 Calories

Fall Roasted Vegetables

Servings: 4
Cooking Time: 45 Minutes

Ingredients:

- 1 red bell pepper, sliced
- 1 green bell pepper, sliced
- 1 orange bell pepper, sliced
- ½ head broccoli, cut into florets
- 2 zucchinis, sliced
- 2 leeks, chopped
- 4 garlic cloves, halved
- 2 thyme sprigs, chopped
- 1 tsp dried sage, crushed
- 4 tbsp olive oil
- 2 tbsp vinegar
- 4 tbsp tomato puree
- Sea salt and cayenne pepper, to taste

Directions:

1. Set oven to 425 °F. Apply nonstick cooking spray to a rimmed baking sheet. Mix all vegetables with oil, seasonings, and vinegar; shake well. Roast for 40 minutes, flipping once halfway through.

Nutrition Info:

- Per Servings 8.2g Carbs, 2.1g Protein, 14.3g Fat, 165 Calories

Cauliflower Mac And Cheese

Servings: 7
Cooking Time: 45 Minutes
Ingredients:

- 1 cauliflower head, riced
- 1 ½ cups shredded cheese
- 2 tsp paprika
- ¾ tsp rosemary
- 2 tsp turmeric
- 3 eggs
- Olive oil, for frying

Directions:

1. Microwave the cauliflower for 5 minutes. Place it in cheesecloth and squeeze the extra juices out. Place the cauliflower in a bowl. Stir in the rest of the ingredients.
2. Heat the oil in a deep pan until it reaches 360°F. Add the 'mac and cheese' and fry until golden and crispy. Drain on paper towels before serving.

Nutrition Info:

- Per Servings 2g Carbs, 8.6g Protein, 12g Fat, 160 Calories

Bell Pepper Stuffed Avocado

Servings: 8
Cooking Time: 10 Minutes
Ingredients:

- 4 avocados, pitted and halved
- 2 tbsp olive oil
- 3 cups green bell peppers, chopped
- 1 onion, chopped
- 1 tsp garlic puree
- Salt and black pepper, to taste
- 1 tsp deli mustard
- 1 tomato, chopped

Directions:

1. From each half of the avocados, scoop out 2 teaspoons of flesh; set aside.
2. Use a sauté pan to warm oil over medium-high heat. Cook the garlic, onion, and bell peppers until tender. Mix in the reserved avocado. Add in tomato, salt, mustard, and black pepper. Separate the mushroom mixture and mix equally among the avocado halves and serve.

Nutrition Info:

- Per Servings 7.4g Carbs, 2.4g Protein, 23.2g Fat, 255 Calories

Strawberry Mug Cake

Servings: 8
Cooking Time: 3 Mins
Ingredients:

- 2 slices fresh strawberry
- 1 teaspoon chia seeds
- 1 teaspoon poppy seeds
- What you'll need from the store cupboard:
- 1/4 teaspoon baking powder
- 3 leaves fresh mint
- 2 tablespoons cream of coconut

Directions:

1. Add all the ingredients together in a mug, stir until finely combined.
2. Cook in microwave at full power for 3 minutes then allow to cool before you serve.

Nutrition Info:

- Per Servings 4.7g Carbs, 2.4g Protein, 12g Fat, 196 Calories

Mushroom & Jalapeño Stew

Servings: 4
Cooking Time: 50 Minutes
Ingredients:

- 2 tsp olive oil
- 1 cup leeks, chopped
- 1 garlic clove, minced
- ½ cup celery, chopped
- ½ cup carrot, chopped
- 1 green bell pepper, chopped
- 1 jalapeño pepper, chopped
- 2 ½ cups mushrooms, sliced
- 1 ½ cups vegetable stock
- 2 tomatoes, chopped
- 2 thyme sprigs, chopped
- 1 rosemary sprig, chopped
- 2 bay leaves
- ½ tsp salt
- ¼ tsp ground black pepper
- 2 tbsp vinegar

Directions:

1. Set a pot over medium-high heat and warm oil. Add in garlic and leeks and sauté until soft and translucent. Add in the pepper, celery, mushrooms, and carrots.
2. Cook as you stir for 12 minutes; stir in a splash of vegetable stock to ensure there is no sticking. Stir in the rest of the ingredients. Set heat to medium; allow to simmer for 25 to 35 minutes or until cooked through. Divide into individual bowls and serve while warm.

Nutrition Info:

- Per Servings 9g Carbs, 2.7g Protein, 2.7g Fat, 65 Calories

Stir Fried Bok Choy

Servings: 4
Cooking Time: 15 Minutes
Ingredients:

- 4 cloves of garlic, minced
- 1 onion, chopped
- 2 heads bok choy, rinsed and chopped
- 2 tablespoons sesame oil
- 2 tablespoons sesame seeds, toasted
- 3 tablespoons oil
- Salt and pepper to taste

Directions:
1. Heat the oil in a pot for 2 minutes.
2. Sauté the garlic and onions until fragrant, around 3 minutes.
3. Stir in the bok choy, salt, and pepper.
4. Cover pan and cook for 5 minutes.
5. Stir and continue cooking for another 3 minutes.
6. Drizzle with sesame oil and sesame seeds on top before serving.

Nutrition Info:
- Per Servings 5.2g Carbs, 21.5g Protein, 28.4g Fat, 358 Calories

Garlic Lemon Mushrooms

Servings: 4
Cooking Time: 20 Minutes
Ingredients:
- 1/4 cup lemon juice
- 3 tablespoons minced fresh parsley
- 3 garlic cloves, minced
- 1-pound large fresh mushrooms
- 4 tablespoons olive oil
- Pepper to taste

Directions:
1. For the dressing, whisk together the first 5 ingredients. Toss mushrooms with 2 tablespoons dressing.
2. Grill mushrooms, covered, over medium-high heat until tender, 5-7 minutes per side. Toss with remaining dressing before serving.

Nutrition Info:
- Per Servings 6.8g Carbs, 4g Protein, 14g Fat, 160 Calories

Avocado And Tomato Burritos

Servings: 4
Cooking Time: 5 Minutes
Ingredients:
- 2 cups cauli rice
- Water for sprinkling
- 6 zero carb flatbread
- 2 cups sour cream sauce
- 1 ½ cups tomato herb salsa
- 2 avocados, peeled, pitted, sliced

Directions:
1. Pour the cauli rice in a bowl, sprinkle with water, and soften in the microwave for 2 minutes.
2. On flatbread, spread the sour cream all over and distribute the salsa on top. Top with cauli rice and scatter the avocado evenly on top. Fold and tuck the burritos and cut into two.

Nutrition Info:
- Per Servings 6g Carbs, 8g Protein, 25g Fat, 303 Calories

Tofu Sesame Skewers With Warm Kale Salad

Servings: 4
Cooking Time: 2 Hours 40 Minutes
Ingredients:
- 14 oz Firm tofu
- 4 tsp sesame oil
- 1 lemon, juiced
- 5 tbsp sugar-free soy sauce
- 3 tsp garlic powder
- 4 tbsp coconut flour
- ½ cup sesame seeds
- Warm Kale Salad:
- 4 cups chopped kale
- 2 tsp + 2 tsp olive oil
- 1 white onion, thinly sliced
- 3 cloves garlic, minced
- 1 cup sliced white mushrooms
- 1 tsp chopped rosemary
- Salt and black pepper to season
- 1 tbsp balsamic vinegar

Directions:
1. In a bowl, mix sesame oil, lemon juice, soy sauce, garlic powder, and coconut flour. Wrap the tofu in a paper towel, squeeze out as much liquid from it, and cut it into strips. Stick on the skewers, height wise. Place onto a plate, pour the soy sauce mixture over, and turn in the sauce to be adequately coated. Cover the dish with cling film and marinate in the fridge for 2 hours.
2. Heat the griddle pan over high heat. Pour the sesame seeds in a plate and roll the tofu skewers in the seeds for a generous coat. Grill the tofu in the griddle pan to be golden brown on both sides, about 12 minutes in total.
3. Heat 2 tablespoons of olive oil in a skillet over medium heat and sauté onion to begin browning for 10 minutes with continuous stirring. Add the remaining olive oil and mushrooms. Continue cooking for 10 minutes. Add garlic, rosemary, salt, pepper, and balsamic vinegar. Cook for 1 minute.
4. Put the kale in a salad bowl; when the onion mixture is ready, pour it on the kale and toss well. Serve the tofu skewers with the warm kale salad and a peanut butter dipping sauce.

Nutrition Info:
- Per Servings 6.1g Carbs, 5.6g Protein, 12.9g Fat, 263 Calories

Zucchini Garlic Fries

Servings: 6
Cooking Time: 25 Minutes
Ingredients:
- ¼ teaspoon garlic powder
- ½ cup almond flour
- 2 large egg, beaten
- 3 medium zucchinis, sliced into fry sticks

- 3 tablespoons olive oil
- Salt and pepper to taste

Directions:
1. Preheat oven to 400oF.
2. Mix all ingredients in a bowl until the zucchini fries are well coated.
3. Place fries on a cookie sheet and spread evenly.
4. Put in the oven and cook for 15 minutes.
5. Stir fries, continue baking for an additional 10 minutes.

Nutrition Info:
- Per Servings 0.5g Carbs, 2g Protein, 8g Fat, 80 Calories

Classic Tangy Ratatouille

Servings: 6
Cooking Time: 47 Minutes
Ingredients:
- 2 eggplants, chopped
- 3 zucchinis, chopped
- 2 red onions, diced
- 1 can tomatoes
- 2 red bell peppers, cut in chunks
- 1 yellow bell pepper, cut in chunks
- 3 cloves garlic, sliced
- ½ cup basil leaves, chop half
- 4 sprigs thyme
- 1 tbsp balsamic vinegar
- 2 tbsp olive oil
- ½ lemon, zested

Directions:
1. In a casserole pot, heat the olive oil and sauté the eggplants, zucchinis, and bell peppers over medium heat for 5 minutes. Spoon the veggies into a large bowl.
2. In the same pan, sauté garlic, onions, and thyme leaves for 5 minutes and return the cooked veggies to the pan along with the canned tomatoes, balsamic vinegar, chopped basil, salt, and pepper to taste. Stir and cover the pot, and cook the ingredients on low heat for 30 minutes.
3. Open the lid and stir in the remaining basil leaves, lemon zest, and adjust the seasoning. Turn the heat off. Plate the ratatouille and serve with some low carb crusted bread.

Nutrition Info:
- Per Servings 5.6g Carbs, 1.7g Protein, 12.1g Fat, 154 Calories

Cauliflower Fritters

Servings: 6
Cooking Time: 15 Minutes
Ingredients:
- 1 large cauliflower head, cut into florets
- 2 eggs, beaten
- ½ teaspoon turmeric
- 1 large onion, peeled and chopped
- ½ teaspoon salt
- ¼ teaspoon black pepper
- 6 tablespoons oil

Directions:

1. Place the cauliflower florets in a pot with water.
2. Bring to a boil and drain once cooked.
3. Place the cauliflower, eggs, onion, turmeric, salt, and pepper into the food processor.
4. Pulse until the mixture becomes coarse.
5. Transfer into a bowl. Using your hands, form six small flattened balls and place in the fridge for at least 1 hour until the mixture hardens.
6. Heat the oil in a skillet and fry the cauliflower patties for 3 minutes on each side.
7. Serve and enjoy.

Nutrition Info:
- Per Servings 2.28g Carbs, 3.9g Protein, 15.3g Fat, 157 Calories

Curried Tofu

Servings: 6
Cooking Time: 15 Minutes
Ingredients:
- 2 cloves of garlic, minced
- 1 onion, cubed
- 12-ounce firm tofu, drained and cubed
- 1 teaspoon curry powder
- 1 tablespoon soy sauce
- ¼ teaspoon pepper
- 5 tablespoons olive oil

Directions:
1. Heat the oil in a skillet over medium flame.
2. Sauté the garlic and onion until fragrant.
3. Stir in the tofu and stir for 3 minutes.
4. Add the rest of the ingredients and adjust the water.
5. Close the lid and allow simmering for 10 minutes.
6. Serve and enjoy.

Nutrition Info:
- Per Servings 4.4g Carbs, 6.2g Protein, 14.1g Fat, 148 Calories

Greek-style Zucchini Pasta

Servings: 4
Cooking Time: 15 Minutes
Ingredients:
- ¼ cup sun-dried tomatoes
- 5 garlic cloves, minced
- 2 tbsp butter
- 1 cup spinach
- 2 large zucchinis, spiralized
- ¼ cup crumbled feta
- ¼ cup Parmesan cheese, shredded
- 10 kalamata olives, halved
- 2 tbsp olive oil
- 2 tbsp chopped parsley

Directions:
1. Heat the olive oil in a pan over medium heat. Add zoodles, butter, garlic, and spinach. Cook for about 5 minutes. Stir in the olives, tomatoes, and parsley. Cook for 2 more minutes. Add in the cheeses and serve.

Nutrition Info:
- Per Servings 6.5g Carbs, 6.5g Protein, 19.5g Fat, 231 Calories

Spicy Cauliflower Steaks With Steamed Green Beans

Servings: 4
Cooking Time: 20 Minutes
Ingredients:
- 2 heads cauliflower, sliced lengthwise into 'steaks'
- ¼ cup olive oil
- ¼ cup chili sauce
- 2 tsp erythritol
- Salt and black pepper to taste
- 2 shallots, diced
- 1 bunch green beans, trimmed
- 2 tbsp fresh lemon juice
- 1 cup water
- Dried parsley to garnish

Directions:
1. In a bowl, mix the olive oil, chili sauce, and erythritol. Brush the cauliflower with the mixture. Place them on the grill, close the lid, and grill for 6 minutes. Flip the cauliflower, cook further for 6 minutes.
2. Bring the water to boil over high heat, place the green beans in a sieve and set over the steam from the boiling water. Cover with a clean napkin to keep the steam trapped in the sieve. Cook for 6 minutes. After, remove to a bowl and toss with lemon juice.
3. Remove the grilled caulis to a plate; sprinkle with salt, pepper, shallots, and parsley. Serve with the steamed green beans.

Nutrition Info:
- Per Servings 4g Carbs, 2g Protein, 9g Fat, 118 Calories

Sautéed Celeriac With Tomato Sauce

Servings: 4
Cooking Time: 20 Minutes
Ingredients:
- 2 tbsp olive oil
- 1 garlic clove, crushed
- 1 celeriac, sliced
- ¼ cup vegetable stock
- Sea salt and black pepper, to taste
- For the Sauce
- 2 tomatoes, halved
- 2 tbsp olive oil
- ½ cup onions, chopped
- 2 cloves garlic, minced
- 1 chili, minced
- 1 bunch fresh basil, chopped
- 1 tbsp fresh cilantro, chopped
- Salt and black pepper, to taste

Directions:
1. Set a pan over medium-high heat and warm olive oil. Add in garlic and sauté for 1 minute. Stir in celeriac slices, stock and cook until softened. Sprinkle with black pepper and salt; kill the heat. Brush olive oil to the tomato halves. Microwave for 15 minutes; get rid of any excess liquid.
2. Remove the cooked tomatoes to a food processor; add the rest of the ingredients for the sauce and puree to obtain the desired consistency. Serve the celeriac topped with tomato sauce.

Nutrition Info:
- Per Servings 3g Carbs, 0.9g Protein, 13.6g Fat, 135 Calories

Zesty Frittata With Roasted Chilies

Servings: 4
Cooking Time: 17 Minutes
Ingredients:
- 2 large green bell peppers, seeded, chopped
- 4 red and yellow chilies, roasted
- 2 tbsp red wine vinegar
- 1 knob butter, melted
- 8 sprigs parsley, chopped
- 8 eggs, cracked into a bowl
- 4 tbsp olive oil
- ½ cup grated Parmesan
- ¼ cup crumbled goat cheese
- 4 cloves garlic, minced
- 1 cup loosely filled salad leaves

Directions:
1. Preheat the oven to 400°F. With a knife, seed the chilies, cut into long strips, and pour into a bowl.
2. Mix in the vinegar, butter, half of the parsley, half of the olive oil, and garlic; set aside. In another bowl, whisk the eggs with salt, pepper, bell peppers, parmesan, and the remaining parsley.
3. Now, heat the remaining oil in the cast iron over medium heat and pour the egg mixture along with half of the goat cheese. Let cook for 3 minutes and when it is near done, sprinkle the remaining goat cheese on it, and transfer the cast iron to the oven.
4. Bake the frittata for 4 more minutes, remove and drizzle with the chili oil. Garnish the frittata with salad greens and serve for lunch.

Nutrition Info:
- Per Servings 2.3g Carbs, 6.4g Protein, 10.3g Fat, 153 Calories

Colorful Vegan Soup

Servings: 6
Cooking Time: 25 Minutes
Ingredients:
- 2 tsp olive oil
- 1 red onion, chopped
- 2 cloves garlic, minced
- 1 celery stalk, chopped
- 1 head broccoli, chopped

- 1 carrot, sliced
- 1 cup spinach, torn into pieces
- 1 cup collard greens, chopped
- Sea salt and black pepper, to taste
- 2 thyme sprigs, chopped
- 1 rosemary sprig, chopped
- 2 bay leaves
- 6 cups vegetable stock
- 2 tomatoes, chopped
- 1 cup almond milk
- 1 tbsp white miso paste
- ½ cup arugula

Directions:

1. Place a large pot over medium-high heat and warm oil. Add in carrots, celery, onion, broccoli, garlic, and sauté until soft.

2. Place in spinach, salt, rosemary, tomatoes, bay leaves, ground black pepper, collard greens, thyme, and vegetable stock. On low heat, simmer the mixture for 15 minutes while the lid is slightly open.

3. Stir in white miso paste, watercress, and almond milk and cook for 5 more minutes.

Nutrition Info:

- Per Servings 9g Carbs, 2.9g Protein, 11.4g Fat, 142 Calories

Cilantro-lime Guacamole

Servings: 4
Cooking Time: 10 Minutes
Ingredients:

- 3 avocados, peeled, pitted, and mashed
- 1 lime, juiced
- 1/2 cup diced onion
- 3 tablespoons chopped fresh cilantro
- 2 Roma (plum) tomatoes, diced
- 1 teaspoon salt
- 1 teaspoon minced garlic
- 1 pinch ground cayenne pepper (optional)
- 1 teaspoon minced garlic

Directions:

1. In a mixing bowl, mash the avocados with a fork. Sprinkle with salt and lime juice.

2. Stir together diced onion, tomatoes, cilantro, pepper and garlic.

3. Serve immediately, or refrigerate until ready to serve.

Nutrition Info:

- Per Servings 8g Carbs, 19g Protein, 22.2g Fat, 362 Calories

Roasted Brussels Sprouts With Sunflower Seeds

Servings: 6
Cooking Time: 45 Minutes
Ingredients:

- Nonstick cooking spray

- 3 pounds brussels sprouts, halved
- ¼ cup olive oil
- Salt and ground black pepper, to taste
- 1 tsp sunflower seeds
- 2 tbsp fresh chives, chopped

Directions:

1. Set oven to 390ºF. Apply a nonstick cooking spray to a rimmed baking sheet. Arrange sprout halves on the baking sheet. Shake in black pepper, salt, sunflower seeds, and olive oil.

2. Roast for 40 minutes, until the cabbage becomes soft. Apply a garnish of fresh chopped chives.

Nutrition Info:

- Per Servings 8g Carbs, 2.1g Protein, 17g Fat, 186 Calories

Stuffed Portobello Mushrooms

Servings: 2
Cooking Time: 30 Minutes
Ingredients:

- 4 portobello mushrooms, stems removed
- 2 tbsp olive oil
- 2 cups lettuce
- 1 cup crumbled blue cheese

Directions:

1. Preheat the oven to 350ºF. Fill the mushrooms with blue cheese and place on a lined baking sheet; bake for 20 minutes. Serve with lettuce drizzled with olive oil.

Nutrition Info:

- Per Servings 5.5g Carbs, 14g Protein, 29g Fat, 334 Calories

Scrambled Eggs With Mushrooms And Spinach

Servings: 2
Cooking Time: 15 Minutes
Ingredients:

- 2 large eggs
- 1 teaspoon butter
- 1/2 cup thinly sliced fresh mushrooms
- 1/2 cup fresh baby spinach, chopped
- 2 tablespoons shredded provolone cheese
- 1/8 teaspoon salt
- 1/8 teaspoon pepper

Directions:

1. In a small bowl, whisk eggs, salt, and pepper until blended. In a small nonstick skillet, heat butter over medium-high heat. Add mushrooms; cook and stir 3-4 minutes or until tender. Add spinach; cook and stir until wilted. Reduce heat to medium.

2. Add egg mixture; cook and stir just until eggs are thickened and no liquid egg remains. Stir in cheese.

Nutrition Info:

- Per Servings 2g Carbs, 14g Protein, 11g Fat, 162 Calories

Creamy Vegetable Stew

Servings: 4
Cooking Time: 32 Minutes
Ingredients:

- 2 tbsp ghee
- 1 tbsp onion garlic puree
- 4 medium carrots, peeled and chopped
- 1 large head cauliflower, cut into florets
- 2 cups green beans, halved
- Salt and black pepper to taste
- 1 cup water
- 1 ½ cups heavy cream

Directions:

1. Melt ghee in a saucepan over medium heat and sauté onion-garlic puree to be fragrant, 2 minutes.
2. Stir in carrots, cauliflower, and green beans, salt, and pepper, add the water, stir again, and cook the vegetables on low heat for 25 minutes to soften. Mix in the heavy cream to be incorporated, turn the heat off, and adjust the taste with salt and pepper. Serve the stew with almond flour bread.

Nutrition Info:

- Per Servings 6g Carbs, 8g Protein, 26.4g Fat, 310 Calories

Herb Butter With Parsley

Servings: 1
Cooking Time: 0 Minutes
Ingredients:

- 5 oz. butter, at room temperature
- 1 garlic clove, pressed
- ½ tbsp garlic powder
- 4 tbsp fresh parsley, finely chopped
- 1 tsp lemon juice
- ½ tsp salt

Directions:

1. In a bowl, stir all ingredients until completely combined. Set aside for 15 minutes or refrigerate it before serving.

Nutrition Info:

- Per Servings 1g Carbs, 1g Protein, 28g Fat, 258 Calories

Fried Tofu With Mushrooms

Servings: 2
Cooking Time: 40 Minutes
Ingredients:

- 12 ounces extra firm tofu, pressed and cubed
- 1 ½ tbsp flax seed meal
- Salt and black pepper, to taste
- 1 tsp garlic clove, minced
- ½ tsp paprika
- 1 tsp onion powder
- ½ tsp ground bay leaf
- 1 tbsp olive oil
- 1 cup mushrooms, sliced
- 1 jalapeño pepper, deveined, sliced

Directions:

1. In a container, add onion powder, tofu, salt, paprika, black pepper, flaxseed, garlic paste, and bay leaf. While the container is closed, toss the mixture to coat, and allow to marinate for 30 minutes.
2. In a pan, warm oil over medium heat. Cook mushrooms and tofu for 6 minutes, stirring continuously.

Nutrition Info:

- Per Servings 8.1g Carbs, 15.6g Protein, 15.9g Fat, 223 Calories

Guacamole

Servings: 2
Cooking Time: 0 Minutes
Ingredients:

- 2 medium ripe avocados
- 1 tablespoon lemon juice
- 1/4 cup chopped tomatoes
- 4 tablespoons olive oil
- 1/4 teaspoon salt
- Pepper to taste

Directions:

1. Peel and chop avocados; place them in a small bowl. Sprinkle with lemon juice.
2. Add tomatoes and salt.
3. Season with pepper to taste and mash coarsely with a fork. Refrigerate until serving.

Nutrition Info:

- Per Servings 10g Carbs, 6g Protein, 56g Fat, 565 Calories

Walnut Tofu Sauté

Servings: 4
Cooking Time: 15 Minutes
Ingredients:

- 1 tbsp olive oil
- 1 block firm tofu, cubed
- 1 tbsp tomato paste with garlic and onion
- 1 tbsp balsamic vinegar
- Pink salt and black pepper to taste
- ½ tsp mixed dried herbs
- 1 cup chopped raw walnuts

Directions:

1. Heat the oil in a skillet over medium heat and cook the tofu for 3 minutes while stirring to brown.
2. Mix the tomato paste with the vinegar and add to the tofu. Stir, season with salt and black pepper, and cook for another 4 minutes.
3. Add the herbs and walnuts. Stir and cook on low heat for 3 minutes to be fragrant. Spoon to a side of squash mash and a sweet berry sauce to serve.

Nutrition Info:

- Per Servings 4g Carbs, 18g Protein, 24g Fat, 320 Calories

Greek Styled Veggie-rice

Servings: 3
Cooking Time: 20 Minutes
Ingredients:

- 3 tbsp chopped fresh mint
- 1 small tomato, chopped
- 1 head cauliflower, cut into large florets
- ¼ cup fresh lemon juice
- ½ yellow onion, minced
- pepper and salt to taste
- ¼ cup extra virgin olive oil

Directions:

1. In a bowl, mix lemon juice and onion and leave for 30 minutes. Then drain onion and reserve the juice and onion bits.
2. In a blender, shred cauliflower until the size of a grain of rice.
3. On medium fire, place a medium nonstick skillet and for 8-10 minutes cook cauliflower while covered.
4. Add grape tomatoes and cook for 3 minutes while stirring occasionally.
5. Add mint and onion bits. Cook for another three minutes.
6. Meanwhile, in a small bowl whisk pepper, salt, 3 tbsp reserved lemon juice, and olive oil until well blended.
7. Remove cooked cauliflower, transfer to a serving bowl, pour lemon juice mixture, and toss to mix.
8. Before serving, if needed season with pepper and salt to taste.

Nutrition Info:

- Per Servings 4.0g Carbs, 2.3g Protein, 9.5g Fat, 120 Calories

Spiced Cauliflower & Peppers

Servings: 4
Cooking Time: 35 Minutes
Ingredients:

- 1 pound cauliflower, cut into florets
- 2 bell peppers, halved
- ¼ cup olive oil
- Sea salt and black pepper, to taste
- ½ tsp cayenne pepper
- 1 tsp curry powder

Directions:

1. Set oven to 425 °F. Line a parchment paper to a large baking sheet. Sprinkle olive oil to the peppers and cauliflower alongside curry powder, black pepper, salt, and cayenne pepper.
2. Set the vegetables on the baking sheet. Roast for 30 minutes as you toss in intervals until they start to brown. Serve alongside mushroom pate or homemade tomato dip!

Nutrition Info:

- Per Servings 7.4g Carbs, 3g Protein, 13.9g Fat, 166 Calories

Cremini Mushroom Stroganoff

Servings: 4

Cooking Time: 15 Minutes
Ingredients:

- 3 tbsp butter
- 1 white onion, chopped
- 4 cups cremini mushrooms, cubed
- 2 cups water
- ½ cup heavy cream
- ½ cup grated Parmesan cheese
- 1 ½ tbsp dried mixed herbs
- Salt and black pepper to taste

Directions:

1. Melt the butter in a saucepan over medium heat, sauté the onion for 3 minutes until soft.
2. Stir in the mushrooms and cook until tender, about 3 minutes. Add the water, mix, and bring to boil for 4 minutes until the water reduces slightly.
3. Pour in the heavy cream and parmesan cheese. Stir to melt the cheese. Also, mix in the dried herbs. Season with salt and pepper, simmer for 40 seconds and turn the heat off.
4. Ladle stroganoff over a bed of spaghetti squash and serve.

Nutrition Info:

- Per Servings 1g Carbs, 5g Protein, 28g Fat, 284 Calories

Vegan Mushroom Pizza

Servings: 4
Cooking Time: 35 Minutes
Ingredients:

- 2 tsp ghee
- 1 cup chopped button mushrooms
- ½ cup sliced mixed colored bell peppers
- Pink salt and black pepper to taste
- 1 almond flour pizza bread
- 1 cup tomato sauce
- 1 tsp vegan Parmesan cheese
- Vegan Parmesan cheese for garnish

Directions:

1. Melt ghee in a skillet over medium heat, sauté the mushrooms and bell peppers for 10 minutes to soften. Season with salt and black pepper. Turn the heat off.
2. Put the pizza bread on a pizza pan, spread the tomato sauce all over the top and scatter vegetables evenly on top. Season with a little more salt and sprinkle with parmesan cheese.
3. Bake for 20 minutes until the vegetables are soft and the cheese has melted and is bubbly. Garnish with extra parmesan cheese. Slice pizza and serve with chilled berry juice.

Nutrition Info:

- Per Servings 8g Carbs, 15g Protein, 20g Fat, 295 Calories

Vegetarian Burgers

Servings: 2
Cooking Time: 20 Minutes
Ingredients:
- 1 garlic cloves, minced
- 2 portobello mushrooms, sliced
- 1 tbsp coconut oil, melted
- 1 tbsp chopped basil
- 1 tbsp oregano
- 2 eggs, fried
- 2 low carb buns
- 2 tbsp mayonnaise
- 2 lettuce leaves

Directions:
1. Combine the melted coconut oil, garlic, herbs, and salt, in a bowl. Place the mushrooms in the bowl and coat well. Preheat the grill to medium heat. Grill the mushrooms for 2 minutes per side.
2. Cut the low carb buns in half. Add the lettuce leaves, grilled mushrooms, eggs, and mayonnaise. Top with the other bun half.

Nutrition Info:
- Per Servings 8.5g Carbs, 23g Protein, 55g Fat, 637 Calories

Kale Cheese Waffles

Servings: 4
Cooking Time: 45 Minutes
Ingredients:
- 2 green onions
- 1 tbsp olive oil
- 2 eggs
- ⅓ cup Parmesan cheese
- 1 cup kale, chopped
- 1 cup mozzarella cheese
- ½ cauliflower head
- 1 tsp garlic powder
- 1 tbsp sesame seeds
- 2 tsp chopped thyme

Directions:
1. Place the chopped cauliflower in the food processor and process until rice is formed. Add kale, spring onions, and thyme to the food processor. Pulse until smooth. Transfer to a bowl. Stir in the rest of the ingredients and mix to combine.
2. Heat waffle iron and spread in the mixture, evenly. Cook following the manufacturer's instructions.

Nutrition Info:
- Per Servings 3.6g Carbs, 16g Protein, 20.2g Fat, 283 Calories

Wild Mushroom And Asparagus Stew

Servings: 4
Cooking Time: 25 Minutes
Ingredients:
- 2 tbsp olive oil

- 1 cup onions, chopped
- 2 garlic cloves, pressed
- ½ cup celery, chopped
- 2 carrots, chopped
- 1 cup wild mushrooms, sliced
- 2 tbsp dry white wine
- 2 rosemary sprigs, chopped
- 1 thyme sprig, chopped
- 4 cups vegetable stock
- ½ tsp chili pepper
- 1 tsp smoked paprika
- 2 tomatoes, chopped
- 1 tbsp flax seed meal

Directions:
1. Set a stockpot over medium heat and warm oil. Add in onions and cook until tender.
2. Place in carrots, celery, and garlic and cook until soft for 4 more minutes. Add in mushrooms; cook the mixture the liquid is lost; set the vegetables aside. Stir in wine to deglaze the stockpot's bottom. Place in thyme and rosemary. Pour in tomatoes, vegetable stock, paprika, and chili pepper; add in reserved vegetables and allow to boil.
3. On low heat, allow the mixture to simmer for 15 minutes while covered. Stir in flax seed meal to thicken the stew. Plate into individual bowls and serve.

Nutrition Info:
- Per Servings 9.5g Carbs, 2.1g Protein, 7.3g Fat, 114 Calories

Morning Granola

Servings: 8
Cooking Time: 1 Hour
Ingredients:
- 1 tbsp coconut oil
- ⅓ cup almond flakes
- ½ cups almond milk
- 2 tbsp sugar
- 1/8 tsp salt
- 1 tsp lime zest
- 1/8 tsp nutmeg, grated
- ½ tsp ground cinnamon
- ½ cup pecans, chopped
- ½ cup almonds, slivered
- 2 tbsp pepitas
- 3 tbsp sunflower seeds
- ¼ cup flax seed

Directions:
1. Set a deep pan over medium-high heat and warm the coconut oil. Add almond flakes and toast for 1 to 2 minutes. Stir in the remaining ingredients. Set oven to 300ºF. Lay the mixture in an even layer onto a baking sheet lined with a parchment paper. Bake for 1 hour, making sure that you shake gently in intervals of 15 minutes. Serve alongside additional almond milk.

Nutrition Info:

- Per Servings 9.2g Carbs, 5.1g Protein, 24.3g Fat, 262 Calories

Grated Cauliflower With Seasoned Mayo

Servings: 2
Cooking Time: 15 Mins
Ingredients:
- 1 lb grated cauliflower
- 3 oz. butter
- 4 eggs
- 3 oz. pimientos de padron or poblano peppers
- ½ cup mayonnaise
- 1 tsp olive oil
- Salt and pepper
- 1 tsp garlic powder (optional)

Directions:
1. In a bowl, whisk together the mayonnaise and garlic and set aside.
2. Rinse, trim and grate the cauliflower using a food processor or grater.
3. Melt a generous amount of butter and fry grated cauliflower for about 5 minutes. Season salt and pepper to taste.
4. Fry poblanos with oil until lightly crispy. Then fry eggs as you want and sprinkle salt and pepper over them.
5. Serve with poblanos and cauliflower. Drizzle some mayo mixture on top.

Nutrition Info:
- Per Servings 9g Carbs, 17g Protein, 87g Fat, 898 Calories

Creamy Kale And Mushrooms

Servings: 3
Cooking Time: 15 Minutes
Ingredients:
- 3 cloves of garlic, minced
- 1 onion, chopped
- 1 bunch kale, stems removed and leaves chopped
- 3 white button mushrooms, chopped
- 1 cup heavy cream
- 5 tablespoons oil
- Salt and pepper to taste

Directions:
1. Heat oil in a pot.
2. Sauté the garlic and onion until fragrant for 2 minutes.
3. Stir in mushrooms. Season with pepper and salt. Cook for 8 minutes.
4. Stir in kale and coconut milk. Simmer for 5 minutes.
5. Adjust seasoning to taste.

Nutrition Info:
- Per Servings 7.9g Carbs, 6.0g Protein, 35.5g Fat, 365 Calories

Parmesan Roasted Cabbage

Servings: 4

Cooking Time: 25 Minutes
Ingredients:
- Cooking spray
- 1 large head green cabbage
- 4 tbsp melted butter
- 1 tsp garlic powder
- Salt and black pepper to taste
- 1 cup grated Parmesan cheese
- Grated Parmesan cheese for topping
- 1 tbsp chopped parsley to garnish

Directions:
1. Preheat oven to 400ºF, line a baking sheet with foil, and grease with cooking spray.
2. Stand the cabbage and run a knife from the top to bottom to cut the cabbage into wedges. Remove stems and wilted leaves. Mix the butter, garlic, salt, and black pepper until evenly combined.
3. Brush the mixture on all sides of the cabbage wedges and sprinkle with parmesan cheese.
4. Place on the baking sheet, and bake for 20 minutes to soften the cabbage and melt the cheese. Remove the cabbages when golden brown, plate and sprinkle with extra cheese and parsley. Serve warm with pan-glazed tofu.

Nutrition Info:
- Per Servings 4g Carbs, 17.5g Protein, 19.3g Fat, 268 Calories

Pumpkin Bake

Servings: 6
Cooking Time: 45 Minutes
Ingredients:
- 3 large Pumpkins, peeled and sliced
- 1 cup almond flour
- 1 cup grated mozzarella cheese
- 2 tbsp olive oil
- ½ cup chopped parsley

Directions:
1. Preheat the oven to 350ºF. Arrange the pumpkin slices in a baking dish, drizzle with olive oil, and bake for 35 minutes. Mix the almond flour, cheese, and parsley and when the pumpkin is ready, remove it from the oven, and sprinkle the cheese mixture all over. Place back in the oven and grill the top for 5 minutes.

Nutrition Info:
- Per Servings 5.7g Carbs, 2.7g Protein, 4.8g Fat, 125 Calories

Creamy Cucumber Avocado Soup

Servings: 4
Cooking Time: 15 Minutes
Ingredients:
- 4 large cucumbers, seeded, chopped
- 1 large avocado, peeled and pitted
- Salt and black pepper to taste
- 2 cups water
- 1 tbsp cilantro, chopped

- 3 tbsp olive oil
- 2 limes, juiced
- 2 tsp minced garlic
- 2 tomatoes, evenly chopped
- 1 chopped avocado for garnish

Directions:

1. Pour the cucumbers, avocado halves, salt, pepper, olive oil, lime juice, cilantro, water, and garlic in the food processor. Puree the ingredients for 2 minutes or until smooth.

2. Pour the mixture in a bowl and top with avocado and tomatoes. Serve chilled with zero-carb bread.

Nutrition Info:

- Per Servings 4.1g Carbs, 3.7g Protein, 7.4g Fat, 170 Calories

Vegan Cheesy Chips With Tomatoes

Servings: 6
Cooking Time: 15 Minutes
Ingredients:

- 5 tomatoes, sliced
- ¼ cup olive oil
- 1 tbsp seasoning mix
- For Vegan cheese
- ½ cup pepitas seeds
- 1 tbsp nutritional yeast
- Salt and black pepper, to taste
- 1 tsp garlic puree

Directions:

1. Over the sliced tomatoes, drizzle olive oil. Set oven to 200°F.

2. In a food processor, add all vegan cheese ingredients and pulse until the desired consistency is attained. Combine vegan cheese and seasoning mixture. Toss in seasoned tomato slices to coat.

3. Set the tomato slices on the prepared baking pan and bake for 10 minutes.

Nutrition Info:

- Per Servings 7.2g Carbs, 4.6g Protein, 14g Fat, 161 Calories

Morning Coconut Smoothie

Servings: 4
Cooking Time: 5 Minutes
Ingredients:

- ½ cup water
- 1 ½ cups coconut milk
- 1 cup frozen cherries
- 4 cup fresh blueberries
- ¼ tsp vanilla extract
- 1 tbsp vegan protein powder

Directions:

1. Using a blender, combine all the ingredients and blend well until you attain a uniform and creamy consistency. Divide in glasses and serve!

Nutrition Info:

- Per Servings 14.9g Carbs, 2.6g Protein, 21.7g Fat, 247 Calories

Spicy Tofu With Worcestershire Sauce

Servings: 4
Cooking Time: 25 Minutes
Ingredients:

- 2 tbsp olive oil
- 14 ounces block tofu, pressed and cubed
- 1 celery stalk, chopped
- 1 bunch scallions, chopped
- 1 tsp cayenne pepper
- 1 tsp garlic powder
- 2 tbsp Worcestershire sauce
- Salt and black pepper, to taste
- 1 pound green cabbage, shredded
- ½ tsp turmeric powder
- ¼ tsp dried basil

Directions:

1. Set a large skillet over medium-high heat and warm 1 tablespoon of olive oil. Stir in tofu cubes and cook for 8 minutes. Place in scallions and celery; cook for 5 minutes until soft

2. Stir in cayenne, Worcestershire sauce, pepper, salt, and garlic; cook for 3 more minutes; set aside.

3. In the same pan, warm the remaining 1 tablespoon of oil. Add in shredded cabbage and the remaining seasonings and cook for 4 minutes. Mix in tofu mixture and serve while warm.

Nutrition Info:

- Per Servings 8.3g Carbs, 8.1g Protein, 10.3g Fat, 182 Calories

Cream Of Zucchini And Avocado

Servings: 4
Cooking Time: 35 Minutes
Ingredients:

- 3 tsp vegetable oil
- 1 onion, chopped
- 1 carrot, sliced
- 1 turnip, sliced
- 3 cups zucchinis, chopped
- 1 avocado, peeled and diced
- ¼ tsp ground black pepper
- 4 vegetable broth
- 1 tomato, pureed

Directions:

1. In a pot, warm the oil and sauté onion until translucent, about 3 minutes. Add in turnip, zucchini, and carrot and cook for 7 minutes; add black pepper for seasoning.

2. Mix in pureed tomato, and broth; and boil. Change heat to low and allow the mixture to simmer for 20 minutes. Lift from the heat. In batches, add the soup and avocado to a blender. Blend until creamy and smooth.

Nutrition Info:

- Per Servings 11g Carbs, 2.2g Protein, 13.4g Fat, 165 Calories

Garlic And Greens

Servings: 4
Cooking Time: 20 Minutes
Ingredients:
- 1-pound kale, trimmed and torn
- 1/4 cup chopped oil-packed sun-dried tomatoes
- 5 garlic cloves, minced
- 2 tablespoons minced fresh parsley
- 1/4 teaspoon salt
- 3 tablespoons olive oil

Directions:
1. In a 6-qt. stockpot, bring 1 inch. of water to a boil. Add kale; cook, covered, 10-15 minutes or until tender. Remove with a slotted spoon; discard cooking liquid.
2. In the same pot, heat oil over medium heat. Add tomatoes and garlic; cook and stir 1 minute. Add kale, parsley and salt; heat through, stirring occasionally.

Nutrition Info:
- Per Servings 9g Carbs, 6g Protein, 13g Fat, 160 Calories

Cheesy Cauliflower Falafel

Servings: 4
Cooking Time: 15 Minutes
Ingredients:
- 1 head cauliflower, cut into florets
- ⅓ cup silvered ground almonds
- ½ tsp mixed spice
- Salt and chili pepper to taste
- 3 tbsp coconut flour
- 3 fresh eggs
- 4 tbsp ghee

Directions:
1. Blend the cauli florets in a food processor until a grain meal consistency is formed. Pour the puree in a bowl, add the ground almonds, mixed spice, salt, chili pepper, and coconut flour, and mix until evenly combined.
2. Beat the eggs in a bowl until creamy in color and mix with the cauli mixture. Shape ¼ cup each into patties and set aside.
3. Melt ghee in a frying pan over medium heat and fry the patties for 5 minutes on each side to be firm and browned. Remove onto a wire rack to cool, share into serving plates, and top with tahini sauce.

Nutrition Info:
- Per Servings 2g Carbs, 8g Protein, 26g Fat, 315 Calories

Bianca Pizza

Servings: 1
Cooking Time: 17 Minutes
Ingredients:
- 2 large eggs
- 1 tbsp water
- ½ jalapeño, diced
- 1 ounce Monterey Jack cheese, shredded
- 1 tbsp chopped green onions
- 1 cup egg Alfredo sauce
- ¼ tsp cumin
- 2 tbsp olive oil

Directions:
1. Preheat the oven to 350ºF.
2. Heat the olive oil in a skillet. Whisk the eggs along with water and cumin. Pour the eggs into the skillet. Cook until set. Top with the alfredo sauce and jalapeno. Sprinkle the green onions and cheese over. Place in the oven and bake for 5 minutes.

Nutrition Info:
- Per Servings 2g Carbs, 22g Protein, 55g Fat, 591 Calories

Briam With Tomato Sauce

Servings: 4
Cooking Time: 70 Minutes
Ingredients:
- 3 tbsp olive oil
- 1 large eggplant, halved and sliced
- 1 large onion, thinly sliced
- 3 cloves garlic, sliced
- 5 tomatoes, diced
- 3 rutabagas, peeled and diced
- 1 cup sugar-free tomato sauce
- 4 zucchinis, sliced
- ¼ cup water
- Salt and black pepper to taste
- 1 tbsp dried oregano
- 2 tbsp chopped parsley

Directions:
1. Preheat the oven to 400ºF. Heat the olive oil in a skillet over medium heat and cook the eggplants in it for 6 minutes to brown on the edges. After, remove to a medium bowl.
2. Sauté the onion and garlic in the oil for 3 minutes and add them to the eggplants. Turn the heat off.
3. In the eggplants bowl, mix in the tomatoes, rutabagas, tomato sauce, and zucchinis. Add the water and stir in the salt, pepper, oregano, and parsley. Pour the mixture in the casserole dish. Place the dish in the oven and bake for 45 to 60 minutes. Serve the briam warm on a bed of cauli rice.

Nutrition Info:
- Per Servings 12.5g Carbs, 11.3g Protein, 12g Fat, 365 Calories

Coconut Cauliflower Rice

Servings: 3
Cooking Time: 15 Minutes
Ingredients:
- 1 head cauliflower, grated
- ½ cup heavy cream
- ¼ cup butter, melted
- 3 cloves of garlic, minced
- 1 onion, chopped
- Salt and pepper to taste

Directions:
1. Place a nonstick saucepan on high fire and heat cream and butter.
2. Saute onion and garlic for 3 minutes.
3. Stir in grated cauliflower. Season with pepper and salt.
4. Cook until cauliflower is tender, around 5 minutes.
5. Turn off fire and let it set for 5 minutes.
6. Serve and enjoy.

Nutrition Info:
- Per Servings 9g Carbs, 3g Protein, 23g Fat, 246 Calories

Vegetable Tempeh Kabobs

Servings: 4
Cooking Time: 2 Hours 26 Minutes
Ingredients:
- 10 oz tempeh, cut into chunks
- 1 ½ cups water
- 1 red onion, cut into chunks
- 1 red bell pepper, cut chunks
- 1 yellow bell pepper, cut into chunks
- 2 tbsp olive oil
- 1 cup sugar-free barbecue sauce

Directions:
1. Bring the water to boil in a pot over medium heat and once it has boiled, turn the heat off, and add the tempeh. Cover the pot and let the tempeh steam for 5 minutes to remove its bitterness.
2. Drain the tempeh after. Pour the barbecue sauce in a bowl, add the tempeh to it, and coat with the sauce. Cover the bowl and marinate in the fridge for 2 hours.
3. Preheat a grill to 350ºF, and thread the tempeh, yellow bell pepper, red bell pepper, and onion.
4. Brush the grate of the grill with olive oil, place the skewers on it, and brush with barbecue sauce. Cook the kabobs for 3 minutes on each side while rotating and brushing with more barbecue sauce.
5. Once ready, transfer the kabobs to a plate and serve with lemon cauli couscous and a tomato sauce.

Nutrition Info:
- Per Servings 3.6g Carbs, 13.2g Protein, 15g Fat, 228 Calories

Zucchini Lasagna With Ricotta And Spinach

Servings: 4
Cooking Time: 50 Minutes
Ingredients:
- Cooking spray
- 2 zucchinis, sliced
- Salt and black pepper to taste
- 2 cups ricotta cheese
- 2 cups shredded mozzarella cheese
- 3 cups tomato sauce
- 1 cup packed baby spinach

Directions:
1. Preheat oven to 370ºF and grease a baking dish with cooking spray.
2. Put the zucchini slices in a colander and sprinkle with salt. Let sit and drain liquid for 5 minutes and pat dry with paper towels. Mix the ricotta, mozzarella, salt, and pepper to evenly combine and spread ¼ cup of the mixture in the bottom of the baking dish.
3. Layer ⅓ of the zucchini slices on top spread 1 cup of tomato sauce over, and scatter a ⅓ cup of spinach on top. Repeat the layering process two more times to exhaust the ingredients while making sure to layer with the last ¼ cup of cheese mixture finally.
4. Grease one end of foil with cooking spray and cover the baking dish with the foil. Bake for 35 minutes, remove foil, and bake further for 5 to 10 minutes or until the cheese has a nice golden brown color. Remove the dish, sit for 5 minutes, make slices of the lasagna, and serve warm.

Nutrition Info:
- Per Servings 2g Carbs, 7g Protein, 39g Fat, 390 Calories

Zucchini Noodles

Servings: 6
Cooking Time: 15 Mins
Ingredients:
- 2 cloves garlic, minced
- 2 medium zucchini, cut into noodles with a spiralizer
- 12 zucchini blossoms, pistils removed; cut into strips
- 6 fresh basil leaves, cut into strips, or to taste
- 4 tablespoons olive oil
- Salt to taste

Directions:
1. In a large skillet over low heat, cook garlic in olive oil for 10 minutes until slightly browned. Add in zucchini and zucchini blossoms, stir well.
2. Toss in green beans and season with salt to taste; sprinkle with basil and serve.

Nutrition Info:
- Per Servings 13.5g Carbs, 5.7g Protein, 28.1g Fat, 348 Calories

Cauliflower Risotto With Mushrooms

Servings: 4
Cooking Time: 15 Minutes
Ingredients:

- 2 shallots, diced
- 3 tbsp olive oil
- ¼ cup veggie broth
- ⅓ cup Parmesan cheese
- 4 tbsp butter
- 3 tbsp chopped chives
- 2 pounds mushrooms, sliced
- 4 ½ cups riced cauliflower

Directions:

1. Heat 2 tbsp. oil in a saucepan. Add the mushrooms and cook over medium heat for about 3 minutes. Remove from the pan and set aside.
2. Heat the remaining oil and cook the shallots for 2 minutes. Stir in the cauliflower and broth, and cook until the liquid is absorbed. Stir in the rest of the ingredients.

Nutrition Info:

- Per Servings 8.4g Carbs, 11g Protein, 18g Fat, 264 Calories

Grilled Cheese The Keto Way

Servings: 1
Cooking Time: 15 Minutes

Ingredients:

- 2 eggs
- ½ tsp baking powder
- 2 tbsp butter
- 2 tbsp almond flour
- 1 ½ tbsp psyllium husk powder
- 2 ounces cheddar cheese

Directions:

1. Whisk together all ingredients except 1 tbsp. butter and cheddar cheese. Place in a square oven-proof bowl, and microwave for 90 seconds. Flip the bun over and cut in half.
2. Place the cheddar cheese on one half of the bun and top with the other. Melt the remaining butter in a skillet. Add the sandwich and grill until the cheese is melted and the bun is crispy.

Nutrition Info:

- Per Servings 6.1g Carbs, 25g Protein, 51g Fat, 623 Calories

Mushroom & Cauliflower Bake

Servings: 4
Cooking Time: 30 Minutes
Ingredients:

- Cooking spray
- 1 head cauliflower, cut into florets
- 8 ounces mushrooms, halved
- 2 garlic cloves, smashed
- 2 tomatoes, pureed
- ¼ cup coconut oil, melted

- 1 tsp chili paprika paste
- ¼ tsp marjoram
- ½ tsp curry powder
- Salt and black pepper, to taste

Directions:

1. Set oven to 390ºF. Apply a cooking spray to a baking dish. Lay mushrooms and cauliflower in the baking dish. Around the vegetables, scatter smashed garlic. Place in the pureed tomatoes. Sprinkle over melted coconut oil and place in chili paprika paste, curry, black pepper, salt, and marjoram. Roast for 25 minutes, turning once. Place in a serving plate and serve with green salad.

Nutrition Info:

- Per Servings 11.6g Carbs, 5g Protein, 6.7g Fat, 113 Calories

Keto Cauliflower Hash Browns

Servings: 4
Cooking Time: 30 Mins
Ingredients:

- 1 lb cauliflower
- 3 eggs
- ½ yellow onion, grated
- 2 pinches pepper
- 4 oz. butter, for frying
- What you'll need from the store cupboard:
- 1 tsp salt

Directions:

1. Rinse, trim and grate the cauliflower using a food processor or grater.
2. In a large bowl, add the cauliflower onion and pepper, tossing evenly. Set aside for 5 to 10 minutes.
3. In a large skillet over medium heat, heat a generous amount of butter on medium heat. The cooking process will go quicker if you plan to have room for 3–4 pancakes at a time. Use the oven on low heat to keep the first batches of pancakes warm while you make the others.
4. Place scoops of the grated cauliflower mixture in the frying pan and flatten them carefully until they measure about 3 to 4 inches in diameter.
5. Fry for 4 to 5 minutes on each side. Adjust the heat to make sure they don't burn. Serve.

Nutrition Info:

- Per Servings 5g Carbs, 7g Protein, 26g Fat, 282 Calories

Grilled Parmesan Eggplant

Servings: 4
Cooking Time: 15 Minutes
Ingredients:

- 1 medium-sized eggplant
- 1 log fresh mozzarella cheese, cut into sixteen slices
- 1 small tomato, cut into eight slices
- 1/2 cup shredded Parmesan cheese
- Chopped fresh basil or parsley
- 1/2 teaspoon salt

- 1 tablespoon olive oil
- 1/2 teaspoon pepper

Directions:

1. Trim ends of the eggplant; cut eggplant crosswise into eight slices. Sprinkle with salt; let stand 5 minutes.

2. Blot eggplant dry with paper towels; brush both sides with oil and sprinkle with pepper. Grill, covered, over medium heat 4-6 minutes on each side or until tender. Remove from grill.

3. Top eggplant with mozzarella cheese, tomato, and Parmesan cheese. Grill, covered, 1-2 minutes longer or until cheese begins to melt. Top with basil.

Nutrition Info:

- Per Servings 10g Carbs, 26g Protein, 31g Fat, 449 Calories

Walnuts With Tofu

Servings: 4

Cooking Time: 13 Minutes

Ingredients:

- 3 tsp olive oil
- 1 cup extra firm tofu, cubed
- ¼ cup walnuts, chopped
- 1 ½ tbsp coconut aminos
- 3 tbsp vegetable broth
- ½ tsp smashed garlic
- 1 tsp cayenne pepper
- ½ tsp turmeric powder
- Sea salt and black pepper, to taste
- 2 tsp sunflower seeds

Directions:

1. Set a frying pan over medium heat. Warm the oil. Add in tofu and fry as you stir until they brown. Pour in the walnuts; turn temperature to higher and cook for 2 minutes. Stir in the remaining ingredients, set heat to medium-low and cook for 5 more minutes. Drizzle with hot sauce and serve!

Nutrition Info:

- Per Servings 5.3g Carbs, 8.3g Protein, 21.6g Fat, 232 Calories

Cauliflower Gouda Casserole

Servings: 4

Cooking Time: 21 Minutes

Ingredients:

- 2 heads cauliflower, cut into florets
- ⅓ cup butter, cubed
- 2 tbsp melted butter
- 1 white onion, chopped
- Pink salt and black pepper to taste
- ¼ almond milk
- ½ cup almond flour
- 1 ½ cup grated gouda cheese
- Water for sprinkling

Directions:

1. Preheat oven to 350ºF and put the cauli florets in a large microwave-safe bowl. Sprinkle with water, and steam in the microwave for 4 to 5 minutes.

2. Melt the ⅓ cup of butter in a saucepan over medium heat and sauté the onion for 3 minutes. Add the cauliflower, season with salt and black pepper and mix in almond milk. Simmer for 3 minutes.

3. Mix the remaining melted butter with almond flour. Stir into the cauliflower as well as half of the cheese. Sprinkle the top with the remaining cheese and bake for 10 minutes until the cheese has melted and golden brown on the top. Plate the bake and serve with arugula salad.

Nutrition Info:

- Per Servings 4g Carbs, 12g Protein, 15g Fat, 215 Calories

Asparagus And Tarragon Flan

Servings: 4

Cooking Time: 65 Minutes

Ingredients:

- 16 asparagus, stems trimmed
- 1 cup water
- ½ cup whipping cream
- 1 cup almond milk
- 2 eggs + 2 egg yolks, beaten in a bowl
- 2 tbsp chopped tarragon, fresh
- Salt and black pepper to taste
- A small pinch of nutmeg
- 2 tbsp grated Parmesan cheese
- 3 cups water
- 2 tbsp butter, melted
- 1 tbsp butter, softened

Directions:

1. Pour the water and some salt in a pot, add the asparagus, and bring them to boil over medium heat on a stovetop for 6 minutes. Drain the asparagus; cut their tips and reserve for garnishing. Chop the remaining asparagus into small pieces.

2. In a blender, add the chopped asparagus, whipping cream, almond milk, tarragon, ½ teaspoon of salt, nutmeg, pepper, and Parmesan cheese. Process the ingredients on high speed until smooth. Pour the mixture through a sieve into a bowl and whisk the eggs into it.

3. Preheat the oven to 350ºF. Grease the ramekins with softened butter and share the asparagus mixture among the ramekins. Pour the melted butter over each mixture and top with 2-3 asparagus tips. Pour the remaining water into a baking dish, place in the ramekins, and insert in the oven.

4. Bake for 45 minutes until their middle parts are no longer watery. Remove the ramekins and let cool. Garnish the flan with the asparagus tips and serve with chilled white wine.

Nutrition Info:

- Per Servings 2.5g Carbs, 12.5g Protein, 11.6g Fat, 264 Calories

Chapter 9. Desserts And Drinks

Blackcurrant Iced Tea

Servings: 4
Cooking Time: 8 Minutes
Ingredients:
- 6 unflavored tea bags
- 2 cups water
- ½ cup sugar-free blackcurrant extract
- Swerve to taste
- Ice cubes for serving
- Lemon slices to garnish, cut on the side

Directions:
1. Pour the ice cubes in a pitcher and place it in the fridge.
2. Bring the water to boil in a saucepan over medium heat for 3 minutes and turn the heat off. Stir in the sugar to dissolve and steep the tea bags in the water for 2 minutes.
3. Remove the bags after and let the tea cool down. Stir in the blackcurrant extract until well incorporated, remove the pitcher from the fridge, and pour the mixture over the ice cubes.
4. Let sit for 3 minutes to cool and after, pour the mixture into tall glasses. Add some more ice cubes, place the lemon slices on the rim of the glasses, and serve the tea cold.

Nutrition Info:
- Per Servings 5g Carbs, 0g Protein, 0g Fat, 22 Calories

Baby Kale And Yogurt Smoothie

Servings: 1
Cooking Time: 0 Minutes
Ingredients:
- ½ cup whole milk yogurt
- ½ cup baby kale greens
- 1 packet Stevia, or more to taste
- 3 tbsps MCT oil
- ½ tbsp sunflower seeds
- 1 cup water

Directions:
1. Add all ingredients in a blender.
2. Blend until smooth and creamy.
3. Serve and enjoy.

Nutrition Info:
- Per Servings 2.6g Carbs, 11.0g Protein, 26.2g Fat, 329 Calories

Lemon Gummies

Servings: 4
Cooking Time: 15 Minutes
Ingredients:
- 1/4 cup fresh lemon juice
- 2 Tablespoons gelatin powder
- 2 Tablespoons stevia, to taste
- ½ cup half and half
- 1 Tablespoon water

Directions:
1. In a small saucepan, heat up water and lemon juice.
2. Slowly stir in the gelatin powder and the rest of the ingredients. Heating and mixing well until dissolved.
3. Pour into silicone molds.
4. Freeze or refrigerate for 2+ hours until firm.

Nutrition Info:
- Per Servings 1.0g Carbs, 3.0g Protein, 7g Fat, 88 Calories

Avocado And Greens Smoothie

Servings: 1
Cooking Time: 0 Minutes
Ingredients:
- ½ cup coconut milk
- ¼ avocado fruit
- ½ cup spring mix greens
- 3 tbsps avocado oil
- 1 ½ cups water
- 2 packets Stevia, or as needed

Directions:
1. Add all ingredients in a blender.
2. Blend until smooth and creamy.
3. Serve and enjoy.

Nutrition Info:
- Per Servings 10.3g Carbs, 3.8g Protein, 77.4g Fat, 764 Calories

Cinnamon Cookies

Servings: 4
Cooking Time: 25 Minutes
Ingredients:
- 2 cups almond flour
- ½ tsp baking soda
- ¾ cup sweetener
- ½ cup butter, softened
- A pinch of salt
- Coating:
- 2 tbsp erythritol sweetener
- 1 tsp cinnamon

Directions:
1. Preheat your oven to 350ºF. Combine all cookie ingredients in a bowl. Make 16 balls out of the mixture and flatten them with hands. Combine the cinnamon and erythritol. Dip the cookies in the cinnamon mixture and arrange them on a lined cookie sheet. Cook for 15 minutes, until crispy.

Nutrition Info:
- Per Servings 1.5g Carbs, 3g Protein, 13g Fat, 131 Calories

Brownie Mug Cake

Servings: 1
Cooking Time: 5 Minutes
Ingredients:

- 1 egg, beaten
- ¼ cup almond flour
- ¼ teaspoon baking powder
- 1 ½ tablespoons cacao powder
- 2 tablespoons stevia powder
- A pinch of salt
- 1 teaspoon cinnamon powder
- ¼ teaspoon vanilla extract (optional)

Directions:
1. Combine all ingredients in a bowl until well-combined.
2. Transfer in a heat-proof mug.
3. Place the mug in a microwave.
4. Cook for 2 minutes. Let it sit for another 2 minutes to continue cooking.
5. Serve and enjoy.

Nutrition Info:
- Per Servings 4.1g Carbs, 9.1g Protein, 11.8g Fat, 159 Calories

Berry Merry

Servings: 4
Cooking Time: 6 Minutes
Ingredients:

- 1 ½ cups blackberries
- 1 cup strawberries + extra for garnishing
- 1 cup blueberries
- 2 small beets, peeled and chopped
- 2/3 cup ice cubes
- 1 lime, juiced

Directions:
1. For the extra strawberries for garnishing, make a single deep cut on their sides; set aside.
2. Add the blackberries, strawberries, blueberries, beet, and ice into the smoothie maker and blend the ingredients at high speed until smooth and frothy, for about 60 seconds.
3. Add the lime juice, and puree further for 30 seconds. Pour the drink into tall smoothie glasses, fix the reserved strawberries on each glass rim, stick a straw in, and serve the drink immediately.

Nutrition Info:
- Per Servings 8g Carbs, 2.7g Protein, 3g Fat, 83 Calories

Keto Lemon Custard

Servings: 8
Cooking Time: 50 Minutes
Ingredients:

- 1 Lemon
- 6 large eggs
- 2 tbsp lemon zest
- 1 cup Lakanto
- 2 cups heavy cream

Directions:
1. Preheat oven to 300oF.
2. Mix all ingredients.
3. Pour mixture into ramekins.
4. Put ramekins into a dish with boiling water.
5. Bake in the oven for 45-50 minutes.
6. Let cool then refrigerate for 2 hours.
7. Use lemon slices as garnish.

Nutrition Info:
- Per Servings 4.0g Carbs, 7.0g Protein, 21.0g Fat, 233 Calories

Coconut-mocha Shake

Servings: 1
Cooking Time: 0 Minutes
Ingredients:

- 2 tbsp cocoa powder
- 1 tbsp coconut flakes, unsweetened
- 2 packet Stevia, or more to taste
- 1 cup brewed coffee, chilled
- 3 tbsps coconut oil

Directions:
1. Add all ingredients in a blender.
2. Blend until smooth and creamy.
3. Serve and enjoy.

Nutrition Info:
- Per Servings 9g Carbs, 2.4g Protein, 43.7g Fat, 402 Calories

Cardamom-cinnamon Spiced Coco-latte

Servings: 1
Cooking Time: 0 Minutes
Ingredients:

- ½ cup coconut milk
- ¼ tsp cardamom powder
- 1 tbsp chocolate powder
- 1 ½ cups brewed coffee, chilled
- 1 tbsp coconut oil
- ¼ tsp cinnamon
- ¼ tsp nutmeg

Directions:
1. Add all ingredients in a blender.
2. Blend until smooth and creamy.
3. Serve and enjoy.

Nutrition Info:
- Per Servings 7.5g Carbs, 3.8g Protein, 38.7g Fat, 362 Calories

Vanilla Jello Keto Way

Servings: 6
Cooking Time: 6 Minutes
Ingredients:
- 1 cup heavy cream
- 1 teaspoon vanilla extract
- 2 tablespoons gelatin powder, unsweetened
- 3 tablespoons erythritol
- 1 cup boiling water

Directions:
1. Place the boiling water in a small pot and bring to a simmer.
2. Add the gelatin powder and allow to dissolve.
3. Stir in the rest of the ingredients.
4. Pour the mixture into jello molds.
5. Place in the fridge to set for 2 hours.

Nutrition Info:
- Per Servings 5.2g Carbs, 3.3g Protein, 7.9g Fat, 105 Calories

Italian Greens And Yogurt Shake

Servings: 1
Cooking Time: 0 Minutes
Ingredients:
- ½ cup half and half
- ½ cup Italian greens
- 1 packet Stevia, or more to taste
- 1 tbsp hemp seeds
- 3 tbsp coconut oil
- 1 cup water

Directions:
1. Add all ingredients in a blender.
2. Blend until smooth and creamy.
3. Serve and enjoy.

Nutrition Info:
- Per Servings 10.3g Carbs, 5.2g Protein, 46.9g Fat, 476 Calories

Granny Smith Apple Tart

Servings: 8
Cooking Time: 65 Minutes
Ingredients:
- 6 tbsp butter
- 2 cups almond flour
- 1 tsp cinnamon
- ⅓ cup sweetener
- Filling:
- 2 cups sliced Granny Smith
- ¼ cup butter
- ¼ cup sweetener
- ½ tsp cinnamon
- ½ tsp lemon juice
- Topping:
- ¼ tsp cinnamon
- 2 tbsp sweetener

Directions:
1. Preheat your oven to 370ºF and combine all crust ingredients in a bowl. Press this mixture into the bottom of a greased pan. Bake for 5 minutes.
2. Meanwhile, combine the apples and lemon juice in a bowl and let them sit until the crust is ready. Arrange them on top of the crust. Combine the rest of the filling ingredients, and brush this mixture over the apples. Bake for about 30 minutes.
3. Press the apples down with a spatula, return to oven, and bake for 20 more minutes. Combine the cinnamon and sweetener, in a bowl, and sprinkle over the tart.
4. Note: Granny Smith apples have just 9.5g of net carbs per 100g. Still high for you? Substitute with Chayote squash, which has the same texture and rich nutrients, and just around 4g of net carbs .

Nutrition Info:
- Per Servings 6.7g Carbs, 7g Protein, 26g Fat, 302 Calories

Coffee Fat Bombs

Servings: 6
Cooking Time: 3 Minutes + Cooling Time
Ingredients:
- 1 ½ cups mascarpone cheese
- ½ cup melted butter
- 3 tbsp unsweetened cocoa powder
- ¼ cup erythritol
- 6 tbsp brewed coffee, room temperature

Directions:
1. Whisk the mascarpone cheese, butter, cocoa powder, erythritol, and coffee with a hand mixer until creamy and fluffy, for 1 minute. Fill into muffin tins and freeze for 3 hours until firm.

Nutrition Info:
- Per Servings 2g Carbs, 4g Protein, 14g Fat, 145 Calories

Fast 'n Easy Cookie In A Mug

Servings: 1
Cooking Time: 5 Minutes
Ingredients:
- 1 tablespoon butter
- 3 tablespoons almond flour
- 1 tablespoon erythritol
- 1 egg yolk
- 1/8 teaspoon vanilla extract
- A dash of cinnamon
- A pinch of salt

Directions:
1. Mix all ingredients in a microwave-safe mug.
2. Nuke in the microwave for 3 minutes.
3. Let it rest for a minute.
4. Serve and enjoy.

Nutrition Info:

- Per Servings 1.4g Carbs, 3.5g Protein, 17.8g Fat, 180 Calories

Coconut Bars

Servings: 4
Cooking Time: 3 Hours
Ingredients:
- 3 ½ ounces ghee
- 10 saffron threads
- 1 ⅓ cups coconut milk
- 1 ¾ cups shredded coconut
- 4 tbsp sweetener
- 1 tsp cardamom powder

Directions:
1. Combine the shredded coconut with 1 cup of the coconut milk. In another bowl, mix together the remaining coconut milk with the sweetener and saffron. Let sit for 30 minutes.
2. Heat the ghee in a wok. Add the coconut mixture as well as the saffron threads, and cook for 5 minutes on low heat, mixing continuously. Stir in the cardamom and cook for another 5 minutes.
3. Spread the mixture onto a small container and freeze for 2 hours. Cut into bars and enjoy!

Nutrition Info:
- Per Servings 1.4g Carbs, 2g Protein, 22g Fat, 215 Calories

Hazelnut-lettuce Yogurt Shake

Servings: 1
Cooking Time: 0 Minutes
Ingredients:
- 1 cup whole milk yogurt
- 1 cup lettuce chopped
- 1 tbsp Hazelnut chopped
- 1 packet Stevia, or more to taste
- 1 tbsp olive oil
- 1 cup water

Directions:
1. Add all ingredients in a blender.
2. Blend until smooth and creamy.
3. Serve and enjoy.

Nutrition Info:
- Per Servings 8.8g Carbs, 9.4g Protein, 22.2g Fat, 282 Calories

Berry Tart

Servings: 4
Cooking Time: 45 Minutes
Ingredients:
- 4 eggs
- 2 tsp coconut oil
- 2 cups berries
- 1 cup coconut milk
- 1 cup almond flour
- ¼ cup sweetener

- ½ tsp vanilla powder
- 1 tbsp powdered sweetener
- A pinch of salt

Directions:
1. Preheat the oven to 350ºF. Place all ingredients except coconut oil, berries, and powdered sweetener, in a blender; blend until smooth. Gently fold in the berries. Grease a baking dish with the oil. Pour the mixture into the prepared pan and bake for 35 minutes. Sprinkle with powdered sugar to serve.

Nutrition Info:
- Per Servings 4.9g Carbs, 15g Protein, 26.5g Fat, 305 Calories

Choco-chia Pudding

Servings: 4
Cooking Time: 5 Minutes
Ingredients:
- ¼ cup fresh or frozen raspberries
- 1 scoop chocolate protein powder
- 1 cup unsweetened almond milk
- 3 tbsp Chia seeds
- 1 tsp Stevia (optional)
- 5 tablespoons coconut oil

Directions:
1. Mix the chocolate protein powder and almond milk.
2. Add the chia seeds and mix well with a whisk or a fork. Add the coconut oil.
3. Flavor with Stevia depending on the desired sweetness.
4. Let it rest for 5 minutes and continue stirring.
5. Serve and enjoy.

Nutrition Info:
- Per Servings 10g Carbs, 11.5g Protein, 19.6g Fat, 243.5 Calories

Almond Choco Shake

Servings: 1
Cooking Time: 0 Minutes
Ingredients:
- ½ cup heavy cream, liquid
- 1 tbsp cocoa powder
- 1 packet Stevia, or more to taste
- 5 almonds, chopped
- 1 ½ cups water
- 3 tbsp coconut oil

Directions:
1. Add all ingredients in a blender.
2. Blend until smooth and creamy.
3. Serve and enjoy.

Nutrition Info:
- Per Servings 9.7g Carbs, 11.9g Protein, 45.9g Fat, 485 Calories

Chocolate Marshmallows

Servings: 4
Cooking Time: 30 Minutes
Ingredients:
- 2 tbsp unsweetened cocoa powder
- ½ tsp vanilla extract
- ½ cup swerve
- 1 tbsp xanthan gum mixed in 1 tbsp water
- A pinch Salt
- 6 tbsp Cool water
- 2 ½ tsp Gelatin powder
- Dusting:
- 1 tbsp unsweetened cocoa powder
- 1 tbsp swerve confectioner's sugar

Directions:
1. Line the loaf pan with parchment paper and grease with cooking spray; set aside. In a saucepan, mix the swerve, 2 tbsp of water, xanthan gum mixture, and salt. Place the pan over medium heat and bring to a boil. Insert the thermometer and let the ingredients simmer to 238 F, for 7 minutes.
2. In a small bowl, add 2 tbsp of water and sprinkle the gelatin on top. Let sit there without stirring to dissolve for 5 minutes. While the gelatin dissolves, pour the remaining water in a small bowl and heat in the microwave for 30 seconds. Stir in cocoa powder and mix it into the gelatin.
3. When the sugar solution has hit the right temperature, gradually pour it directly into the gelatin mixture while continuously whisking. Beat for 10 minutes to get a light and fluffy consistency.
4. Next, stir in the vanilla and pour the blend into the loaf pan. Let the marshmallows set for 3 hours and then use an oiled knife to cut it into cubes; place them on a plate. Mix the remaining cocoa powder and confectioner's sugar together. Sift it over the marshmallows.

Nutrition Info:
- Per Servings 5.1g Carbs, 0.5g Protein, 2.2g Fat, 55 Calories

No Nuts Fudge

Servings: 15
Cooking Time: 4 Hours
Ingredients:
- ¼ cup cocoa powder
- ½ teaspoon baking powder
- 1 stick of butter, melted
- 4 tablespoons erythritol
- 6 eggs, beaten
- Salt to taste.

Directions:
1. Mix all ingredients in a slow cooker.
2. Add a pinch of salt.
3. Mix until well combined.
4. Cover pot.
5. Press the low settings and adjust the time to 4 hours.

Nutrition Info:

- Per Servings 1.3g Carbs, 4.3g Protein, 12.2g Fat, 132 Calories

Eggnog Keto Custard

Servings: 8
Cooking Time: 10 Minutes
Ingredients:
- ¼ tsp nutmeg
- ¼ Truvia
- ½ cup heavy whipping cream
- 1 cup half and half
- 4 eggs

Directions:
1. Blend all ingredients together.
2. Pour evenly into 6 ramekins (microwave safe).
3. Microwave at 50% power for 4 minutes then stir thoroughly.
4. Microwave for another 3-4 minutes at 50% power then stir well again.
5. Serve either cool or hot.

Nutrition Info:
- Per Servings 1.0g Carbs, 3.0g Protein, 6.0g Fat, 70 Calories

Strawberry Vanilla Extract Smoothie

Servings: 3
Cooking Time: 5 Mins
Ingredients:
- 1 cup almond milk
- 14 frozen strawberries
- 1 1/2 teaspoons stevia
- What you'll need from the store cupboard:
- 1/2 teaspoon vanilla extract

Directions:
1. Place almond milk and strawberries in a blender, blend until creamy. Add vanilla and stevia if desired, blend again and serve.

Nutrition Info:
- Per Servings 5g Carbs, 12.8g Protein, 18.8g Fat, 240.4 Calories

Coconut-melon Yogurt Shake

Servings: 1
Cooking Time: 0 Minutes
Ingredients:
- ¼ cup half and half
- 3 tbsp coconut oil
- ½ cup melon, slices
- 1 tbsp coconut flakes, unsweetened
- 1 tbsp chia seeds
- 1 ½ cups water
- 1 packet Stevia, or more to taste

Directions:
1. Add all ingredients in a blender.
2. Blend until smooth and creamy.
3. Serve and enjoy.

Nutrition Info:
- Per Servings 8g Carbs, 2.4g Protein, 43g Fat, 440 Calories

Raspberry Sorbet

Servings: 1
Cooking Time: 3 Minutes
Ingredients:
- ¼ tsp vanilla extract
- 1 packet gelatine, without sugar
- 1 tbsp heavy whipping cream
- ⅓ cup boiling water
- 2 tbsp mashed raspberries
- 1 ½ cups crushed Ice
- ⅓ cup cold water

Directions:
1. Combine the gelatin and boiling water, until completely dissolved; then transfer to a blender. Add the remaining ingredients. Blend until smooth and freeze for at least 2 hours.

Nutrition Info:
- Per Servings 3.7g Carbs, 4g Protein, 10g Fat, 173 Calories

Chocolate Chip Cookies

Servings: 4
Cooking Time: 20 Minutes
Ingredients:
- 1 cup butter, softened
- 2 cups swerve brown sugar
- 3 eggs
- 2 cups almond flour
- 2 cups unsweetened chocolate chips

Directions:
1. Preheat oven to 350ºF and line a baking sheet with parchment paper.
2. Whisk the butter and sugar with a hand mixer for 3 minutes or until light and fluffy. Add the eggs one at a time, and scrape the sides as you whisk. Mix in the almond flour in low speed until well combined.
3. Fold in the chocolate chips. Scoop 3 tablespoons each on the baking sheet creating spaces between each mound and bake for 15 minutes to swell and harden. Remove, cool and serve.

Nutrition Info:
- Per Servings 8.9g Carbs, 6.3g Protein, 27g Fat, 317 Calories

Nutty Arugula Yogurt Smoothie

Servings: 1
Cooking Time: 0 Minutes
Ingredients:
- 1 cup whole milk yogurt
- 1 cup baby arugula
- 3 tbsps avocado oil
- 2 tbsps macadamia nuts

- 1 packet Stevia, or more to taste
- 1 cup water

Directions:
1. Add all ingredients in a blender.
2. Blend until smooth and creamy.
3. Serve and enjoy.

Nutrition Info:
- Per Servings 9.4g Carbs, 9.3g Protein, 51.5g Fat, 540 Calories

Green And Fruity Smoothie

Servings: 2
Cooking Time: 0 Minutes
Ingredients:
- 1 cup spinach, packed
- ½ cup strawberries, chopped
- ½ avocado, peeled, pitted, and frozen
- 1 tbsp almond butter
- ¼ cup packed kale, stem discarded, and leaves chopped
- 1 cup ice-cold water
- 5 tablespoons MCT oil or coconut oil

Directions:
1. Blend all ingredients in a blender until smooth and creamy.
2. Serve and enjoy.

Nutrition Info:
- Per Servings 10g Carbs, 1.6g Protein, 47.3g Fat, 459 Calories

Hazelnut And Coconut Shake

Servings: 1
Cooking Time: 0 Minutes
Ingredients:
- ¼ coconut milk
- ¼ cup hazelnut, chopped
- 2 tbsps MCT oil or coconut oil
- 1 ½ cups water
- 1 packet Stevia, optional

Directions:
1. Add all ingredients in a blender.
2. Blend until smooth and creamy.
3. Serve and enjoy.

Nutrition Info:
- Per Servings 8.9g Carbs, 6.5g Protein, 62.1g Fat, 591 Calories

Strawberry-choco Shake

Servings: 1
Cooking Time: 0 Minutes
Ingredients:
- ½ cup heavy cream, liquid
- 1 tbsp cocoa powder
- 1 packet Stevia, or more to taste
- 4 strawberries, sliced
- 1 tbsp coconut flakes, unsweetened
- 1 ½ cups water

- 3 tbsps coconut oil

Directions:
1. Add all ingredients in a blender.
2. Blend until smooth and creamy.
3. Serve and enjoy.

Nutrition Info:
- Per Servings 10.1g Carbs, 2.6g Protein, 65.3g Fat, 610 Calories

Vanilla Bean Frappuccino

Servings: 4
Cooking Time: 6 Minutes
Ingredients:
- 3 cups unsweetened vanilla almond milk, chilled
- 2 tsp swerve
- 1 ½ cups heavy cream, cold
- 1 vanilla bean
- ¼ tsp xanthan gum
- Unsweetened chocolate shavings to garnish

Directions:
1. Combine the almond milk, swerve, heavy cream, vanilla bean, and xanthan gum in the blender, and process on high speed for 1 minute until smooth. Pour into tall shake glasses, sprinkle with chocolate shavings, and serve immediately.

Nutrition Info:
- Per Servings 6g Carbs, 15g Protein, 14g Fat, 193 Calories

Blackberry Cheese Vanilla Blocks

Servings: 5
Cooking Time: 20mins
Ingredients:
- ½ cup blackberries
- 6 eggs
- 4 oz mascarpone cheese
- 1 tsp vanilla extract
- 4 tbsp stevia
- 8 oz melted coconut oil
- ½ tsp baking powder

Directions:
1. Except for blackberries, blend all ingredients in a blender until smooth.
2. Combine blackberries with blended mixture and transfer to a baking dish.
3. Bake blackberries mixture in the oven at 320°F for 20 minutes. Serve.

Nutrition Info:
- Per Servings 15g Carbs, 13g Protein, 4g Fat, 199 Calories

Eggless Strawberry Mousse

Servings: 6
Cooking Time: 6 Minutes + Cooling Time
Ingredients:
- 2 cups chilled heavy cream
- 2 cups fresh strawberries, hulled

- 5 tbsp erythritol
- 2 tbsp lemon juice
- ¼ tsp strawberry extract
- 2 tbsp sugar-free strawberry preserves

Directions:
1. Beat the heavy cream, in a bowl, with a hand mixer at high speed until a stiff peak forms, for about 1 minute; refrigerate immediately. Puree the strawberries in a blender and pour into a saucepan.
2. Add erythritol and lemon juice, and cook on low heat for 3 minutes while stirring continuously. Stir in the strawberry extract evenly, turn off heat and allow cooling. Fold in the whipped cream until evenly incorporated, and spoon into six ramekins. Refrigerate for 4 hours to solidify.
3. Garnish with strawberry preserves and serve immediately.

Nutrition Info:
- Per Servings 5g Carbs, 5g Protein, 24g Fat, 290 Calories

Dark Chocolate Mousse With Stewed Plums

Servings: 6
Cooking Time: 45 Minutes
Ingredients:
- 12 oz unsweetened chocolate
- 8 eggs, separated into yolks and whites
- 2 tbsp salt
- ¾ cup swerve sugar
- ½ cup olive oil
- 3 tbsp brewed coffee
- Stewed Plums
- 4 plums, pitted and halved
- ½ stick cinnamon
- ½ cup swerve
- ½ cup water
- ½ lemon, juiced

Directions:
1. Put the chocolate in a bowl and melt in the microwave for 1 ½ minutes. In a separate bowl, whisk the yolks with half of the swerve until a pale yellow has formed, then, beat in the salt, olive oil, and coffee. Mix in the melted chocolate until smooth.
2. In a third bowl, whisk the whites with the hand mixer until a soft peak has formed. Sprinkle the remaining swerve sugar over and gently fold in with a spatula. Fetch a tablespoon full of the chocolate mixture and fold in to combine. Pour in the remaining chocolate mixture and whisk to mix.
3. Pour the mousse into 6 ramekins, cover with plastic wrap, and refrigerate overnight. The next morning, pour water, swerve, cinnamon, and lemon juice in a saucepan and bring to a simmer for 3 minutes, occasionally stirring to ensure the swerve has dissolved and a syrup has formed.
4. Add the plums and poach in the sweetened water for 18 minutes until soft. Turn the heat off and discard the

cinnamon stick. Spoon a plum each with syrup on the chocolate mousse and serve.

Nutrition Info:

- Per Servings 6.9g Carbs, 9.5g Protein, 23g Fat, 288 Calories

Coconut Macadamia Nut Bombs

Servings: 4
Cooking Time: 0 Mins
Ingredients:

- 2 packets stevia
- 5 tbsps unsweetened coconut powder
- 10 tbsps coconut oil
- 3 tbsps chopped macadamia nuts
- Salt to taste

Directions:

1. Heat the coconut oil in a pan over medium heat. Add coconut powder, stevia and salt, stirring to combined well; then remove from heat.
2. Spoon mixture into a lined mini muffin pan. Place in the freezer for a few hours.
3. Sprinkle nuts over the mixture before serving.

Nutrition Info:

- Per Servings 0.2g Carbs, 1.1g Protein, 15.2g Fat, 143 Calories

Blueberry Tart With Lavender

Servings: 6
Cooking Time: 2 Hours 25 Minutes
Ingredients:

- 1 large low carb pie crust
- 1 ½ cups heavy cream
- 2 tbsp swerve
- 1 tbsp culinary lavender
- 1 vanilla, seeds extracted
- 2 cups fresh blueberries
- Erythritol for topping

Directions:

1. Preheat the oven to 400ºF. Place the pie crust with its pan on a baking tray and bake in the oven for 30 minutes, until golden brown; remove and let cool.
2. Mix the heavy cream and lavender in a saucepan. Set the pan over medium heat and bring the mixture to a boil; turn the heat off and let cool. Refrigerate for 1 hour to infuse the cream.
3. Remove the cream from the fridge and strain through a colander into a bowl to remove the lavender pieces. Mix swerve and vanilla into the cream, and pour into the cooled crust. Scatter the blueberries on and refrigerate the pie for 45 minutes. Remove and top with erythritol, before slicing.

Nutrition Info:

- Per Servings 10.7g Carbs, 3.3g Protein, 16.4g Fat, 198 Calories

Green Tea Brownies With Macadamia Nuts

Servings: 4
Cooking Time: 28 Minutes
Ingredients:

- 1 tbsp green tea powder
- ¼ cup unsalted butter, melted
- 4 tbsp swerve confectioner's sugar
- A pinch of salt
- ¼ cup coconut flour
- ½ tsp low carb baking powder
- 1 egg
- ¼ cup chopped macadamia nuts

Directions:

1. Preheat the oven to 350ºF and line a square baking dish with parchment paper. Pour the melted butter into a bowl, add sugar and salt, and whisk to combine. Crack the egg into the bowl.
2. Beat the mixture until the egg has incorporated. Pour the coconut flour, green tea, and baking powder into a fine-mesh sieve and sift them into the egg bowl; stir. Add the nuts, stir again, and pour the mixture into the lined baking dish. Bake for 18 minutes, remove and slice into brownie cubes. Serve warm.

Nutrition Info:

- Per Servings 2.2g Carbs, 5.2g Protein, 23.1g Fat, 248 Calories

Vanilla Flan With Mint

Servings: 4
Cooking Time: 10 Minutes
Ingredients:

- ⅓ cup erythritol, for caramel
- 2 cups almond milk
- 4 eggs
- 1 tbsp vanilla
- 1 tbsp lemon zest
- ½ cup erythritol, for custard
- 2 cup heavy whipping cream
- Mint leaves, to serve

Directions:

1. Heat the erythritol for the caramel in a deep pan. Add 2-3 tablespoons of water, and bring to a boil. Reduce the heat and cook until the caramel turns golden brown. Divide between 4-6 metal tins. Set aside and let them cool.
2. In a bowl, mix the eggs, remaining erythritol, lemon zest, and vanilla. Add the almond milk and beat again until well combined.
3. Pour the custard into each caramel-lined ramekin and place them into a deep baking tin. Fill over the way with the remaining hot water. Bake at 345 ºF for 45-50 minutes. Using tongs, take out the ramekins and let them cool for at least 4 hours in the fridge. Run a knife slowly around the edges to invert onto a dish. Serve with dollops of whipped cream, scattered with mint leaves.

Nutrition Info:
- Per Servings 1.7g Carbs, 7.6g Protein, 26g Fat, 269 Calories

Smarties Cookies

Servings: 8
Cooking Time: 10 Mins
Ingredients:
- 1/4 cup. butter
- 1/2 cup. almond flour
- 1 tsp. vanilla essence
- 12 oz. bag of smarties
- 1 cup. stevia
- 1/4 tsp. baking powder

Directions:
1. Sift in flour and baking powder in a bowl, then stir through butter and mix until well combined.
2. Whisk in stevia and vanilla essence , stir until thick.
3. Then add the smarties and use your hand to mix and divide into small balls.
4. Bake until completely cooked, about 10 minutes. Let it cool and serve.

Nutrition Info:
- Per Servings 20.77g Carbs, 3.7g Protein, 11.89g Fat, 239 Calories

Lemon Cheesecake Mousse

Servings: 4
Cooking Time: 5 Minutes +cooling Time
Ingredients:
- 24 oz cream cheese, softened
- 2 cups swerve confectioner's sugar
- 2 lemons, juiced and zested
- Pink salt to taste
- 1 cup whipped cream + extra for garnish

Directions:
1. Whip the cream cheese in a bowl with a hand mixer until light and fluffy. Mix in the sugar, lemon juice, and salt. Fold in the whipped cream to evenly combine.
2. Spoon the mousse into serving cups and refrigerate to thicken for 1 hour. Swirl with extra whipped cream and garnish lightly with lemon zest. Serve immediately.

Nutrition Info:
- Per Servings 3g Carbs, 12g Protein, 18g Fat, 223 Calories

Strawberry Yogurt Shake

Servings: 1
Cooking Time: 0 Minutes
Ingredients:
- ½ cup whole milk yogurt
- 4 strawberries, chopped
- 1 tbsp cocoa powder
- 3 tbsp coconut oil
- 1 tbsp pepitas
- 1 ½ cups water

- 1 packet Stevia, or more to taste

Directions:
1. Add all ingredients in a blender.
2. Blend until smooth and creamy.
3. Serve and enjoy.

Nutrition Info:
- Per Servings 10.5g Carbs, 7.7g Protein, 49.3g Fat, 496 Calories

Boysenberry And Greens Shake

Servings: 1
Cooking Time: 0 Minutes
Ingredients:
- ¼ cup coconut milk
- 2 tbsps Boysenberry
- 2 packets Stevia, or as needed
- ¼ cup Baby Kale salad mix
- 3 tbsps MCT oil
- 1 ½ cups water

Directions:
1. Add all ingredients in a blender.
2. Blend until smooth and creamy.
3. Serve and enjoy.

Nutrition Info:
- Per Servings 3.9g Carbs, 1.7g Protein, 55.1g Fat, 502 Calories

Lychee And Coconut Lassi

Servings: 4
Cooking Time: 2 Hours 28 Minutes
Ingredients:
- 2 cups lychee pulp, seeded
- 2 ½ cups coconut milk
- 4 tsp swerve
- 2 limes, zested and juiced
- 1 ½ cups plain yogurt
- 1 lemongrass, white part only, crushed
- Toasted coconut shavings for garnish

Directions:
1. In a saucepan, add the lychee pulp, coconut milk, swerve, lemongrass, and lime zest. Stir and bring to boil on medium heat for 2 minutes, = stirring continually. Then reduce the heat, and simmer for 1 minute. Turn the heat off and let the mixture sit for 15 minutes.
2. Remove the lemongrass and pour the mixture into a smoothie maker or a blender, add the yogurt and lime juice, and process the ingredients until smooth, for about 60 seconds.
3. Pour into a jug and refrigerate for 2 hours until cold; stir. Serve garnished with coconut shavings.

Nutrition Info:
- Per Servings 1.5g Carbs, 5.3g Protein, 26.1g Fat, 285 Calories

Blueberry And Greens Smoothie

Servings: 1
Cooking Time: 0 Minutes
Ingredients:
- ¼ cup coconut milk
- 2 tbsps blueberries
- ½ cup arugula
- 1 tbsp hemp seeds
- 2 packets Stevia, or as needed
- 1 ½ cups water
- 3 tbsps coconut oil

Directions:
1. Add all ingredients in a blender.
2. Blend until smooth and creamy.
3. Serve and enjoy.

Nutrition Info:
- Per Servings 10.4g Carbs, 3.6g Protein, 59.8g Fat, 572 Calories

Nutty Choco Milk Shake

Servings: 1
Cooking Time: 0 Minutes
Ingredients:
- ¼ cup half and half
- 1 tbsp cocoa powder
- 1 packet Stevia, or more to taste
- 4 pecans
- 1 tbsp macadamia oil
- 1 ½ cups water
- 3 tbsp coconut oil

Directions:
1. Add all ingredients in a blender.
2. Blend until smooth and creamy.
3. Serve and enjoy.

Nutrition Info:
- Per Servings 9.4g Carbs, 4.8g Protein, 73g Fat, 689 Calories

Ice Cream Bars Covered With Chocolate

Servings: 15
Cooking Time: 4 Hours And 20 Minutes
Ingredients:
- Ice Cream:
- 1 cup heavy whipping cream
- 1 tsp vanilla extract
- ¾ tsp xanthan gum
- ½ cup peanut butter
- 1 cup half and half
- 1 ½ cups almond milk
- ⅓ tsp stevia powder
- 1 tbsp vegetable glycerin
- 3 tbsp xylitol
- Chocolate:

- ¾ cup coconut oil
- ¼ cup cocoa butter pieces, chopped
- 2 ounces unsweetened chocolate
- 3 ½ tsp THM super sweet blend

Directions:
1. Blend all ice cream ingredients until smooth. Place in an ice cream maker and follow the instructions. Spread the ice cream into a lined pan, and freezer for about 4 hours.
2. Combine all chocolate ingredients in a microwave-safe bowl and heat until melted. Allow cooling. Remove the ice cream from the freezer and slice into bars. Dip them into the cooled chocolate mixture and return to the freezer for about 10 minutes before serving.

Nutrition Info:
- Per Servings 5g Carbs, 4g Protein, 32g Fat, 345 Calories

Lemony-avocado Cilantro Shake

Servings: 1
Cooking Time: 0 Minutes
Ingredients:
- ½ cup half and half
- 1 packet Stevia, or more to taste
- ¼ avocado, meat scooped
- 1 tbsp chopped cilantro
- 3 tbsps coconut oil
- 1 ½ cups water

Directions:
1. Add all ingredients in a blender.
2. Blend until smooth and creamy.
3. Serve and enjoy.

Nutrition Info:
- Per Servings 8.4g Carbs, 4.4g Protein, 49g Fat, 501 Calories

Spicy Cheese Crackers

Servings: 4
Cooking Time: 10 Mins
Ingredients:
- 3/4 cup almond flour
- 1 egg
- 2 tablespoons cream cheese
- 2 cups shredded Parmesan cheese
- 1/2 teaspoon red pepper flakes
- 1 tablespoon dry ranch salad dressing mix

Directions:
1. Preheat oven to 425 degrees F.
2. Combine Parmesan and cream cheese in a microwave safe bowl and microwave in 30 second intervals. Add the cheese to mix well, and whisk along the almond flour, egg, ranch seasoning, and red pepper flakes, stirring occasionally.
3. Transfer the dough in between two parchment-lined baking sheets. Form the dough into rolls by cutting off plum-sized pieces of dough with dough cutter into 1-inch square pieces, yielding about 60 pieces.

4. Place crackers to a baking sheet lined parchment. Bake for 5 minutes, flipping halfway, then continue to bake for 5 minutes more. Chill before serving.

Nutrition Info:
- Per Servings 18g Carbs, 17g Protein, 4g Fat, 235 Calories

Chia And Blackberry Pudding

Servings: 2
Cooking Time: 10 Minutes
Ingredients:
- 1 cup full-fat natural yogurt
- 2 tsp swerve
- 2 tbsp chia seeds
- 1 cup fresh blackberries
- 1 tbsp lemon zest
- Mint leaves, to serve

Directions:
1. Mix together the yogurt and the swerve. Stir in the chia seeds. Reserve 4 blackberries for garnish and mash the remaining ones with a fork until pureed. Stir in the yogurt mixture
2. Chill in the fridge for 30 minutes. When cooled, divide the mixture between 2 glasses. Top each with a couple of raspberries, mint leaves, lemon zest and serve.

Nutrition Info:
- Per Servings 4.7g Carbs, 7.5g Protein, 10g Fat, 169 Calories

Coco-ginger Fat Bombs

Servings: 10
Cooking Time: 10 Minutes
Ingredients:
- 1 cup coconut oil
- 1 cup shredded coconut
- 1 teaspoon erythritol
- 1 teaspoon ginger powder
- ¼ cup water

Directions:
1. Add all ingredients and pour ¼ cup water in a saucepan on the medium-low fire.
2. Stir constantly for 10 minutes.
3. Turn off and scoop small balls from the mixture.
4. Allow to set in the fridge for 1 hour.

Nutrition Info:
- Per Servings 2.2g Carbs, 0.5g Protein, 12.8g Fat, 126 Calories

Crispy Zucchini Chips

Servings: 5
Cooking Time: 20 Mins
Ingredients:
- 1 large egg, beaten
- 1 cup. almond flour
- 1 medium zucchini, thinly sliced
- 3/4 cup Parmesan cheese, grated
- Cooking spray

Directions:
1. Preheat oven to 400 degrees F. Line a baking pan with parchment paper.
2. In a bowl, mix together Parmesan cheese and almond flour.
3. In another bowl whisk the egg. Dip each zucchini slice in the egg, then the cheese mixture until finely coated.
4. Spray zucchini slices with cooking spray and place in the prepared oven.
5. Bake for 20 minutes until crispy. Serve.

Nutrition Info:
- Per Servings 16.8g Carbs, 10.8g Protein, 6g Fat, 215.2 Calories

Chocolate Hazelnut Bites

Servings: 9
Cooking Time: 0 Minutes
Ingredients:
- 1 carton spreadable cream cheese
- 1 cup semisweet chocolate chips, melted
- 1/2 cup Nutella
- 2-1/4 cups graham cracker crumbs
- 2 cups chopped hazelnuts, toasted
- 5 tablespoons butter

Directions:
1. Beat cream cheese, melted chocolate chips, and Nutella until blended. Stir in cracker crumbs. Refrigerate until firm enough to roll, about 30 minutes.
2. Shape mixture into 1-in. balls; roll in chopped hazelnuts. Make an indentation in the center of each with the end of a wooden spoon handle. Fill with a hazelnut. Store between layers of waxed paper in an airtight container in the refrigerator.

Nutrition Info:
- Per Servings 10g Carbs, 2.7g Protein, 14g Fat, 176 Calories

White Choco Fatty Fudge

Servings: 6
Cooking Time: 10 Minutes
Ingredients:
- 1/4 cup coconut butter
- 1/4 cup cashew butter
- 2 tbsp cacao butter
- 1/4 teaspoon vanilla powder
- 10–12 drops liquid stevia, or to taste
- 2 tbsp coconut oil

Directions:
1. Over low heat, place a small saucepan and melt coconut oil, cacao butter, cashew butter, and coconut butter.
2. Remove from the heat and stir in the vanilla and stevia.
3. Pour into a silicone mold and place it in the freezer for 30 minutes.
4. Store in the fridge for a softer consistency.

Nutrition Info:

- Per Servings 1.7g Carbs, 0.2g Protein, 23.7g Fat, 221 Calories

Raspberry Nut Truffles

Servings: 4
Cooking Time: 6 Minutes + Cooling Time
Ingredients:
- 2 cups raw cashews
- 2 tbsp flax seed
- 1 ½ cups sugar-free raspberry preserves
- 3 tbsp swerve
- 10 oz unsweetened chocolate chips
- 3 tbsp olive oil

Directions:
1. Line a baking sheet with parchment paper and set aside. Grind the cashews and flax seeds in a blender for 45 seconds until smoothly crushed; add the raspberry and 2 tbsp of swerve.
2. Process further for 1 minute until well combined. Form 1-inch balls of the mixture, place on the baking sheet, and freeze for 1 hour or until firmed up.
3. Melt the chocolate chips, oil, and 1tbsp of swerve in a microwave for 1 ½ minutes. Toss the truffles to coat in the chocolate mixture, put on the baking sheet, and freeze further for at least 2 hours.

Nutrition Info:
- Per Servings 3.5g Carbs, 12g Protein, 18.3g Fat, 251 Calories

Minty-coco And Greens Shake

Servings: 1
Cooking Time: 0 Minutes
Ingredients:
- ½ cup coconut milk
- 2 peppermint leaves
- 2 packets Stevia, or as needed
- 1 cup 50/50 salad mix
- 1 tbsp coconut oil
- 1 ½ cups water

Directions:
1. Add all ingredients in a blender.
2. Blend until smooth and creamy.
3. Serve and enjoy.

Nutrition Info:
- Per Servings 5.8g Carbs, 2.7g Protein, 37.8g Fat, 344 Calories

Coconut Fat Bombs

Servings: 4
Cooking Time: 22 Minutes +cooling Time
Ingredients:
- 2/3 cup coconut oil, melted
- 1 can coconut milk
- 18 drops stevia liquid
- 1 cup unsweetened coconut flakes

Directions:

1. Mix the coconut oil with the milk and stevia to combine. Stir in the coconut flakes until well distributed. Pour into silicone muffin molds and freeze for 1 hour to harden.

Nutrition Info:
- Per Servings 2g Carbs, 4g Protein, 19g Fat, 214 Calories

Lettuce Green Shake

Servings: 1
Cooking Time: 0 Minutes
Ingredients:
- ¾ cup whole milk yogurt
- 2 cups 5-lettuce mix salad greens
- 3 tbsp MCT oil
- 1 tbsp chia seeds
- 1 ½ cups water
- 1 packet Stevia, or more to taste

Directions:
1. Add all ingredients in a blender.
2. Blend until smooth and creamy.
3. Serve and enjoy.

Nutrition Info:
- Per Servings 6.1g Carbs, 8.1g Protein, 47g Fat, 483 Calories

Walnut Cookies

Servings: 12
Cooking Time: 25 Minutes
Ingredients:
- 1 egg
- 2 cups ground pecans
- ¼ cup sweetener
- ½ tsp baking soda
- 1 tbsp butter
- 20 walnuts halves

Directions:
1. Preheat the oven to 350°F. Mix the ingredients, except the walnuts, until combined. Make 20 balls out of the mixture and press them with your thumb onto a lined cookie sheet. Top each cookie with a walnut half. Bake for about 12 minutes.

Nutrition Info:
- Per Servings 0.6g Carbs, 1.6g Protein, 11g Fat, 101 Calories

No Bake Lemon Cheese-stard

Servings: 8
Cooking Time: 0 Minutes
Ingredients:
- 1 tsp vanilla flavoring
- 1 tbsp lemon juice
- 2 oz heavy cream
- 8 oz softened cream cheese
- 1 tsp liquid low carb sweetener (Splenda)
- 1 tsp stevia

Directions:

1. Mix all ingredients in a large mixing bowl until the mixture has a pudding consistency.
2. Pour the mixture to small serving cups and refrigerate for a few hours until it sets.
3. Serve chilled.
Nutrition Info:
- Per Servings 1.4g Carbs, 2.2g Protein, 10.7g Fat, 111 Calories

Cream Cheese 'n Coconut Cookies

Servings: 15
Cooking Time: 17 Minutes
Ingredients:
- 1 Egg
- 1/2 cup Butter softened
- 1/2 cup Coconut Flour
- 1/2 cup Erythritol or other sugar substitutes
- 3 tablespoons Cream cheese, softened
- 1 teaspoon Vanilla extract
- 1/4 teaspoon salt
- 1/2 teaspoon baking powder

Directions:
1. In a mixing bowl, whisk well erythritol, cream cheese, and butter.
2. Add egg and vanilla. Beat until thoroughly combined.
3. Mix in salt, baking powder, and coconut flour.
4. On an 11x13-inch piece of wax paper, place the batter. Mold into a log shape and then twist the ends to secure. Refrigerate for an hour and then slice into 1-inch circles.
5. When ready, preheat oven to 350oF and line a baking sheet with foil. Place cookies at least 1/2-inch apart.
6. Pop in the oven and bake until golden brown, around 17 minutes.
7. Serve and enjoy.
Nutrition Info:
- Per Servings 3.0g Carbs, 1.0g Protein, 8.0g Fat, 88 Calories

Almond Butter Fat Bombs

Servings: 4
Cooking Time: 3 Minutes + Cooling Time
Ingredients:
- ½ cup almond butter
- ½ cup coconut oil
- 4 tbsp unsweetened cocoa powder
- ½ cup erythritol

Directions:
1. Melt butter and coconut oil in the microwave for 45 seconds, stirring twice until properly melted and mixed. Mix in cocoa powder and erythritol until completely combined.
2. Pour into muffin moulds and refrigerate for 3 hours to harden.
Nutrition Info:
- Per Servings 2g Carbs, 4g Protein, 18.3g Fat, 193 Calories

Cinnamon And Turmeric Latte

Servings: 4
Cooking Time: 7 Minutes
Ingredients:
- 3 cups almond milk
- ⅓ tsp cinnamon powder
- 1 cup brewed coffee
- ½ tsp turmeric powder
- 1 ½ tsp erythritol
- Cinnamon sticks to garnish

Directions:
1. In the blender, add the almond milk, cinnamon powder, coffee, turmeric, and erythritol. Blend the ingredients at medium speed for 45 seconds and pour the mixture into a saucepan.
2. Set the pan over low heat and heat through for 5 minutes; do not boil. Keep swirling the pan to prevent from boiling. Turn the heat off, and serve in latte cups, with a cinnamon stick in each one.
Nutrition Info:
- Per Servings 0.3g Carbs, 3.9g Protein, 12g Fat, 132 Calories

Chocolate Bark With Almonds

Servings: 12
Cooking Time: 1 Hour 15 Minutes
Ingredients:
- ½ cup toasted almonds, chopped
- ½ cup butter
- 10 drops stevia
- ¼ tsp salt
- ½ cup unsweetened coconut flakes
- 4 ounces dark chocolate

Directions:
1. Melt together the butter and chocolate, in the microwave, for 90 seconds. Remove and stir in stevia.
2. Line a cookie sheet with waxed paper and spread the chocolate evenly. Scatter the almonds on top, coconut flakes, and sprinkle with salt. Refrigerate for one hour.
Nutrition Info:
- Per Servings 1.9g Carbs, 1.9g Protein, 15.3g Fat, 161 Calories

Strawberry And Yogurt Smoothie

Servings: 3
Cooking Time: 5 Minutes
Ingredients:
- 1/2 cup yogurt
- 1 cup strawberries
- 1 teaspoon almond milk
- 1 teaspoon lime juice
- 1 1/2 teaspoons stevia

Directions:
1. Place all ingredients in a blender, blender until finely smooth. Serve and enjoy.
Nutrition Info:

- Per Servings 6.3g Carbs, 4.6g Protein, 12.4g Fat, 155.2 Calories

Almond Milk Hot Chocolate

Servings: 4
Cooking Time: 7 Minutes
Ingredients:
- 3 cups almond milk
- 4 tbsp unsweetened cocoa powder
- 2 tbsp swerve
- 3 tbsp almond butter
- Finely chopped almonds to garnish

Directions:
1. In a saucepan, add the almond milk, cocoa powder, and swerve. Stir the mixture until the sugar dissolves. Set the pan over low to heat through for 5 minutes, without boiling.
2. Swirl the mix occasionally. Turn the heat off and stir in the almond butter to be incorporated. Pour the hot chocolate into mugs and sprinkle with chopped almonds. Serve warm.

Nutrition Info:
- Per Servings 0.6g Carbs, 4.5g Protein, 21.5g Fat, 225 Calories

Sea Salt 'n Macadamia Choco Barks

Servings: 10
Cooking Time: 5 Minutes
Ingredients:
- 1 teaspoon sea salt flakes
- 1/4 cup macadamia nuts, crushed
- 2 Tablespoons erythritol or stevia, to taste
- 3.5 oz 100% dark chocolate, broken into pieces
- 2 Tablespoons coconut oil, melted

Directions:
1. Melt the chocolate and coconut oil over a very low heat.
2. Remove from heat. Stir in sweetener.
3. Pour the mixture into a loaf pan and place in the fridge for 15 minutes.
4. Scatter the crushed macadamia nuts on top along with the sea salt. Lightly press into the chocolate.
5. Place back into the fridge or freezer for 2 hours.

Nutrition Info:
- Per Servings 1.0g Carbs, 2.0g Protein, 8.0g Fat, 84 Calories

Raspberry And Greens Shake

Servings: 1
Cooking Time: 0 Minutes
Ingredients:
- ½ cup half and half
- 1 packet Stevia, or more to taste
- 4 raspberries, fresh
- 1 tbsp macadamia oil
- 1 cup Spinach
- 1 cup water

Directions:
1. Add all ingredients in a blender.
2. Blend until smooth and creamy.
3. Serve and enjoy.

Nutrition Info:
- Per Servings 2.7g Carbs, 1.4g Protein, 15.5g Fat, 151 Calories

Strawberry Vanilla Shake

Servings: 4
Cooking Time: 2 Minutes
Ingredients:
- 2 cups strawberries, stemmed and halved
- 12 strawberries to garnish
- ½ cup cold unsweetened almond milk
- 2/3 tsp vanilla extract
- ½ cup heavy whipping cream
- 2 tbsp swerve

Directions:
1. Process the strawberries, milk, vanilla extract, whipping cream, and swerve in a large blender for 2 minutes; work in two batches if needed . The shake should be frosty.
2. Pour into glasses, stick in straws, garnish with strawberry halves, and serve.

Nutrition Info:
- Per Servings 3.1g Carbs, 16g Protein, 22.6g Fat, 285 Calories

Raspberry Creamy Smoothie

Servings: 1
Cooking Time: 0 Minutes
Ingredients:
- ¼ cup coconut milk
- 1 ½ cups brewed coffee, chilled
- 2 tbsps raspberries
- 2 tbsps avocado meat
- 1 tsp chia seeds
- 2 packets Stevia or more to taste
- 3 tbsps coconut oil

Directions:
1. Add all ingredients in a blender.
2. Blend until smooth and creamy.
3. Serve and enjoy.

Nutrition Info:
- Per Servings 8.2g Carbs, 4.9g Protein, 33.2g Fat, 350 Calories

21 day meal plan

Day 1
Breakfast: Sweet And Hot Nuts 16
Lunch: Simple Pulled Pork 31
Dinner: Vegetable Burritos 100

Day 2
Breakfast: Soy Garlic Mushrooms 16
Lunch: Grilled Fennel Cumin Lamb Chops 31
Dinner: Zucchini Boats 100

Day 3
Breakfast: Pecorino-mushroom Balls 16
Lunch: Hot Pork With Dill Pickles 31
Dinner: Cauliflower Mash 101

Day 4
Breakfast: Cheesy Green Bean Crisps 16
Lunch: Peanut Butter Pork Stir-fry 32
Dinner: Cauliflower & Hazelnut Salad 101

Day 5
Breakfast: Middle Eastern Style Tuna Salad 16
Lunch: Pork Chops With Cranberry Sauce 32
Dinner: Chard Swiss Dip 101

Day 6
Breakfast: Mixed Roast Vegetables 17
Lunch: Pork Wraps 32
Dinner: Vegetable Tempura 101

Day 7
Breakfast: Parmesan Crackers With Guacamole 17
Lunch: Broccoli & Ground Beef Casserole 32
Dinner: Tasty Cauliflower Dip 102

Day 8
Breakfast: Walnut Butter On Cracker 17
Lunch: One Pot Tomato Pork Chops Stew 33
Dinner: Garlicky Bok Choy 102

Day 9
Breakfast: Coconut And Chocolate Bars 17
Lunch: Pulled Pork With Avocado 33
Dinner: Fall Roasted Vegetables 102

Day 10
Breakfast: Stuffed Jalapeno 18
Lunch: Pancetta Sausage With Kale 33
Dinner: Cauliflower Mac And Cheese 103

Day 11
Breakfast: Parmesan Crackers 18

Lunch: Beef Steak Filipino Style 34
Dinner: Bell Pepper Stuffed Avocado 103

Day 12
Breakfast: Ricotta And Pomegranate 18
Lunch: Beef Stew With Bacon 34
Dinner: Strawberry Mug Cake 103

Day 13
Breakfast: Apricot And Soy Nut Trail Mix 18
Lunch: Cocoa-crusted Pork Tenderloin 34
Dinner: Mushroom & Jalapeño Stew 103

Day 14
Breakfast: Old Bay Chicken Wings 19
Lunch: Garlic Pork Chops 35
Dinner: Stir Fried Bok Choy 103

Day 15
Breakfast: Choco And Coconut Bars 19
Lunch: Thai Beef With Shiitake Mushrooms 35
Dinner: Garlic Lemon Mushrooms 104

Day 16
Breakfast: Zucchini And Cheese Gratin 19
Lunch: Pork Sausage With Spinach 35
Dinner: Avocado And Tomato Burritos 104

Day 17
Breakfast: Chicken Enchilada Dip 20
Lunch: Moroccan Beef Stew 35
Dinner: Zucchini Garlic Fries 104

Day 18
Breakfast: Crispy Keto Pork Bites 20
Lunch: Warm Rump Steak Salad 35
Dinner: Classic Tangy Ratatouille 105

Day 19
Breakfast: Baked Cheese & Spinach Balls 20
Lunch: Asian-style Beef Steak 36
Dinner: Cauliflower Fritters 105

Day 20
Breakfast: Fat Burger Bombs 20
Lunch: Garlic Crispy Pork Loin 36
Dinner: Curried Tofu 105

Day 21
Breakfast: Tuna Topped Pickles 20
Lunch: Beef Enchilada Stew 36
Dinner: Greek-style Zucchini Pasta 105

INDEX

B

Baby Carrot

Beef And Ale Pot Roast 44

Baby Spinach

Chicken And Spinach Stir Fry 48

Sausage Links With Tomatoes & Pesto 47

Green Minestrone Soup 91

Spinach Turnip Salad With Bacon 25

Scrambled Eggs With Mushrooms And Spinach 107

Bacon

Bacon Chicken Alfredo 63

Chicken With Parmesan Topping 51

Bacon And Chicken Cottage Pie 63

Beef Stew With Bacon 34

Juicy Pork Medallions 39

Pork Wraps 32

Crispy Bacon Salad With Mozzarella & Tomato 94

Bacon And Spinach Salad 94

Chicken Stock And Green Bean Soup 99

Grilled Cheese Bacon Jalapeno 27

Fat Burger Bombs 20

Party Bacon And Pistachio Balls 31

Bacon Mashed Cauliflower 23

Spinach Turnip Salad With Bacon 25

Bacon-wrapped Jalapeño Peppers 21

Cheese-jalapeno Mushrooms 27

Sicilian-style Zoodle Spaghetti 81

Bacon Strip

Coconut Aminos Chicken Bake 62

Bacon Chowder 89

Creamy Cauliflower Soup With Bacon Chips 92

Green Salad With Bacon And Blue Cheese 91

Bacon Tomato Salad 88

Bacon And Pea Salad 90

Bacon Jalapeno Poppers 29

Cobb Salad With Blue Cheese Dressing 24

Cod With Balsamic Tomatoes 76

Bacon Wrapped Mahi-mahi 79

Baguette

Nutty Avocado Crostini With Nori 24

Bay Leaf

Chicken Cacciatore 56

Chicken With Asparagus & Root Vegetables 58

One Pot Tomato Pork Chops Stew 33

Beef Bourguignon 37

Cajun Pork 42

Power Green Soup 91

Chicken Stock And Green Bean Soup 99

Bean

Green Salad 98

Green Mackerel Salad 95

Roasted String Beans, Mushrooms & Tomato Plate 17

Cheesy Green Bean Crisps 16

Creamy Vegetable Stew 108

Beef

Garlic Beef & Egg Frittata 37

Beef And Butternut Squash Stew 38

Homemade Classic Beef Burgers 46

Cherry-balsamic Sauced Beef 40

Slow-cooked Beef Moroccan Style 38

Keto Beefy Burritos 39

Beef Cheeseburger Casserole 40

Beef Stew With Bacon 34

Ground Beef And Cabbage Stir Fry 47

Broccoli & Ground Beef Casserole 32

Herby Beef & Veggie Stew 44

Russian Beef Gratin 45

Beef Tripe In Vegetable Sauté 47

Beef Cotija Cheeseburger 48

Beef Zucchini Boats 46

Beef Enchilada Stew 36

Soy-glazed Meatloaf 40

Jalapeno Beef Pot Roasted 38

Caribbean Beef 46

Old-style Beef Stew 41

Beef Bourguignon 37

Beef Reuben Soup 100

Tomato Hamburger Soup 98

Cranberry Sauce Meatballs 26

Fat Burger Bombs 20

Beef Steak

Beef Steak Filipino Style 34

Thai Beef With Shiitake Mushrooms 35

Asian-style Beef Steak 36

Beef Tenderloin Steak

Bistro Beef Tenderloin 36

Beet

Berry Merry 118

Black Olives

Chicken With Anchovy Tapenade 60

Greek Chicken Stew 57

Tuna Salad With Lettuce & Olives 91

Salmon Panzanella 67

Blackberry

Blackberry Cheese Vanilla Blocks 123

Chia And Blackberry Pudding 127

Blue Cheese

Cheesy Avocado Dip 86

Green Salad With Bacon And Blue Cheese 91

Garlic Chicken Salad 96

Cobb Salad With Blue Cheese Dressing 24

Stuffed Portobello Mushrooms 107

Blueberry

Blueberry Tart With Lavender 124

Broccoli

Chicken, Broccoli & Cashew Stir-fry 62

Creamy Stewed Chicken 52

Cheesy Turkey And Broccoli Traybake 51

Broccoli & Ground Beef Casserole 32

Creamy Soup With Greens 87

Mushroom-broccoli Soup 87

Power Green Soup 91

Green Minestrone Soup 91

Colorful Vegan Soup 106

Brown Onion

Beef Stew With Bacon 34

Brussels Sprout

Turkey Burgers With Fried Brussels Sprouts 58

Lemon Pork Chops With Buttered Brussels Sprouts 34

Brussels Sprouts Salad With Pecorino Romano 97

Citrusy Brussels Sprouts Salad 99

Kale And Brussels Sprouts 98

Mixed Roast Vegetables 17

Balsamic Brussels Sprouts With Prosciutto 19

Roasted Brussels Sprouts With Sunflower Seeds 107

Buttermilk

Beef Tripe In Vegetable Sauté 47

Butternut Squash

Chicken & Squash Traybake 49

Beef And Butternut Squash Stew 38

Butternut Squash And Cauliflower Stew 101

C

Cabbage

Chicken And Green Cabbage Casserole 50

Beef Cheeseburger Casserole 40

Pork And Cabbage Soup 41

Chicken Cabbage Soup 88

Spicy Tofu With Worcestershire Sauce 112

Parmesan Roasted Cabbage 111

Asian-style Fish Salad 81

Calamari Ring

Baked Calamari And Shrimp 81

Carrot

Lamb Stew With Veggies 43

Herby Beef & Veggie Stew 44

Beef And Ale Pot Roast 44

Parsnip And Carrot Fries With Aioli 30

Creamy Vegetable Stew 108

Wild Mushroom And Asparagus Stew 110

Cashew

Chicken, Broccoli & Cashew Stir-fry 62

Raspberry Nut Truffles 128

Cauliflower Rice

Cranberry Sauce Meatballs 26

Cheddar Cheese

Coconut Aminos Chicken Bake 62

Slow-cooked Mexican Turkey Soup 62

Quattro Formaggi Chicken 57

Cheddar Chicken Tenders 65

Chicken And Green Cabbage Casserole 50

Chicken Cauliflower Bake 51

Bacon And Chicken Cottage Pie 63

Pork Burger Salad With Yellow Cheddar 93

Grilled Cheese Bacon Jalapeno 27

Duo-cheese Chicken Bake 26

Cheddar Cheese Chips 30

Stuffed Jalapeno 18

Garlicky Cheddar Biscuits 28

Grilled Cheese The Keto Way 115

Cherry Tomato

Sausage Links With Tomatoes & Pesto 47

Easy Tomato Salad 87

Spaghetti Squash With Eggplant & Parmesan 102

Simply Steamed Alaskan Cod 71

Chia Seeds

Chia And Blackberry Pudding 127

Chicken Breast

Lemon Threaded Chicken Skewers 64

Chicken And Mushrooms 60

Cilantro Chicken Breasts With Mayo-avocado Sauce 63

Bacon Chicken Alfredo 63

Coconut Aminos Chicken Bake 62

Spicy Chicken Kabobs 65

Creamy Stewed Chicken 52

Chicken With Anchovy Tapenade 60

Rosemary Grilled Chicken 64

Chicken And Zucchini Bake 59

Red Wine Chicken 57

Quattro Formaggi Chicken 57

Pacific Chicken 52

Chicken And Green Cabbage Casserole 50

Smoky Paprika Chicken 54

Pesto Chicken 49

Fried Chicken With Coconut Sauce 64

Chicken And Spinach Stir Fry 48

Chicken Skewers With Celery Fries 61

Chicken Pesto 50

Chicken And Spinach 48

Chicken With Parmesan Topping 51

Greek Chicken Stew 57

Sweet Garlic Chicken Skewers 59

Yummy Chicken Queso 56

Poulet En Papiotte 55

Chicken Stroganoff 50

Easy Chicken Chili 54

Spinach & Ricotta Stuffed Chicken Breasts 61

Oregano & Chili Flattened Chicken 64

Roasted Stuffed Chicken With Tomato Basil Sauce 60

Greek Chicken With Capers 60

Chicken Goujons With Tomato Sauce 52

Chicken Breasts With Walnut Crust 54

Chicken And Mushrooms 60

Stewed Italian Chicken 49

Bacon And Chicken Cottage Pie 63

Chicken With Asparagus & Root Vegetables 58

Spicy Chicken Bean Soup 90

Cobb Egg Salad In Lettuce Cups 90

Chicken Cabbage Soup 88

Garlic Chicken Salad 96

Cobb Salad With Blue Cheese Dressing 24

Chicken Drumstick

Chicken Paella With Chorizo 62

Chicken Cacciatore 56

Chicken Sausage

Marinara Chicken Sausage 54

Chicken Tender

Cheddar Chicken Tenders 65

Italian-style Chicken Wraps 22

Chicken Thighs

Chicken In White Wine Sauce 59

Fennel Shredded Chicken 49

Lemon & Rosemary Chicken In A Skillet 61

Zesty Grilled Chicken 56

Chicken & Squash Traybake 49

Roasted Chicken With Tarragon 52

One-pot Chicken With Mushrooms And Spinach 55

Oven-baked Skillet Lemon Chicken 65

Easy Chicken Vindaloo 57

Chicken In Creamy Spinach Sauce 57

Eggplant & Tomato Braised Chicken Thighs 53

Thyme Chicken Thighs 65

Mexican Soup 94

Caesar Salad With Chicken And Parmesan 94

Chicken Wing

Parmesan Wings With Yogurt Sauce 63

Air Fryer Garlic Chicken Wings 27

Old Bay Chicken Wings 19

Teriyaki Chicken Wings 26

Chocolate

Reese Cups 23

Sea Salt 'n Macadamia Choco Barks 130

Dark Chocolate Mousse With Stewed Plums 123

Chocolate Chip Cookies 122

Chocolate Bark With Almonds 129

Keto Cauliflower Hash Browns 115

Zesty Frittata With Roasted Chilies 106

Smoked Mackerel Patties 79

Yummy Shrimp Fried Rice 79

Creamy Hoki With Almond Bread Crust 74

Dark Chocolate Mousse With Stewed Plums 123

No Nuts Fudge 121

Berry Tart 120

Fast 'n Easy Cookie In A Mug 119

Blackberry Cheese Vanilla Blocks 123

Chocolate Chip Cookies 122

Keto Lemon Custard 118

Eggnog Keto Custard 121

Vanilla Flan With Mint 124

Eggplant

Eggplant & Tomato Braised Chicken Thighs 53

Baba Ganoush Eggplant Dip 22

Grilled Parmesan Eggplant 115

Classic Tangy Ratatouille 105

Spaghetti Squash With Eggplant & Parmesan 102

Enoki Mushroom

Asian Seafood Stir-fry 74

F

Feta Cheese

Feta Avocado Dip 85

Greek Chicken Stew 57

Balsamic Cucumber Salad 96

Zucchini Gratin With Feta Cheese 29

Cheesy Lettuce Rolls 22

Zucchini Gratin With Feta Cheese 29

Cheesy Lettuce Rolls 22

Baked Fish With Feta And Tomato 78

Firm Tofu

Tofu Stuffed Peppers 29

Tofu Sesame Skewers With Warm Kale Salad 104

Walnuts With Tofu 116

Green Onion

Coconut Aminos Chicken Bake 62

Duck & Vegetable Casserole 51

Warm Rump Steak Salad 35

Thai Beef With Shiitake Mushrooms 35

Italian Sausage Stew 47

Middle Eastern Style Tuna Salad 16

Cauliflower & Hazelnut Salad 101

Kale Cheese Waffles 110

Avocado Tuna Boats 75

Cedar Salmon With Green Onion 78

Green Pepper

Homemade Cold Gazpacho Soup 92

Ground Turkey

Turkey Burgers With Fried Brussels Sprouts 58

H

Habanero Pepper

Caribbean Beef 46

Halibut Fillet

Halibut En Papillote 72

Lemon Chili Halibut 72

Halibut With Pesto 67

Ham

Pacific Chicken 52

Hazelnut

Cauliflower & Hazelnut Salad 101

Spicy Sea Bass With Hazelnuts 70

Chocolate Hazelnut Bites 127

Hazelnut And Coconut Shake 122

Heavy Cream

Chicken Pesto 50

Chicken In Creamy Spinach Sauce 57

Beef Reuben Soup 100

Creamy Vegetable Stew 108

Creamy Kale And Mushrooms 111

Butternut Squash And Cauliflower Stew 101

Angel Hair Shirataki With Creamy Shrimp 73

Vanilla Jello Keto Way 119

Vanilla Bean Frappuccino 123

No Bake Lemon Cheese-stard 128

Blueberry Tart With Lavender 124

Eggless Strawberry Mousse 124

Keto Lemon Custard 118

Hoki Fillet

Creamy Hoki With Almond Bread Crust 74

I

Italian Pork Sausage

Pork Sausage With Spinach 35

Italian Sausage

Italian Sausage Stew 47

J

Jack Cheese

Cheesy Turkey And Broccoli Traybake 51

Sausage Links With Tomatoes & Pesto 47

Lettuce Taco Carnitas 41

Onion Cheese Muffins 23

Bianca Pizza 113

Jalapeno Pepper

Grilled Cheese Bacon Jalapeno 27

Jalapeno Popper Spread 28

Stuffed Jalapeno 18

Cheese-jalapeno Mushrooms 27

Jumbo Shrimp

Coconut, Green Beans, And Shrimp Curry Soup 96

Blue Cheese Shrimps 78

K

Kale

Buttered Duck Breast 56

Turkey, Coconut And Kale Chili 55

Pancetta Sausage With Kale 33

Keto Beefy Burritos 39

Kale And Brussels Sprouts 98

Bacon-flavored Kale Chips 28

Garlic Flavored Kale Taters 25

Garlic And Greens 113

Kale Cheese Waffles 110

Tofu Sesame Skewers With Warm Kale Salad 104

Creamy Kale And Mushrooms 111

L

Lamb

Lamb Stew With Veggies 43

Lamb Shashlyk 46

Lamb Chop

Grilled Fennel Cumin Lamb Chops 31

Grilled Lamb On Lemony Sauce 36

Lettuce

Cobb Egg Salad In Lettuce Cups 90

Bacon And Spinach Salad 94

Fruit Salad With Poppy Seeds 93

Middle Eastern Style Tuna Salad 16

Cobb Salad With Blue Cheese Dressing 24

Vegetarian Burgers 110

Stuffed Portobello Mushrooms 107

Avocado Salad With Shrimp 76

Hazelnut-lettuce Yogurt Shake 120

London Broil

Moroccan Beef Stew 35

Cherry-balsamic Sauced Beef 40

Beef Enchilada Stew 36

M

Macadamia Nut

Sea Salt 'n Macadamia Choco Barks 130

Coconut Macadamia Nut Bombs 124

Mascarpone Cheese

Quattro Formaggi Chicken 57

Turkey Pastrami & Mascarpone Cheese Pinwheels 19

Coffee Fat Bombs 119

Blackberry Cheese Vanilla Blocks 123

Mexican Cheese

Beef Enchilada Stew 36

Monterey Jack Cheese

Lettuce Taco Carnitas 41

Beef Zucchini Boats 46

Bianca Pizza 113

Mozzarella Cheese

Bacon Chicken Alfredo 63

Chicken And Zucchini Bake 59

Quattro Formaggi Chicken 57

Turkey Enchilada Bowl 50

Bacon And Chicken Cottage Pie 63

Marinara Chicken Sausage 54

Broccoli & Ground Beef Casserole 32

Crispy Bacon Salad With Mozzarella & Tomato 94

Mediterranean Salad 88

Tuna Caprese Salad 95

Strawberry, Mozzarella Salad 99

Zucchini Lasagna With Ricotta And Spinach 114

Grilled Parmesan Eggplant 115

Pumpkin Bake 111

O

Okra
Italian Sausage Stew 47

P

Pancetta
Chicken In White Wine Sauce 59
Pancetta Sausage With Kale 33
Beef Bourguignon 37

Parmesan Cheese
Caesar Salad Dressing 83
Parmesan Crackers 18
Jalapeno Popper Spread 28
Parmesan Crackers With Guacamole 17
Easy Baked Parmesan Chips 28
Parmesan Roasted Cabbage 111
Spicy Cheese Crackers 126
Crispy Zucchini Chips 127

Parsnip
Parsnip And Carrot Fries With Aioli 30

Pea
Bacon And Pea Salad 90

Peanut
Pumpkin & Meat Peanut Stew 99
Asian Seafood Stir-fry 74

Pecan
Cajun Spiced Pecans 29

Roasted Pepper
Brazilian Moqueca (shrimp Stew) 89
Cauliflower & Hazelnut Salad 101

Pie Crust
Blueberry Tart With Lavender 124

Plain Yogurt
Parmesan Wings With Yogurt Sauce 63
Lychee And Coconut Lassi 125

Plum
Dark Chocolate Mousse With Stewed Plums 123

Pork Belly
Crispy Keto Pork Bites 20

Pork Chop
Herb Pork Chops With Raspberry Sauce 39

Oregano Pork Chops With Spicy Tomato Sauce 42
Simple Pulled Pork 31
One Pot Tomato Pork Chops Stew 33
Mushroom Pork Chops 42
Pork Chops And Peppers 42
Garlic Pork Chops 35
Hot Pork With Dill Pickles 31

Pork Loin Chop
Pork Chops With Cranberry Sauce 32
Balsamic Grilled Pork Chops 48

Pork Sausage
Sausage Links With Tomatoes & Pesto 47
Pancetta Sausage With Kale 33
Pork Sausage With Spinach 35
Smoked Pork Sausages With Mushrooms 43
Pork Sausage Bake 45

Pork Tenderloin
Cocoa-crusted Pork Tenderloin 34
Juicy Pork Medallions 39

Portobello Mushroom
Smoked Pork Sausages With Mushrooms 43
Pecorino-mushroom Balls 16
Vegetarian Burgers 110
Stuffed Portobello Mushrooms 107

Prawn
Arugula Prawn Salad With Mayo Dressing 96
Avocado & Cauliflower Salad With Prawns 80

Prosciutto
Mozzarella & Prosciutto Wraps 25
Balsamic Brussels Sprouts With Prosciutto 19
Roasted Stuffed Piquillo Peppers 23
Italian-style Chicken Wraps 22

Provolone Cheese
Quattro Formaggi Chicken 57
Cheddar Cheese Chips 30
Italian-style Chicken Wraps 22

Prune
Moroccan Beef Stew 35

Pumpkin
Pumpkin Bake 111

Pumpkin Puree
Pumpkin & Meat Peanut Stew 99

Pumpkin Seed

Apricot And Soy Nut Trail Mix 18

R

Radish

Roasted Chicken With Tarragon 52

Pancetta Sausage With Kale 33

Spinach Turnip Salad With Bacon 25

Asian-style Fish Salad 81

Raspberry

Raspberry Nut Truffles 128

Herb Pork Chops With Raspberry Sauce 39

Raspberry And Greens Shake 130

Choco-chia Pudding 120

Raspberry Sorbet 122

Red Bell Pepper

Spicy Chicken Kabobs 65

Pork Sausage With Spinach 35

Caribbean Beef 46

Pork Sausage Bake 45

Italian Sausage Stew 47

Zucchini Gratin With Feta Cheese 29

Fall Roasted Vegetables 102

Vegetable Tempura 101

Vegetable Tempeh Kabobs 114

Seared Scallops With Chorizo And Asiago Cheese 66

Tuna Steaks With Shirataki Noodles 80

Red Cabbage

Brussels Sprouts Salad With Pecorino Romano 97

Red Cabbage Tilapia Taco Bowl 77

Red Chili

Oregano Pork Chops With Spicy Tomato Sauce 42

Squid Salad With Mint, Cucumber & Chili Dressing 22

Red Onion

Beef And Ale Pot Roast 44

Balsamic Cucumber Salad 96

Pork Burger Salad With Yellow Cheddar 93

Pesto Tomato Cucumber Salad 98

Homemade Cold Gazpacho Soup 92

Traditional Greek Salad 98

Bacon And Pea Salad 90

Classic Tangy Ratatouille 105

Seared Scallops With Chorizo And Asiago Cheese 66

Red Pepper

Pesto Arugula Salad 99

Homemade Cold Gazpacho Soup 92

Baked Fish With Feta And Tomato 78

Rice

Chicken Paella With Chorizo 62

Beef Cheeseburger Casserole 40

Beef And Egg Rice Bowls 37

Cranberry Sauce Meatballs 26

Avocado And Tomato Burritos 104

Red Cabbage Tilapia Taco Bowl 77

Ricotta Cheese

Easy Chicken Meatloaf 59

Spinach & Ricotta Stuffed Chicken Breasts 61

Ricotta And Pomegranate 18

Baked Cheese & Spinach Balls 20

Zucchini Lasagna With Ricotta And Spinach 114

Roma Tomato

Chicken Cacciatore 56

Baked Fish With Feta And Tomato 78

S

Salad Green

Green Salad With Bacon And Blue Cheese 91

Green Mackerel Salad 95

Strawberry, Mozzarella Salad 99

Middle Eastern Style Tuna Salad 16

Lettuce Green Shake 128

Salmon

Salmon Salad With Walnuts 97

Chili-garlic Salmon 75

Dilled Salmon In Creamy Sauce 69

Chipotle Salmon Asparagus 72

Seasoned Salmon With Parmesan 70

Avocado And Salmon 66

Baked Salmon With Pistachio Crust 75

Salmon Panzanella 67

Steamed Mustard Salmon 69

Pistachio-crusted Salmon 69

Sour Cream Salmon With Parmesan 76

Salmon And Cauliflower Rice Pilaf 80

Cedar Salmon With Green Onion 78

Lemon Marinated Salmon With Spices 67

Asian-style Fish Salad 81

Parmesan Fish Bake 71

Salmon With Pepita And Lime 77

Scallop

Asian Seafood Stir-fry 74

Seared Scallops With Chorizo And Asiago Cheese 66

Serrano Pepper

Easy Chicken Chili 54

Shiitake Mushroom

Vegetarian Fish Sauce 84

Thai Beef With Shiitake Mushrooms 35

Shrimp

Shrimp With Avocado & Cauliflower Salad 97

Coconut, Green Beans, And Shrimp Curry Soup 96

Lobster Salad With Mayo Dressing 95

Brazilian Moqueca (shrimp Stew) 89

Cilantro Shrimp 75

Steamed Asparagus And Shrimps 79

Grilled Shrimp With Chimichurri Sauce 78

Yummy Shrimp Fried Rice 79

Bang Bang Shrimps 73

Rosemary-lemon Shrimps 69

Chili-lime Shrimps 68

Sautéed Savory Shrimps 66

Lemon Garlic Shrimp 80

Baked Calamari And Shrimp 81

Shrimp In Curry Sauce 72

Lemon-rosemary Shrimps 82

Shrimp And Cauliflower Jambalaya 68

Blue Cheese Shrimps 78

Avocado Salad With Shrimp 6

Sushi Shrimp Rolls 82

Angel Hair Shirataki With Creamy Shrimp 73

Skirt Steak

Adobo Beef Fajitas 39

Beef And Egg Rice Bowls 37

Smoked Mackerel

Smoked Mackerel Patties 79

Smoked Sausage

Smoked Pork Sausages With Mushrooms 43

Sour Cream

Sour Cream And Cucumbers 95

Sour Cream Salmon With Parmesan 76

Spinach

Chicken And Spinach Stir Fry 48

One-pot Chicken With Mushrooms And Spinach 55

Spinach & Ricotta Stuffed Chicken Breasts 61

Roasted Stuffed Chicken With Tomato Basil Sauce 60

Chicken In Creamy Spinach Sauce 57

Chicken Cauliflower Bake 51

Sausage Links With Tomatoes & Pesto 47

Spicy Pork Stew With Spinach 40

Pork Sausage With Spinach 35

Bacon And Spinach Salad 94

Strawberry Salad With Spinach, Cheese & Almonds 91

Spinach Fruit Salad With Seeds 89

Baked Cheese & Spinach Balls 20

Spinach Turnip Salad With Bacon 25

Scrambled Eggs With Mushrooms And Spinach 107

Green And Fruity Smoothie 122

Squash

Chicken & Squash Traybake 49

Chicken Goujons With Tomato Sauce 52

Beef And Butternut Squash Stew 38

Creamy Squash Bisque 88

Mixed Roast Vegetables 17

Spaghetti Squash With Eggplant & Parmesan 102

Vegetable Tempura 101

Butternut Squash And Cauliflower Stew 101

Strawberry

Strawberry Mug Cake 103

Sweet Onion

Smoked Pork Sausages With Mushrooms 43

Sour Cream And Cucumbers 95

Swiss Cheese

Fruit Salad With Poppy Seeds 93

T

Tiger Prawn

Arugula Prawn Salad With Mayo Dressing 96

Tilapia Fillet

Steamed Chili-rubbed Tilapia 66

Five-spice Steamed Tilapia 74

Tilapia With Olives & Tomato Sauce 78

Buttery Almond Lemon Tilapia 70

Red Cabbage Tilapia Taco Bowl 77

Tofu

Tofu Stuffed Peppers 29
Tofu Sesame Skewers With Warm Kale Salad 104
Chard Swiss Dip 101
Spicy Tofu With Worcestershire Sauce 112
Walnuts With Tofu 116
Fried Tofu With Mushrooms 108
Zucchini Boats 100
Curried Tofu 105
Walnut Tofu Sauté 108

Trout

Trout And Fennel Parcels 66

Tuna

Tuna Salad With Lettuce & Olives 91
Asparagus Niçoise Salad 87
Tuna Caprese Salad 95
Middle Eastern Style Tuna Salad 16
Dill Pickles With Tuna-mayo Topping 26
Tuna Topped Pickles 20
Avocado Tuna Boats 75
Tuna Steaks With Shirataki Noodles 80

Tuna Steak

Tuna Steaks With Shirataki Noodles 80

Turkey

Turkey Burgers With Fried Brussels Sprouts 58
Slow-cooked Mexican Turkey Soup 62
Cheesy Turkey And Broccoli Traybake 51
Turkey Enchilada Bowl 50
Turkey, Coconut And Kale Chili 55
Tender Turkey Breast 55
Turkey Pastrami & Mascarpone Cheese Pinwheels 19

Turnip

Chicken With Asparagus & Root Vegetables 58
Creamy Cauliflower Soup With Chorizo Sausage 87

Spinach Turnip Salad With Bacon 25
Cream Of Zucchini And Avocado 112
Smoked Mackerel Patties 79

W

Walnut

Chicken Breasts With Walnut Crust 54
Salmon Salad With Walnuts 97
Walnuts With Tofu 116
Walnut Tofu Sauté 108
Walnut Cookies 128

Y

Yellow Onion

Greek Styled Veggie-rice 109

Z

Zucchini

Chicken And Zucchini Bake 59
Quattro Formaggi Chicken 57
Chicken Stroganoff 50
Duck & Vegetable Casserole 51
Beef Zucchini Boats 46
Baked Vegetable Side 30
Zucchini Gratin With Feta Cheese 29
Zucchini And Cheese Gratin 19
Fall Roasted Vegetables 102
Zucchini Lasagna With Ricotta And Spinach 114
Greek-style Zucchini Pasta 105
Classic Tangy Ratatouille 105
Cream Of Zucchini And Avocado 112
Zucchini Garlic Fries 104
Zucchini Noodles 114
Briam With Tomato Sauce 113
Sicilian-style Zoodle Spaghetti 81
Crispy Zucchini Chips 127

Printed in Great Britain
by Amazon